# Me[illegible]

# Rev. John Russell

# and His Out-of-Door Life

E. W. L. Davies

Alpha Editions

This edition published in 2020

ISBN : 9789354022722

Design and Setting By
**Alpha Editions**
email - alphaedis@gmail.com

# MEMOIR

OF THE

# REV. JOHN RUSSELL

AND HIS

# OUT-OF-DOOR LIFE

BY

E. W. L. DAVIES M.A.

AUTHOR OF "DARTMOOR DAYS"

A NEW EDITION
WITH ILLUSTRATIONS BY
N. H. J. BAIRD
COLOURED BY HAND.

CHATTO & WINDUS | JAMES G. COMMIN
LONDON. | EXETER.

1902.

# PREFACE.

The Reader will be glad to know, as the Author is to state, that before a line of the first edition of this Memoir was published, the proof-sheets of every chapter were duly submitted to Mr. Russell himself, in order that any statement, affecting directly or indirectly the authenticity of his personal history, might be corrected, refuted, or substantiated by his own hand.

That advantage is lacking only in the final chapter ; which is added to wind up the history of his last years, and at the same time to record—as the Author does with unspeakable regret—the closing scene of his prolonged and active life.

To the present edition is added a series of illustrations by Mr. Baird depicting scenes and incidents in the life of Mr. Russell.

# CONTENTS.

## CHAPTER I.



## CHAPTER II.



## CHAPTER III.

## CHAPTER IV.



## CHAPTER V.



## CHAPTER VI.



## CHAPTER VII.



## CHAPTER VIII.

## CHAPTER IX.



## CHAPTER X.



## CHAPTER XI.



## CHAPTER XII.

## CHAPTER XIII.



## CHAPTER XIV.



## CHAPTER XV.

# ILLUSTRATIONS.

# MEMOIR OF

# THE REV. JOHN RUSSELL.

## CHAPTER I.

JOHN RUSSELL'S EDUCATION UNDER HIS FATHER—IS SENT TO PLYMPTON SCHOOL—HIS FIRST FIGHT WITH J. C. BULTEEL—IS REMOVED TO TIVERTON SCHOOL—KEEPS HOUNDS THERE, AND GETS INTO TROUBLE WITH DR. RICHARDS, THE HEAD MASTER—IS ADMITTED INTO EXETER COLLEGE, OXFORD, IN 1814.

> Boys, to the hunting field! though 'tis November,
> The wind's in the south; but a word ere we start—
> Though keenly excited, I bid you remember
> That hunting's a science, and riding an art.
>
> EGERTON-WARBURTON.

The subject of the present memoir, the Rev. John Russell, was born on the 21st of December, 1795. His father was the well-known rector of Iddesleigh, in the north of Devon, but resided, when John was born, and for a short time afterwards, at Dartmouth, where he took pupils, and at the same time kept hounds. It is recorded of him that not only was he careful to instruct the former in the rudiments of Greek and Latin, but in those of the "noble science;" the full enjoyment of the one being made subservient to the due acquirement of the other.

"Work and play" was the good man's motto; and to carry out this principle he adopted the novel plan of keeping a pony-hunter expressly for the benefit of the boys; and he who managed to gain the highest marks for his work during the week was rewarded with sole possession of the pony on the following hunting-day.

As might be expected, no stimulant could have been more effective: the boys worked like Trojans at their school tasks.

During this eventful era, however, the child "Jack" was in petticoats; and before he became old enough to compete for a mount, his father removed to Southhill Rectory, near Callington. But, inheriting as he did a double portion of that sire's hunting blood, had the chance been given him, it may well be imagined how he would have stepped first and foremost into the academic ring, and how he would have striven, early and late, to secure so glorious a reward. His "Propria quæ maribus," we may be sure, would have been perfect; his knowledge of the Concords and Syntax equally faultless; nor, the victory gained, would he have failed to acknowledge that the day's sport, thus earned, had been doubly sweetened by the very labour he had taken to obtain it.

A Cornish gentleman, whose father had been educated by the elder Russell, writes thus to the author of these memoirs: "My father has long been dead: he sleeps in the Consul's garden at Tangier; but I can well remember the delight with which he was wont to talk of his school days at Dartmouth, and the admiration he felt for his dear old master. Of him he would say: 'He was one of the best classics, one of the best preachers and readers, and by far the boldest hunter in the county of Devon. Not unfrequently, too,' my father would add, 'have I seen the fine old fellow's top-boots peeping out from under his cassock.'"

His son became a fair classical scholar, nothing more; but, otherwise, to no one in the West of England would this description apply with more fidelity than to John Russell; whose fine sonorous voice, distinct enunciation, and earnest exhortations have long established his repute, both in desk and pulpit, as an expounder of truth second to none. A story is told that, on the occasion of his preaching a sermon, either at the re-opening of a church newly restored, or on behalf of the North Devon Hospital (to which, in this way, he has ever been a ready and bountiful contributor,) the late Bishop of Exeter, Henry Phillpotts, travelled a long distance on purpose to hear him. The stout-hearted prelate, himself a master of eloquence, was so taken with the matter of the discourse and the style of its delivery, that he pointedly expressed his commendation of both to those assembled around him at the luncheon-table.

"Yes, my lord," said a lady sitting next to him, who happened to be nearly connected with the preacher, and very well known as a prominent rider in the hunting-field, "yes, Mr. Russell is very good in the wood; but I should like your lordship to see him in the pigskin."

But, having anticipated the period of his middle-life by this anecdote, it will be necessary now to revert to the boy's school days, and follow him through the bright but not unclouded portion of that somewhat eventful time.

An old-established grammar school was that of Plympton, the go-cart of Sir Joshua Reynolds, to which he was first sent. There, it would appear, the head master maintained the block-system in full force; not, however, for the purpose of checking, but rather of expediting the educational progress of his pupils; for, when a boy's head appeared to be too hard to comprehend and remember some crabbed line of Phædrus' Fables or Cæsar's Commentaries, it was duly whacked into him at another more sensitive point.

Such, however, was the training at that time, which scholars like Dean Gaisford, Bishop

Copleston, and the late Mr. Justice Coleridge were probably compelled to submit to, notwithstanding the grand brains with which Nature had blessed those distinguished men.

Here it was he first met his fellow-pupil, John Crocker Bulteel, "the heir-apparent of Flete," afterwards so well known in the county, not only as a popular master of hounds, but as one of the most genial and talented of men. The old borough of Plympton—the stronghold of the Treby family, till the brush of the Reform Bill swept away its charter—was proud enough of its then flourishing grammar school; but prouder still was John Bulteel of being "cock of the walk" over the many juveniles who flocked from all quarters to that establishment.

On more than one occasion he had exhibited a disposition to crow over Russell, but he was very soon taught a lesson that few boys would be likely to forget so long as they lived. Bulteel, at length, brought matters to a crisis by saying something to Russell's disparagement, in his absence, which, of course, was speedily conveyed to him in an exaggerated form by one of his schoolfellows. The offender, however, was not to be found at the moment, so Russell, seeing a book with "J. C. B." inscribed on it, pounced upon it at once, and in his wrath tore it to shreds; this he did under the full conviction that Bulteel, on discovering the outrage, would lose no time in resenting it.

"Who tore this book?" demanded Bulteel, coming in soon after, and viewing the pages of his new Gradus scattered on the school floor, like autumn leaves that strew "the brooks in Vallombrosa."

"I did!" responded Russell, defiantly, as he doubled his fists and prepared for the imminent encounter.

"Then take that," said Bulteel, acting on the principle that "the first blow is half the battle," and hitting him like a flash of lightning on the most prominent feature of Russell's face.

A sharp and severe encounter then followed. Russell, however, at length prevailed, winning, as he would call it, his first spurs, and at the same time securing ever after the unqualified respect of his antagonist as a foeman worthy of his steel.

Soon after he had attained his fourteenth year, John Russell was removed to Tiverton School, then under the able mastership of Dr. Richards, a disciplinarian strict as Draco, who, by the success of his tuition and the obedience he enforced, elevated the standard of his school to a rank equal to that of Reading or Sherborne in their best days. Nor were the worthies of Devon slack in availing themselves of these and other educational advantages offered by Blundell's school; for, when Russell joined, it was swarming with pupils, several of whom represented, more or less directly, a goodly portion of the county families.

He had been but a short time at this Spartan seminary when, daily provoked by the tyranny of a boy called Hunter, a monitor in the first class, and a notorious bully, Russell avowed himself a champion of the oppressed, and, for his own sake and that of others, determined to fight him on the first opportunity. Now, if a junior boy presumed to challenge a monitor, it was regarded as a serious and punishable offence; but if he struck him, so dire an act of insubordination was promptly visited by expulsion.

To bide his time, therefore, was Russell's only safe policy; but the trial of doing so tested his utmost patience; for the longer he managed to submit to Hunter's bullying, the more oppressive and galling it became. The long-deferred chance, however, came at last. Dr. Richards having discovered that several of the boys kept rabbits, gave a peremptory order that they were to be got rid of forthwith. Accordingly, on being dismissed from dinner the owners all, with one exception, posted off to dispose of their rabbits; that exception being Hunter, who, possessing a choice breed, delayed to execute the order, with the intention of asking permission to send them home, on the ground that his rabbits were so valuable.

Russell, in the meantime, observing the monitor's neglect of duty, and ignorant of the cause of it, resolved to see the edict fulfilled to its bitter end, and proceeded at once to do for Hunter what he seemed so loth to do for himself. Russell kept ferrets, and, like most boys of a manly nature, held those who kept rabbits in supreme contempt, denouncing them as milksops, only fit to live and associate with maiden aunts. So it can well be imagined how the spirit of retaliation took instant possession of him, and with what zest he conveyed the rabbits to his ferret-box. As well might the innocent victims have been tossed into a python's den, for they were all dead before the owner became aware of their untimely fate or his own grievous loss.

But he was not long in discovering it; nor was Russell, who avowed himself the perpetrator, slow to discover that the maledictions and fierce threats of Hunter, who swore he would give him a sound thrashing, would all end in smoke, and that, in fact, the bully was what he had suspected him to be, an arrant coward.

Though older and stronger than Russell, and boiling with rage, he dared not strike him, which the junior fully hoped he would have done; but off he started, as fast as his legs could carry him, to tell Dr. Richards, whom he accosted with a torrent of tears, as he met him returning on his brown cob from his daily ride in the country lanes.

"What are you crying for?" inquired the really kind-hearted doctor, touched by the boy's distress, and exhibiting a weakness he rarely showed within the precincts of the school.

"My rabbits, sir," replied Hunter, still blubbering aloud; "Russell has killed them all with his ferrets."

"Killed *your* rabbits," responded the doctor, gravely; "and with ferrets, too? Are they his own ferrets, did you say?"

"Oh yes, sir, his own; he keeps a lot of them," added Hunter, observing that a storm was brewing which would break with awful effect on Russell's head.

On arriving at the school-house the culprit was instantly sent for by Dr. Richards.

"Now, sir," he said, in a voice of thunder, "what right have you to kill Hunter's rabbits, and what reason can you give for committing so gross an outrage on your schoolfellow's property?"

"It was your own order, sir," pleaded Russell, fearlessly, "that all the rabbits should be killed; and as Hunter did not seem inclined to kill his, I did it for him."

"And with your own ferrets, too," added the doctor, seizing Russell by the collar and flogging him with his long, heavy riding-whip, till the whalebone appeared in splinters at its end.

Many a week passed before the marks of that castigation became invisible on Russell's back; but never from that day did he suffer further persecution either from Hunter or any other bully of the school; for, though good-natured to a fault, he was discovered to be too dangerous a customer to trifle with.

Without hunting, Jack Russell could not have lived; and severe as he knew the penalty would be if he were caught indulging in it, still hunting he must have in some shape or other. Then, as ever since, it has been the one master-passion of his life. "Men," some one has truly said, "do not lose their passions till they get their wings;" and certainly from his earliest years Russell's passion for the chase has clung to him closely as his own skin, through good report and evil report, cheering him in storms which few but he would have faced; and in all weather, fair or foul, asserting its ruling, nay, its paramount influence over him even down to the close of his life.

But after that episode with Hunter, either by compulsion, or more likely from inclination, Jack disposed of his ferrets, and took to keeping hounds. He had already won the good-will of the neighbouring farmers by joining them in many a lively rat-hunt among their stacks and barns; in bolting rabbits, too, from their over-stocked hedges he had ever readily lent a useful hand, doing them a substantial service, and treating himself to a labour of love.

This sport, however, such as it was, did not long satisfy the boy's aspirations. He was now sixteen years of age, and craved daily, as he said, "for the ding-dong of hounds," a music to which, by nature, his ear had been so finely attuned. A schoolfellow of his own standing, called Bob Bovey, appears also to have had a strong strain of hunting-blood in his veins; and hearing Russell's oft-expressed wish to keep a few hounds, he came to him one day, and despite the danger of doing so, proposed to join him in starting a pack.

Accordingly, the two boys, forming a joint mastership, were very soon able to muster a scratch lot, consisting of four and a half couple of hounds, which they kept at a blacksmith's on the outskirts of Tiverton town. The worthy Vulcan must have been a kindred spirit, for he seems not only to have given up a linhay adjoining the forge for the use of the hounds, but to have run the risk of incurring Dr. Richard's displeasure and losing his custom, solely for the love of hunting, and the sheer sake of promoting the sport.

Those were glorious days so long as they lasted; the farmers, to a man, seeing the hounds chiefly managed by Russell, giving them a hearty welcome over their land, and supporting them in various ways calculated to show their cordial interest in the welfare of the pack. One, for instance, would say, "he'd a got a hare sitting in fuzzy-park bottom, and ef Maister Rissell wid on'y bring up his cry, he'd turn un out, and they'd have a rare crack o' hunting, sure enow." Another would inform him that "his auld blind maire had mit wi' a mishap, got stogged in a mire, zo he'd a knacked her in th' head, and Maister Rissell was kindly welcome to her vor the dags."

Then, there was no end to the bread-and-cheese and cider, which the hospitable and hound-loving yeomen of that county pressed upon him and his companions, whenever the chase led them within hail of their farm homesteads. Perhaps the happiness of a schoolboy was never more complete. Being a fair classical scholar, and gifted with far more than ordinary abilities, which in any profession might have carried him, but for his devotion to hounds, to the top of the tree, he found no difficulty in satisfying Dr. Richard's class requirements, and at the same time, whenever a half or a whole holiday occurred, in following the pastime he so keenly loved.

The feeling, too, that he was snatching a stolen pleasure might have enhanced

"... that theft of sweet delight"

a hundredfold; but dark clouds were now looming in the horizon, portending a short season and disastrous end to this enjoyable life. A shaft from some hidden enemy (and well for him was it that his name was never discovered) did the mischief. Some one, purporting to be "a friend to good discipline," wrote to Dr. Richards, and communicated the astounding intelligence that a cry of hounds were kept by his scholars, Bovey and Russell, and that the latter, if he was not sole manager, acted at least as huntsman to the pack.

"Ringleader, in fact, of the hunting gang," exclaimed Richards, indignantly, as an expression of grave import darkened his whole countenance. "What! set my discipline at nought, and bring discredit on the honoured name of Blundell?"

He sent for Bovey, and expelled him on the spot. Russell came next, little doubting that he should share a similar fate; as, like a mouse tortured by a cat, he underwent a preliminary examination before the fatal blow fell.

"You keep hounds, don't you?" demanded the autocrat, in a stern and pitiless tone.

"No, sir."

"Do you dare to tell me a lie? Bovey has just told me you do keep them," said

Richards, striking him in his wrath with great violence.

"'Tis no lie, sir," pleaded Russell, pathetically; "for Bovey stole them yesterday, and sent them home to his father at Pear-tree."

"Then that's lucky for you," responded the doctor, "or I'd have expelled you too."

After this narrow escape, Russell, it would appear, was compelled to quench as best he could the latent flame that burned within him, and pay due deference, at least outwardly, to the more than ever strict discipline exacted by Dr. Richards.

It may be inferred, too, that he was now compelled to give more attention to his studies than he had hitherto done; for, soon after his fall as a master of hounds, two prizes were offered for competition—an exhibition of £30 per annum, tenable for four years, and a medal for elocution—both of which he won in a canter, regaining at the same time the favour of Dr. Richards. But, had the worthy man been able to foresee the use Jack made of the first £30 he received as an exhibitioner, he would certainly have denounced him as a most unworthy recipient of Blundell's bounty. Our hero expended it in buying a horse from the Rev. John Froude, of Knowstone; and, as he soon found to his cost, did not get the best of the bargain.

The day, however was nigh at hand when the pent-up flame was destined to be no longer suppressed. Oxford was before him, the seat, in those days, not of learning only, but of much liberty and little restraint.

In 1814, when he had just completed his nineteenth year, he was admitted a commoner at Exeter College, his matriculation being rather a matter of form than dependent on the amount of scholarship he had acquired at Tiverton School. An easy-going head was Dr. Cole, the rector of Exeter at that period; the tutors, too, taking their cue from him, with here and there a sturdy conscientious exception, rarely interfered with the daily life of the undergraduates, so long as chapel and lectures were attended with tolerable regularity.

Consequently, men did much as they liked at all other times; shot, fished, and hunted; boated, sparred, and drove tandem; finishing each day with heavy drinking and convivial songs.

In this land of freedom, emancipated from the Spartan discipline of Dr. Richards, and now his own master, Russell found, to his unspeakable delight, an open and congenial field for the cultivation of that science so deeply implanted in his nature, and in the acquirement of which he had already proved himself so apt a pupil.

Cicero has said that without the divine *afflatus* no one has ever become a distinguished man; and it has been long accepted, but by whose authority I believe is unknown, that a poet must be born a poet, or he can never become one either by education or art. So the talent required by a huntsman must be inborn—the gift of Nature alone—or the very foundation on which he builds, no matter how he may labour, or what experience he may have, will be defective and unreliable to the end.

Endowed, then, by Nature with the first and most essential element required in a huntsman, Russell, as might be expected, lost no chance of improving the gift, and gaining by experience a sound practical knowledge of the infinite mysteries pertaining to the "noble science."

If, however, the University, otherwise so liberal with respect to its pupils, had omitted the duty of providing instruction in that department, Russell, at least, found no lack of first-class professors in the surrounding neighbourhood. Philip Payne and Will Long were at Heythrop, huntsman and first whip to his Grace the sixth Duke of Beaufort, who, in addition to his "home country," hunted the Oxfordshire hills in those days with his grand badger-pies; while at Bicester, Stephen Goodall, and Tom Wingfield, under Sir Thomas Mostyn, possessed a knowledge of woodcraft second to none in Great Britain. Heroes, in fact, were those four men, in their line, worthy of song as the heroes of Homer.

Then there was Mr. John Codrington on the Old Berkshire side, an amateur who, in all the details of field or kennel management, knew scarcely a whit less than his professional fellow-workmen of the Oxfordshire hills and vale. Being a Master of the Meynell School and an ardent promoter of the modern foxhound, Codrington was eminently qualified to give any tyro, who had the luck to hunt with him, most instructive lessons in all that pertained to the newest style of breeding hounds and killing a fox.

No wonder, then, that at the feet of such a Gamaliel, and with such professors so near at hand, Russell should have proved himself a ready and proficient scholar; nor that, with his natural aspirations, quick perception, and decisive action, he should have gained that practical knowledge of the "noble science" which few have attained to and none have surpassed.

It was fortunate for Russell that his passion for hunting was limited by the tide of his exchequer, which, never overflowing, was too often reduced to the lowest ebb; for, had it permitted him to hunt his four or five days a week, it is very questionable if ever he would have passed his final examination, and then taken his degree—an important matter to him, although in those days by no means a difficult task. He himself was wont to say, "It was no marvel Oxford was so learned a place, for men brought up a fair stock of school learning, but carried little away with them."

When tempted by some hunting friend to "send on," perhaps to Bicester-Windmill, or Bradwell Grove—an arrangement involving a heavy expense as to hack, hunter, and groom—Russell would point pathetically to his own broad chest and lament his inability to do so in dolorous tones: "Impossible, my dear fellow; I'm suffering just now from tightness of the chest; it's the old complaint; and my doctor won't let me hunt at any price."

Still, hunting would have its vent, and Jack managed to enjoy a liberal share of hunting, in spite of Plutus and every other impediment.

Russell's first run with the Staghounds.

# CHAPTER II.

Buys his First Horse at Tiverton Fair, and sees his First Stag killed with Lord Fortescue's Hounds—Learns to Spar at Oxford, and Sets-to with Denne and others—Wrestling Matches in Devon and Cornwall his great delight.

> Pastime for princes!—prime sport of our nation!
> Strength in their sinew, and bloom on their cheek;
> Health to the old, to the young recreation;
> All for enjoyment the hunting-field seek.
>
> Egerton-Warburton.

Of the many hunting days enjoyed by Russell in early life, no one stood out in such strong relief as the 30th of September, 1814, for on it he saw his first stag found and killed under somewhat memorable circumstances. The tedium of a long vacation at home, with little or no sport to satisfy the cravings of his nature, was beginning to tell heavily upon him, when one day, as he sat pondering over the beauties of Somerville's Chase, scarcely knowing how else to amuse himself, his father appeared, and with a few magic words put life into him.

"Come, Jack," he said, "my boy. The hounds are going to meet at Baron's Down, and I should like to show you a stag. Tiverton Fair will take place to-morrow; so you shall go there early and buy a horse for yourself; but mind, he must be a well-bred one and up to your weight."

Jack felt as if he should require a strait-waistcoat—almost beside himself—on hearing such joyous news; for of all things on earth a day with the staghounds, and that, too, on his own horse, was then, in the heyday of his youth, the climax of his ambition.

Accordingly, the next morning, long before daylight, he was off for Tiverton Fair, at that time considered the Howden of the West, so far as a goodly show of Exmoor ponies, Devonshire pack-horses, and half-bred hunters could justify such a comparison. Nor did he waste much time in making a selection; a brown mare with big limbs and a lean head, belonging to a dealer named Rookes, caught his eye, and as she proved to be a good mover, and was said to be a five-year-old, he bought her after a few words for £30.

Alas! The mare proved to be only a two-year-old; but, although Russell was unmercifully quizzed as a second Moses of green spectacle celebrity, she turned out to be as honest a beast as ever looked through a bridle.

A saddle and bridle having been readily lent him by a friendly farmer, Jack, unconscious of the tender age of the mare, and relying confidently on his father's promise that "he would send on a fresh horse for him to the meet," rode her along at a hand canter, and without drawing rein from Tiverton town-end to Baron's Down, a distance, by the old road, of at least fifteen miles.

"Never before, and never after," records the son, "do I remember my father failing to fulfil a promise he had made me; but there, at Baron's Down, for some reason which I cannot now remember, the fresh horse did not appear."

The young mare was of course blown, but, happily for the rider, not yet beaten. The harbourer had reported a "warrantable deer;" but the woodland was a deep one in which he had made his lair, and many a change took place before the two couple of tufters could rouse and force the right animal away. By that time the mare, under the freshening influence of gentle exercise and the breezy moor, had fairly recovered herself, and as Jack avowed, was then "fit as a fiddle to go for her life."

But now an awkward accident occurred that suddenly checked, and might have terminated, our hero's career before he had gone ten strides with the hounds. Mr. Stucley Lucas, of Baron's Down, who at a later period became Master of the Staghounds, was riding a race-horse called Erebus, and, as that gentleman was known to be an authority on all matters relating to the moor and the running of the deer, Russell very naturally looked to him as the pilot for the day. The racer, however, appears to have had but little fancy for Jack's company, for, on approaching incautiously within reach of his heels, he was kicked under the stirrup-iron with such force that he was thrown headlong to the ground.

But as the stirrup had acted as a shield to his foot, so the friendly heather, breaking the violence of his fall, saved his bones and enabled him promptly to remount his steed and follow the chase, if not a sadder, certainly a wiser man for the rest of his life.

Jack, now taking his own line, made the best of his way to Hawkridge, from the high ground of which he could view the hounds driving hard, and the field following at a long distance from him; and just as he had determined to start in pursuit, a gentleman trotted up from an opposite direction and counselled him to remain where he was, "for" said he, "they'll be sure to come this way, and you can see the sport better from this point than if you were with them."

Comprehending intuitively that his Mentor spoke with authority, Russell without hesitation adopted this kind advice, and again easing his mare led her to and fro along the ridge, as he feasted his eyes on the wild and stirring scene taking place on the opposite moor.

Russell's patience as a quiet looker-on was not long tried; for even now the heads of the leading hounds were turning towards him, and he could distinctly hear the deep chop of their musical tongues, as, sinking the valley near Tarrsteps, they crossed the Barle and pointed directly for Hawkridge Moor.

Jack was now in his glory, alongside them on a willing steed, and they tearing ahead over the purple heather, as if on the very haunches of their game. With a trimming scent and never a check, it lasted for three long hours, when the deer, to baffle the pack, took soil under Slade Bridge, sinking himself in a deep pool and allowing little more than his nostrils to appear above the wave.

But the stratagem availed him not a rush; some five or six couple of old hounds dashed into the stream, and swimming in full cry, passed over him at first for a hundred or more yards; when James Tout, the huntsman, turned the pack, and then casting them steadily back, they winded him at once in his retreat. Every hound was at him in an instant, and a gambol of porpoises in that moorland stream could scarcely have created a greater commotion. "There stood the stag, beneath them in the stream," writes Charles Kingsley, who must have witnessed a similar turmoil, "his back against the black rock, with its green cushions of dripping velvet, knee-deep in the clear amber water, the hounds around him, some struggling in the deep pool, some rolling and tossing and splashing in a mad half-terrified ring, as he reared in the air on his great haunches, with the sparkling beads running off his red mane, and, dropping on his knees, plunged his antlers among them with blows which would have brought certain death with it if the yielding water had not broken the shock."

With such a scene enacted before his eyes, Jack Russell must have been chained down to remain a passive spectator for a single moment; nor, had Dr. Richards and all the Dons of Oxford been present, could they have restrained the wild impulse he felt to take part in the fray! A struggle it was for life and liberty; the last effort of the noble beast to escape from his foes. Naturally, however, the young hunter's sympathy being wholly with the hounds, in he plunged waist-deep into the flood, eager at once to encourage and help them in the somewhat dangerous work of capturing and killing the deer.

That event speedily followed; and Jack, being duly "blooded" according to the usage of the period, received an impression of stag-hunting, deep-cut, enduring, and only to be effaced when the stream of life ceased to flow in his veins.

The late Earl Fortescue, Lord-Lieutenant of the county, was at that time, from 1812 to 1818, Master of the Staghounds; and "those," Mr. Collyns tells us, "were glorious days; ninety deer, forty-two stags, and forty-eight hinds having fallen in fair chase during the six years of his Mastership.* The halls of Castle Hill rang merrily with the wassail of the hunters, and many a pink issued from the hospitable seats of the neighbouring squires, on the bright autumn morning, to participate in the pleasures of the chase. When a good stag had been killed, the custom was for James Tout, the huntsman, to enter the dining-room at Castle Hill after dinner in full costume, with his horn in his hand, and after he had sounded a Mort, 'Success to stag-hunting' was solemnly drunk by the assembled company in port-wine, after which Tout again retired 'to his own place,' and rested himself after the labours of the day in company with one or two favourites whose escape from the kennel had been connived at. There, before the ample fire, the huntsman dozed away his evening, and killed his deer again; while

"'The staghound, weary with the chase,
Lay stretched upon the rushy floor,
And waged in dreams the forest race
From *Castle Hill* to wild *Exmoor*.'"

* The Devon and Somerset Staghounds, under the able Mastership of Mr. Fenwick Bisset, killed fifty deer (stags and hinds) from August to December, 1876.

The eyes of the noble master, being himself an enthusiastic stag-hunter, must have sparkled with delight on witnessing the daring ardour of the young Oxonian, as he struggled through the deep water to collar the deer, and finally emerged red-handed from the fight. Russell, on that occasion, was not invited to enjoy the princely hospitality of Castle Hill, and to celebrate in due form the death of his first deer; but, if such honour had been done him, certain it is that he would have been the first of the company to forswear the wassail bowl, and to bid one and all an early "good-night." For has not his old friend, the late accomplished and much-beloved Devonshire squire, George Templer of Stover, chronicled his unvarying habit in this respect? In poetic strain he writes thus of him:

> "Another Prime Minister rode from the North,
> Of his talents Southmolton can best tell the worth;
> So prone to the chase that he followed each scent,
> From the stag in the forest to 'bubble-a-vent;'
> More attached to his bed than a lover of wine,
> He was sure to be sound on his pillow at nine."

"Bubble-a-vent" is a term used in otter hunting; when the quarry bolting in a hurry or becoming distressed by the chase, is compelled to vent; and thus, by a chain of silver bubbles rising to the surface, unconsciously reveals his course beneath the turbid wave.

But more of that anon; when Russell himself, a few years afterwards, started a pack of otter-hounds, and, as he says, "did little more than disturb the sleeping echoes of the North Devon combes."

It was but a short time since, namely in 1876, when he was dining with the present Lord Fortescue at Castle Hill, that the remembrance of his first entry with staghounds in 1814 was brought back to his mind with vivid effect after the lapse of so many years. He had said "good night" to his hospitable and kind host, and, homeward bound, was making his way towards the hall door, accompanied by some of the junior members of the family holding on to his skirt, when Lord Ebrington begged him to relate when and where he had seen his first stag killed.

"With your grandfather," was the ready reply; "we found him in Padwells, and killed him on the Barle, under Slade Bridge, on the 30th of September, 1814; and there he is," added Russell, catching sight at that instant of the head and antlers of the very animal, under the frontlet of which appeared a tablet indicating the above particulars.

Those who have once heard Russell tell a story, especially if hunting were the theme, will never forget the charm of his graphic touches, the intensity of his tone, and the point he had the power of imparting to the minutest detail. They will remember it as a picture painted by a master-hand, with its light and shade strong as one of Rembrandt's; a picture true to life as was ever transferred to canvas.

It may well be imagined, then, how effectually those poetic touches must have inspired his youthful hearers with a longing to traverse the same wild moors, to witness the same exciting scenes, and to play their part as their forefathers and he had done, with like energy and like love for the manly game. With hunting blood already running richly in their veins, he must have stirred it to the very depths of their hearts; and, beyond all doubt, the poetry of the scene, the music of the hounds, and the odour of the heather will cling to their memories for many a day to come.

Russell's return to Oxford about the 20th of October brought his stag-hunting to a close for the remainder of that season; but he must have been a gourmand indeed, if the bountiful bill of fare provided by *Alma Mater* did not fully satisfy his physical as well as mental requirements. He had only been a short time in residence at Exeter when a Kentish man, called Denne, of Lydd, a gentleman-commoner of the same college, introduced him to a professor of pugilism, one Rowlands, who, having graduated in the school founded by John

Broughton and the Duke of Cumberland, had come down from Westminster to instruct the youth of Oxford in the then popular art of self-defence.

Jack, now standing just six feet in his shoes, furnished with big limbs, a long reach, and withal a stalwart frame, required little persuasion from his friend Denne to attend and take part in the course of muscular lectures delivered by Rowlands in that gentleman's rooms. Nor was it long ere the professor was able to pronounce him one of his most promising pupils—a compliment duly appreciated by Russell, who, although far from being either a quarrelsome or a pugnacious character, possessed the ambition of Cæsar, if attacked, to prove himself a man to the backbone.

In those days Exeter College teemed with gentlemen-commoners, who, as a rule, were either the eldest sons of large landed proprietors in the West of England, or men already in possession of their paternal acres, to whom the payment of double fees was a matter of less consideration than the distinction conferred by the silk gown and velvet cap, which the University permitted them to wear. They dined, too, at a separate table from the commoners, namely, at the first below the daïs; and, exalted by these and other privileges, here and there a fool would give himself airs and affect to consider the latter simply as beings of an inferior caste, companionship with whom it was his bounden duty to eschew.

Such was Gordon, a gentleman-commoner of Exeter at that time; a conceited young spark, whose chief ambition it was to associate with out-college men, especially those of Christ Church, to quote their sayings and doings at every turn, and, in reference thereto, to institute comparisons far from complimentary to the members of his own college. In fact, he was a tuft-hunter, and doubtless suffered as much contempt from the men whom he courted as from those whose society he would fain have ignored.

Denne, on the other hand, was as fine a specimen of manhood as ever stepped in shoe-leather; independent as Achilles himself, lithe, long-limbed, and of rare muscular development; he might have taken rank among the Promachi of old, so skilled was he in the use of the caestus, and so powerful was his blow. At Eton he had been contemporary with Ball Hughes, the noted dandy of the 7th Hussars; with Harris of Hayne, the ally and strenuous supporter of Russell in after days; and with that far-famed sportsman, Sir Harry Goodricke. Denne was there distinguished as a great football player; but especially as the avenger of the lower boys, who never failed to find shelter under his ægis, when oppressed by the bullies of the upper school. At Oxford, in a town-and-gown row, he had knocked down the ringleader of the mob—a prize-fighting butcher, the terror of the slums—with such force that his comrades who lifted him up carried him to the rear in a state of insensibility, shouting as they did so that a coroner's inquest would sit upon the corpse, and hang Denne for the murder.

The butcher, however, lived to fight at many a town-and-gown row after that day, but never again could be induced to confront Denne in single combat, either by the jeers of the gownsmen or the encouragement of his friends.

It was only at rare intervals that Gordon favoured the hall at Exeter with his company at dinner, for as a general rule he preferred taking that meal with his Christ Church friends, either at Saddler's, the Mitre, or at the Maidenhead Hotel. But dropping in on one occasion, he had scarcely been seated five minutes at table when the "art of sparring" became the subject of conversation, and the insolent tone in which he vaunted the prowess of the Christ Church men, and disparaged that of his own college, so disturbed the usually placid current of Denne's temper, that he challenged him forthwith to arrange a meeting and prove his words.

"Bring your three best men," he said, "from Christ Church to my rooms, and if they can only stand up in a fair set-to against three of Exeter, we'll give your heroes full credit for all you say of them, but not till then."

"Thank you, Denne, for your most courteous insinuation," replied Gordon, curling his upper lip, and speaking in a tone of the bitterest irony; "there will be no difficulty whatever in finding three good men and true to accept your challenge; indeed, a score, if necessary, would be forthcoming, so name your day, and they shall be ready."

It was not usual for the commoners, before the high table had risen, to move from their seats and hold conversation with those at another table, much less with the gentlemen-commoners; but Russell, who was seated at a short distance below the latter, and had overheard all that had passed, could restrain himself no longer. "Don't forget me, Denne," he said, jumping on his legs and stalking up to his friend's side; "I'll be one of the three, mind that, and the sooner we meet the better."

The Fiery Cross of Clan-Alpine was never carried with such speed through the Trossachs as Gordon's message to the Christ Church men; nor did the interest excited by it flag for an instant, till three of them had been chosen, who, in the opinion of all, were best qualified to accept the challenge and carry to the front the colours of the college.

A 'Set-to' with Denne.

On a fixed day, then, soon afterwards, the party on both sides having assembled in Denne's rooms, with Gordon alone to witness the match, Russell was deputed to open the ball, the antagonist selected to meet him being the second best man of the Christ Church lot. It was a brisk set-to while it lasted, but, evidently, a one-sided affair from beginning to end; for Russell's long reach, and quick, straight blows. which fell with tremendous thuds on his adversary's visage, brought the trial to a close in little more than ten minutes.

The latter, admitting himself overmatched, then declined the unequal contest; while Russell, self-reliant and still "fresh as paint," refused to take off his gloves, calling stoutly for the next man to come on. Denne, however, interposed and would have his turn; going in first with No. 1, then No. 3, and finally polishing them both off with as much ease as if they had been two old women.

"Now," said Russell, addressing Gordon aside, "I think you had better take your three fellows home and don't make such fools of them again."

But the meeting did not end there. Denne, willing to show the Christ Church men what a real set-to meant, invited Russell to put on the gloves with him and give them a lesson. Now, Denne being a master-hand at the work, it was no joke setting to with him, for Rowlands himself had acknowledged that he could teach him nothing. Nevertheless, Russell, regardless of the punishment he knew must follow, responded readily to the summons. He stood up, and stopped and countered with the coolness of a professional, but, as he soon found, to little purpose. Denne forced him into a corner, paused a moment, and thus warned him: "Now, Jack, you are going to catch it!"

"Perhaps I am," said the other; "but don't make too sure of that."

The words had scarcely escaped the enclosure of his teeth, ere a tremendous left-hander, coming straight from the shoulder, caught him on the lower jaw with such violence that it sent him reeling against a table, bringing him and it to the ground with a fearful crash. "I really thought," said Russell, relating the story to a friend long afterwards, "that my chin had been knocked away; nor could I masticate a bit of roast beef for many a subsequent day."

On the table that fell with him had stood a brass-bound writing-desk, which, besides the usual materials of such an article, contained a number of letters and notes, curiously folded, and written on coloured and gold-edged paper, while not a few other souvenirs, more or less valuable, were scattered broadcast on the floor. Shocked apparently by this unwonted exposure,

Denne, amid an outburst of laughter, from the Christ Church men, dropped on his knees as if he was shot, and, gathering the precious favours together, crammed them again into the treacherous receptacle, denouncing as he did so, in no measured terms, the ill-luck that had revealed them to view.

Denne, like a good fellow, did his best to solace the wounded pride of his visitors by giving them a sumptuous champagne breakfast; but, "nothing could a charm impart" to Gordon's spirits, who, according to Russell, "carried his tail between his legs like a cur-dog that had been worrying sheep, and from that day never cocked it again."

Prize-fighting was then the order of the day; and a set-to between two professionals of celebrity would bring together men of all ranks, patricians and proletarians, from the most remote parts of England, to witness what it would have been heresy then to call a barbarous exhibition. The vale of Bicester, being on the borders of two counties, was a convenient rendezvous for such encounters; and thither, on the occasion of a grand fight, the University would pour forth its legion of gownsmen; some betting heavily on the event, and some, chiefly amateurs in boxing, going there for the sole purpose of taking a first-class lesson in the "noble art of self-defence."

For such ruffianism, however, Russell had no taste; nor, skilled though he was in sparring, could he ever be induced to ride even so far as Bicester to witness a prize-fight.

"No!" he would say to Denne and others pressing him to accompany them, "if I do get on a horse, it shall be to see a hound with his natural enemy, a fox, before him—a cross-country fight, not one in a ring."

Still, the Greeks of Homer's song never enjoyed the display of athletic skill more emphatically than John Russell; for, when a "turn at wrastling" was about to be played between Cann and Polkinghorn—the champions respectively of Devon and Cornwall—he has ridden a hundred miles in a day to see the manly game come off. Then, if Cann, his compatriot, proved successful in giving his adversary a fair back-fall, *i.e.*, in bringing three points of his back to the earth without touching it with his limbs, every star in the sky would have cheered him on his long ride home; ay, and he would not have failed to describe every feature of the "play" for months afterwards, with sparkling comment and unflagging zest.

Prize-fighting, indeed, popular as it was during the first quarter of the present century, never appears to have taken the same hold of the public mind in Devon and Cornwall as it did in other parts of the United Kingdom.

The worthies of those counties adhered, with better taste, to their ancient and manly game of wrestling, which they rightly regarded as testing to the utmost the strength, skill, and courage of the combatants; but, at the same time, exhibiting none of the brutality that invariably characterized every pugilistic encounter.

During the summer season, but especially at that period of it between the hay and corn harvest, when the cereals were assuming a golden hue, and the orchards bending under their burden of fruit, there was scarcely a large village in the West which did not offer its prizes, and enjoy annually the time-honoured spectacle of a game at wrestling, the players coming from all parts to contend for the mastery.

I have heard Russell relate that, on a certain Sunday while at church in Cornwall, he saw a man posted just outside the churchyard gate; six silver spoons were stuck into the band of his hat, and there he stood, shouting at the top of his voice: "Plaize to tak' notiss. Thaise zix zilver spunes to be wrastled vor next Thursday, at Poughill, and all gen'lemen wrastlers will receive fair play." The man, with the spoons in his hat, then entered the church, went up into the "singing gallery," and hung it on a peg, from which it was perfectly visible to the parson and the greater part of his congregation.

On another occasion in the same locality, but not in the same church, snow lying deep on the ground, the clergyman was reading the second lesson, when a man opened the church door, and, with a loud voice, proclaimed, "I've a got 'un!" and immediately withdrew. But he had sounded the well-known note; every farmer and labourer who possessed a gun soon followed him, and, within a couple of hours, brought to the village inn a fine old fox, dug out and murdered in cold blood.

As in Cornwall, so formerly in the forest of Dartmoor; Tom French, the once notorious vulpicide, was wont to say of a fox, "'Tis a nasty varmint, I tell 'ee, and aufght to be killed on a Sunday, so well as on a week-day;" a doctrine he was not slow to practice, especially when a fall of snow gave him the chance:—

> "While faithless snaws ilk step betray
> Whar *he* has been——."
>
> BURNS.

## CHAPTER III.

A Day with the Heythrop and Sir Thomas Mostyn's Packs—Russell's Terriers—Anecdotes of "Tip" and "Nelson"—The Process of Manufacturing so-called "Fox-terriers" for the Market.

> They champ'd the bit and twitch'd the rein,
> And paw'd the frozen earth in vain;
> Impatient with fleet hoof to scour
> The vale, each minute seem'd an hour.
>
> Egerton-Warburton.

From the period of his first matriculation at Oxford to that on which he donned his bachelor's gown and quitted the University, Russell appears to have kept no regular record of his hunting days. Nevertheless, when in genial company, the sport and incidents of many a run, witnessed at that time and chronicled on the unwritten pages of his memory, were still ever and anon flashed out with the freshness of a schoolboy who has only recently enjoyed his first mount with a pack of hounds. Upwards of sixty years had rolled by since then; yet every detail of those early scenes he still painted in colours so fresh and vivid, that it was difficult to believe they could have occurred in the days "when George the Third was King."

The man who has once heard Russell hold forth on some favourite topic, must indeed have a very defective memory if he ever forget the charm of his earnest, natural manner, or the epigrammatic and pointed style in which he was wont to tell the simplest tale; like the Wedding-guest, the listener "cannot choose but hear," spell-bound at once by his glittering eye and winged words.

To attempt a description of the sport he saw with hounds during his residence at Oxford, in the absence of written records, would be a task beyond the design of the present memoir; but the adventure of one disastrous day, on which he went to a distant meet and never saw a hound, must not be omitted, for it left such an impression on his memory that to his latest hour he spoke of it with mixed feelings of disappointment and remorse.

. The fixture was Sandford Brake; the hounds those of his Grace the sixth Duke of Beaufort, who, as the reader has already been informed, hunted the Oxfordshire hills from Heythrop at one season of the year, and his "home country" from Badminton at another. The fame of the pack, the favourite colour being badger-pie, had at this period traversed the length and breadth of the land. There were no hounds like them; none that combined so perfectly the close hunting and hard driving qualities required in a foxhound; none that surpassed them in power, symmetry, and grandeur of form.

Russell had never yet seen this noble pack; but at every wine and supper party he attended, if there were any hunting men present, the chief theme of their conversation invariably turned on the Beaufort badger-pies; so it may well be imagined how he longed to feast his eyes on so attractive a sight, to watch them at work, and enjoy the sport they so rarely failed to show.

With his head, then, brimful of such anticipations, dry indeed must he have found the task of getting up the Greek lecture over which he was poring, when one morning his friend Peter Jackson, a Yorkshireman devoted to hounds, rushed into his rooms, and exhibiting a card of the hunting appointments, put his finger on "Sandford Brake," and said:

"Now, then, Russell, throw that physic to the dogs; here's a chance of seeing the Heythrop Hounds; let's be off at once to secure the two best nags we can find in Oxford."

No invitation could have been more acceptable.

"With all my heart," responded Russell, chucking his Herodotus to the far end of the room, and starting off, in company with his friend, to Austin's stables, reputed in those days to be the first in Oxford.

Their selection was soon made; Jackson choosing a big thorough-bred chestnut, with sloping shoulders, flat hocks, and rare sinewy thighs; while Russell, fixed on a well-known horse called "Charlie," which, though "speechless in one eye," Austin declared "could see a weak place in a bullfinch better than ever a horse in his stable."

Accordingly, on the day before the meet, Charlie and the chestnut, ridden by a couple of grooms, were duly "sent on" to the Chequers Inn, there to rest for the night, the stables of that hostelry being only at a short distance from the cover-side; while in the morning, if Russell and his friend had been mounted on two fiery dragons, they could scarcely have been carried through the air with more speed and impetuosity than by the two raw-boned hacks which, ewe-necked and clean as Eclipse in their pasterns, bore them to the meet in so short a time.

But, could they have anticipated the fruitlessness of their haste, they might have spared the poor brutes' legs, and their own pockets at the same time; for the roads were hard as iron, and no hounds had as yet arrived. In fact, a keen north wind had set in at daybreak, and although a goodly company had mustered at the cover-side, a feeling of mistrust prevailed, that unless a speedy change took place, hunting would be out of the question for that day.

Now it was, for the first time, that Russell met those celebrated brothers, Mr. Rawlinson, of Chadlington, and Mr. Lindo, a pair of resolute and brilliant horsemen who were not to be beaten in any country. The former will also be remembered as the owner of Revenge and Ruby, and subsequently of Coronation, winner of the Derby in 1841; while, of the latter, it is scarcely too much to say that every hunting man in the kingdom either knew him personally or knew him by his portrait, which, admirably painted by some sporting artist, appeared in all the print-shops of town and country at that period. Even on snuff-boxes Mr. Lindo might have been seen standing up in his stirrups, and going "a slapping pace" on his famous horse the Clipper—a horse so quick at his fences, that it was said he could "go a mile and a half over a country while others were going a mile."

But the man of all others who attracted the admiration of our Oxonians was Sir Henry Peyton, the second baronet of that name. He had driven four greys to the meet, and with characteristic good-nature had entered at once into a horse-and-hound conversation with Russell, whose impatience at not seeing the hounds he had observed with no little sympathy.

"'Tis a north-easter, keen as a knife," said the baronet, pointing with his crop to the very eye of the wind. "Hard lines on you, young fellow, for I dare say you've cut lecture to come here, and now, I fear, the hounds are going to cut you."

"I hope not, Sir Henry; for that would be the unkindest cut of all."

"Never mind! come again; better luck next time. I knew by the going of the near leader that the road was getting harder and harder every yard of the way. I've lately had him nerved; and when there's a touch of frost in the ground he can't keep his secret a bit; but he's all right at other times."

"I can see nothing amiss, Sir Henry," replied Russell, whose interest in that new operation, which he now heard of for the first time, made him forget for a moment the non-arrival of the hounds; "he looks, however, like a hunter all over."

"The cleverest horse across country I ever owned," said the baronet, right pleased with the observant remark. He then took up the foreleg of the leader, and drew Russell's attention to the all but invisible marks of the operator's skill, adding, "It's an ill wind that blows no luck; for he bids fair to be as good in harness as out of it; so I ought not to grumble."

No man of that day, as Russell well knew, could do more with a horse than Sir Henry Peyton. In the saddle or on the box, he was equally at home; the prince of all coachmen, gentle or simple, and as brilliant a performer across country as ever rode to hounds.

A small knot of gentlemen had now gathered round the drag, admiring the well-appointed team, and exchanging short greetings with its pleasant owner, when at length a horseman in green plush, pricking along at a quick trot towards the meet, was viewed in the distance, and at once recognised as Will Long.

"His Grace's compliments to the field," said the well-mannered whip, as he lifted his cap respectfully to one and all, "and begs to say the frost is too hard to take the hounds out of kennel."

"Then," said Russell, in an agony of disappointment, "I hope when you get back that you'll find them all dead on their benches."

It is almost needless to say that, if such a calamity had occurred, no man on earth would have deplored it more than John Russell, as every one who knew the humanity of his nature and his love for a hound will readily understand. Hard words they were, it is true; but, beyond all doubt, they were words only, and not wishes, which he thus allowed himself to blurt out; and, as the keenest remorse overtook him with no limping foot, let us hope that the recording angel has long since blotted out the angry speech for ever. Will Long, however, never forgot it; for, years afterwards, when the "chilling touch of Time" had turned the locks of both of them to silver-grey, and they were returning together to Badminton, after a hard day with the present Duke's hounds, Russell asked him if he remembered the first time they met at Sandford Brake.

"Yes, sir," said Will, "and I'm not likely to forget it. You hoped I should find all the hounds dead upon the benches. But there, I didn't think you meant it."

"Quite right, Will; in two minutes afterwards I could have bitten my tongue out for having made such a speech."

It is impossible to overrate the estimation and respect with which Will Long was regarded, not only by the Beaufort family, but by all who followed him to the chase and enjoyed his cheery company in days gone by; still, brilliant horseman as he was acknowledged to be, I have heard Russell declare that as a practical huntsman he could never hold a candle to old Philip Payne nor to the present Duke. That probably was the case; nevertheless it must not be forgotten that Will Long hunted those hounds with signal success from 1826 down to October, 1855, a period of twenty-nine years; when, overtaken at length by the infirmities of age, he retired from active service, carrying with him his well-earned laurels, and enjoying, by the bounty of his noble master, a comfortable cottage, a steady hunter, and a handsome pension to the last day of his long life. In February, 1877, poor Will was borne to his narrow home —"an earth made for rest"—at the patriarchal age of fourscore years and four. He was buried at Oldbury-on-the-Hill, where Philip Payne lies; and never to its kindred clay were committed the relics of a kindlier spirit or a truer man:—

"Reliquit equos, cornu, canes,
Tandem quiescant ejus manes."

The last time Russell met him he inquired if his brother Michael were yet alive.

"Yes," replied Russell, "and well, too."

"I'm glad to hear that," responded the veteran; "he gave my son Nimrod his first mount, took him out of my wife's arms and held him on the saddle when he was only a month old. Please give him my duty." An early entry this for that well-known huntsman, Nimrod Long.

Among the many hunting friends with whom Russell associated at Oxford, there was no one, perhaps, whose sympathies accorded so closely with his own as did those of Mr. Philip Dauncey, of Little Horwood, a Buckinghamshire gentleman, even then distinguished as a bold rider and thorough houndsman; and who subsequently became widely known as a successful breeder of Guernsey cows, the cream and butter of which obtained such high favour in the royal household. Like tendencies, the love of hunting, with all its accompanying charms, had brought them together on many occasions to the merry cover-side ; but one day, on which they had met Sir Thomas Mostyn's hounds, stood out in strong relief on the tablet of Russell's memory, and probably left a like impression on that of Mr. Dauncey.

Stephen Goodall, a real Titan himself, and the progenitor of a race of Titans—the three Goodalls—of whom the country that bred them may well be proud, was about to draw a small willow spinney on the north side of Bletchington House, when a fox, closely pursued by the Duke of Beaufort's pack, crossed in view of his hounds, and, putting his head like an arrow for Gravenall Wood, led the now united field and packs at a terrific pace over the stiffest portion of the Bicester Vale. The brook is a bumper, even with its banks—that brook which has baptized more Oxford men than any parson in the county—and the hounds, five or six couple abreast, are flinging desperately for the lead, as they make straight for the stream, and dash into it amid a cloud of spray.

"Give them room, gentlemen, do," shouted Will Long to the field, as his horse, pricking his ears and measuring the tide, was the first to sweep over, like a swallow on a summer's eye. Rivalry was running high, and the warning was little heeded by a couple of Heythrop thrusters, who, pressing too closely on Will's heels, gave their horses no chance of distinguishing the water lying on the bank from the real channel of the brook; consequently they floundered headlong into the flood; and, like the famous Brewers, immortalized by Mr. Egerton-Warburton, they very narrowly escaped "a watery *bier*."

Russell and Dauncey were more fortunate; the latter on a game little mare, well bred and stout as whalebone, and the other on old Charlie, taking it evenly in their strides, and landing together on the right side, a bowshot clear of the pack; while Lord Jersey, Sir Henry Peyton, Captain Evans, and Tom Wingfield—men whom nothing but the Styx itself could stop—were the only others well up, as the hounds, now all but mute and carrying a desperate head, were breaking the fence into the lower quarter of Gravenall Wood.

But the fox was sinking; and Will Long, acting as whip and huntsman in one (for Philip Payne, Stephen, and Griff Lloyd had not yet crossed the Rubicon), knew it full well, as he dashed over the cover fence and rang out the death-knell in a strain of ecstatic delight.

"Never before," said Russell, as he described the scene to an old friend, "never before had

I witnessed so glorious a run; and you may well imagine the pride I felt on finding myself in such good company. I could have hugged old Charlie on the spot! And as for Will Long, I looked upon him as something more than mortal—a demigod in disguise."

The Christ Church drag, consisting recently of four and a half couple of hounds with a bag of aniseed or a red herring for their fox, had, I believe, no existence in those days—at all events, I never heard Russell allude to it; but if such had existed, he certainly would have been the last man to join so spurious and questionable a sport. The love of orthodox hunting; the instinct of the hound in its fullest development; the science, in fact, so ably taught by such men as Philip Payne, Stephen Goodall, and Mr. John Codrington, had already taken so strong a hold of his mind and that of his contemporaries, that they were little likely to swerve from the faith and fall into such a heresy.

The use of the hound for the purpose of hunting a red herring was certainly never contemplated by Somerville when he penned—

> "The chase I sing, hounds and their various breed,
> And no less various use."

No! the poet's animated and fine verse applies only, as we know, to the chase of the stag, the fox, the otter, and the hare, those denizens of the stream and forest—the legitimate "beasts of venerie" in all ages. In any pack of Russell's, hunted by him during the last fifty years, the fate of a hound touching on such riot would have been quickly sealed; on returning to his kennel I can almost hear him say to old Will Rawle, his faithful and devoted henchman for forty years, "Will, that hound eats no more of my meal, mind that;" and the culprit would thenceforth disappear from the scene.

In less than ten years, however, after Russell had taken his degree, steeple-chasing, with its concomitant vice of heavy betting, became the popular amusement of the University; and about the same period the drag, established at Christ Church, provided an afternoon "grind" across country for the men, who either were unable to cut college lectures, or cared not a rush whether it was a fox or a red herring they rode after, so long as they had their "grind."

The line of country chosen for the drag was generally a stiff one, and the pace frequently a cracker from first to last, consequently the staying powers of every hack-hunter in Oxford were gauged to a pound; and bitter enough were the complaints of the stable-keepers at the beaten and maimed condition in which their horses were often brought home after a day with the drag.

"No, sir," said Squeaker Smith to a member of Christ Church, surnamed Hard-riding Dick, "no, sir, you ain't a-going to have a horse of mine again in a hurry for that drag; I picked thorns enough to make a crow's nest out of Woodman's legs the last time you rode him, and he never touched a grain of corn for a week afterwards. 'Tisn't hunting, nor 'tisn't hacking; but, to speak plainly, 'tis barbarous cruelty to a noble animal."

Smith was quite right; and Russell, had he been present, would have highly commended the humanity of his decision.

Russell had been in residence some fourteen terms, and was now, with a view to his final examination, busily employed in preparing for the schools and furbishing up his old Tiverton armour, which, he was not slow to discover, had grown somewhat rusty by habitual disuse and the easy conditions of his college life. His degree being of paramount importance to him, the short period that now remained for getting up his books was naturally accompanied by the inevitable doubt and anxiety, which even the ablest scholars are apt to feel at such a time.

It was on a glorious afternoon towards the end of May, when strolling round Magdalen meadow with Horace in hand, but Beckford in his head, he emerged from the classic shade of Addison's Walk, crossed the Cherwell in a punt, and passed over in the direction of Marston, hoping to devote an hour or two to study in the quiet meads of that hamlet, near the charming slopes of Elsfield, or in the deeper and more secluded haunts of Shotover Wood. But before he had reached Marston a milkman met him with a terrier—such an animal as Russell had as yet only seen in his dreams; he halted, as Actæon might have done when he caught sight of Diana disporting in her bath; but, unlike that ill-fated hunter, he never budged from the spot till he had won the prize and secured it for his own. She was called Trump, and became the progenitress of that famous race of terriers which, from that day to the present, have been associated with Russell's name at home and abroad—his able and keen coadjutors in the hunting-field. An oil-painting of Trump is still in existence, and is, I believe, possessed by H.R.H. the Prince of Wales; but as a copy, executed by a fair and talented artist, is now in my possession, and was acknowledged by Russell to be not only an admirable likeness of the original, but equally good as a type of the race in general, I will try, however imperfectly, to describe the portrait as it now lies before me.

In the first place, the colour is white with just a patch of dark tan over each eye and ear, while a similar dot, not larger than a penny piece, marks the root of the tail. The coat, which is thick, close, and a trifle wiry, is well calculated to protect the body from wet and cold, but has no affinity with the long, rough jacket of a Scotch terrier. The legs are straight as arrows, the feet perfect; the loins and conformation of the whole frame indicative of hardihood and endurance; while the size and height of the animal may be compared to that of a full-grown vixen fox.

"I seldom or ever see a real fox-terrier nowadays," said Russell recently to a friend who was inspecting a dog show containing a hundred and fifty entries under that denomination; "they have so intermingled strange blood with the real article, that, if he were not informed, it would puzzle Professor Bell himself to discover what race the so-called fox-terrier belongs to."

"And pray, how is it managed?" inquired the friend, eager to profit by Russell's long experience in such matters. "I can well remember Rubie's and Tom French's Dartmoor terriers, and have myself owned some of that sort worth their weight in gold. True terriers they were, but certainly differing as much from the present show dogs as the wild eglantine differs from a garden rose."

"The process," replied Russell, "is simply as follows: they begin with a smooth bitch terrier; then, to obtain a finer skin, an Italian greyhound is selected for her mate. But as the ears of the produce are an eyesore to the connoisseur, a beagle is resorted to, and then little is seen of that unsightly defect in the next generation. Lastly, to complete the mixture, the bulldog is now called on to give the necessary courage; and the composite animals, thus elaborated, become, after due selection, the sires and dams of the modern fox-terriers. This version of their origin," continued he, "I received from a man well qualified to speak on the subject."

The bulldog blood thus infused imparts courage, it is true, to the so-called terrier; he is matchless at killing any number of rats in a given time; will fight any dog of his weight in a Westminster pit; draw a badger heavier than himself out of his long box; and turn up a tom-cat possessed even of ten lives, before poor pussy can utter a wail. But the ferocity of that blood is in reality ill suited—nay, is fatal—to fox-hunting purposes; for a terrier that goes to ground and fastens on his fox, as one so bred will do, is far more likely to spoil sport than promote it; he goes in to kill, not to bolt, the object of his attack.

Besides, such animals, if more than one slip into a fox-earth, are too apt to forget the game, and fight each other, the death of one being occasionally the result of such encounters. Hence, Russell may well have been proud of the pure pedigree he had so long possessed and so carefully watched over. Tartars they were, and ever have been, beyond all doubt; going up to their fox in any earth, facing him alternately with hard words and harder nips, until at length he is forced to quit his stronghold, and trust to the open for better security.

A fox thus bolted is rarely a pin the worse for the skirmish; he has had fair play given him, and instead of being half strangled, is fit to flee for his life. The hounds, too, have their chance, and the field are not baulked of their expected run.

Russell's country is technically known as a hollow one; that is, a country in which rocky fastnesses and earths, excavated by badgers, abound in every direction. Consequently, on every hunting day a terrier or two invariably accompanied him to the field; and certainly no general ever depended with more trust on the services of an *aide-de-camp* than he on those of his terriers. If in chase they could not always live with the pack, still they stuck to the line, and were sure to be there or thereabouts when they were wanted, if the hounds threw up even for a minute.

"I like them to throw their tongue freely when face to face with their enemy," said

Russell one day, as he stood listening to his famous dog Tip, marking energetically in a long drain some six feet below the surface; "you know then where they are, and what they're about."

The late Earl Fitzhardinge, one of the finest sportsmen of his day, was wont to give a very similar reason for mounting his whips on confirmed roarers.

"I like to know where the beggars are," he would say; "for, with the bagpipes going, I can hear, if I don't see them, in the densest cover."

Entered early, and only at fox, Russell's terriers were as steady from riot as the staunchest of his hounds; so that, running together with them, and never passing over an earth without drawing it, they gave a fox, whether above ground or below it, but a poor chance of not being found, either by one or the other. A squeak from a terrier was the sure signal of a find, and there was not a hound in the pack that would not fly to it, as eagerly as to Russell's horn, or his own wild and marvellous scream.

This steadiness from riot was, of course, the result of early education on one object—the fox; nor did Russell consider it needful to train his terriers by progressive steps, according to the plan adopted by Dandie Dinmont.

"A bonny terrier that, sir; and a fell chiel at the vermin, I warrant him—that is, if he's been weel entered, for it a' lies in that."

"Really, sir," said Brown, "his education has been somewhat neglected, and his chief property is being a pleasant companion."

"Ay, sir! that's a pity, begging your pardon—it's a great pity, that—beast or body, education should aye be minded. I have six terriers at home; forbye twa couple of slow hounds, five grews, and a wheen other dogs. There's Auld Pepper and Auld Mustard, and Young Pepper and Young Mustard, and Little Pepper and Little Mustard. I had them a' regularly entered, first wi' rottens, then wi' stots or weasels, and then wi' the tods and brocks; and now they fear nothing that ever cam' wi' a hairy skin on't."

A hundred anecdotes might be related of the wondrous sagacity displayed in chase by Russell's terriers; but, as Tip's name has been already mentioned, one of his many feats will suffice to show, not merely the large amount of instinctive faculty, but the almost reasoning power with which that dog was endowed. Russell himself told me the story, as, some thirty years ago, in going to cover, he drew my attention to a deep combe not far from Lidcote Hall, the seat of Sir Hugh and the birthplace of poor Amy Robsart.

"Do you see," he said, "that dark patch of hanging gorse, hemmed in on the northern side by yonder knoll? Well, I've seen many a good run from that sheltered nook. On one occasion, however, I had found a fox which, in spite of a trimming scent, contrived to beat us by reaching Gray's Holts, and going to ground before we could catch him." Now those earths are fathomless and interminable as the Catacombs of St. Calixtus. They are so called 'Gray' from the old Devonshire name, signifying a badger, a number of those animals having long occupied that spot. Consequently such a fortress once gained is not easily to be stormed, even by Tip or the stoutest foe.

"Again, we found that fox a second time; and now, while the hounds were in close pursuit and driving hard, to my infinite surprise I saw Tip going off at full speed in quite a different direction."

"He's off, sir, to Gray's Holts; I know he is," shouted Jack Yelland, the whip, as he called my attention to the line of country the dog was then taking.

That proved to be the case. The fox had scarcely been ten minutes on foot when the dog, either by instinct, or, as I believe, by some power akin to reason putting two and two together, came to the conclusion that the real object of the fox was to gain Gray's Holts, although the hounds were by no means pointing in that direction. It was exactly as if the dog had said to himself: 'No, no! You're the same fox, I know, that gave us the slip once before; but you're not going to play us that trick again.'

"Tip's deduction was accurately correct; for the fox, after a turn or two in cover, put his nose directly for Gray's Holts; hoping, beyond a doubt, to gain that city of refuge once more, and then to whisk his brush in the face of his foes. But in this manœuvre he was fairly out-generalled by the dog's tactics. Tip had taken the short cut—the chord of the arc—and, as the hounds raced by at some distance off, there I saw him," continued Russell, "dancing about on Gray's Holts, throwing his tongue frantically, and doing his utmost, by noise and gesture, to scare away the fox from approaching the earths.

"Perfect success crowned the manœuvre: the fox, not daring to face the lion in his path, gave the spot a wide berth; while the hounds, carrying a fine head, passed on to the heather, and after a clinking run killed him on the open moor."

Tip scarcely ever missed a day for several seasons, and never appeared fatigued, though he occasionally went from fifteen to twenty miles to cover. He died at last from asthma in the Chorley earths, Russell having dug up to him and the fox in half an hour; but, to his master's great grief, the poor old dog was quite dead.

Russell looked upon his terriers as his fire-side friends—the *penates* of his home; nor was he ever happier than when to some congenial spirit he was recording the service they had done him in bygone days; and vast indeed was the store from which he drew so many interesting facts connected with their history.

One peculiarity of Tip's, however, must not be omitted: on a hunting morning no man on earth could catch him, after he had once seen Russell with his top-boots on.

Nettle, too, a prodigy of courage and sagacity, would follow no one but her master; and not even him, except the hounds were at his heels; knowing full well that her services were only required in connection with the hunting-field.

Then there was the one-eyed Nelson, a genius in his way; and in point of valour, a worthy namesake of England's immortal hero. Russell had run a fox to ground near Tetcott, the seat of Sir William Molesworth; but tiers of passages, one under the other, rendered the earth so perfect a honeycomb that the terriers were soon puzzled, nor did the diggers know what line to follow; there was scent everywhere. Nelson at length came out, and at some distance off commenced digging eagerly at the greensward: "Here's the fox," said Russell, "under Nelson's nose, or I'll forfeit my head." The dog went in again, and marking hard and sharp, under that very spot, the men broke ground and speedily came upon the fox. Russell then, with his arm bared, drew him forth; and setting him on his legs, treated his field to as merry a ten minutes over that wild country as man's heart could ever wish to enjoy.

## CHAPTER IV.

Is Ordained, and Licensed to his First Curacy—Keeps Otter-hounds at South Molton, and Hunts with Mr. Froude—Anecdotes of that Gentleman and Dr. Phillpotts, the late Bishop of Exeter.

---

Having resided the necessary number of terms required by the University, Russell entered the Schools for his final examination, declaring, as he crossed the awful Quadrangle, that he felt at that moment "very like Atlas, with a world of weight on his shoulders." However that might be, the stock of erudition he had acquired at Tiverton stood him again in good stead, and enabled him, with a very small amount of previous preparation, to sustain the ordeal bravely. His ambition did not prompt him to go up for honours, nor did his name appear in the class list; but, having satisfied the examiners and obtained his pass paper, he turned his back on the Bodleian Library with a grateful and joyous heart.

That night, in accordance with an old University custom, the happy event was celebrated with a grand supper; and if, during the orgies that followed, the toast of fox-hunting, given with nine times nine and three cheers more, did not effectually wake up the Dons, not only of Exeter, but of Lincoln and Jesus, they, too, must have swallowed a magnum of port, or they never could have slept through such a din.

Once more, before he quits the University, but this time with a light and elastic step, if not "with pride in his port," he crossed that same Quadrangle, where

> "Bacon's mansion trembles o'er his head,"

to put on his Bachelor's gown; and being soon afterwards nominated by the Rev. W. B. Stawell to the curacy of George Nympton — a rural parish, with a sparse population, near South Molton—he was ordained a deacon in 1819, and priest in the following year. George Pelham, then Bishop of Exeter, performed the ceremony, in the Chapel Royal, London, where, notwithstanding the long double journeys by coach, and the expenses incidental thereto—a serious tax on a salary of £60 a year—the young candidate was summoned to attend on each occasion.

"The railway between Exeter and London has been a great boon to me," said the late Bishop of Exeter to his son, Charles Phillpotts, "for by it not only do I save time, but I can now travel to town with the utmost comfort for a £5 note; whereas formerly, by sleeping a night in Bath, and posting it the whole way, it cost me £50, and much fatigue on every journey."

That still more primitive Churchman, the judicious Hooker, must have fared far worse than either of his clerical brethren, when he undertook a journey on foot from Oxford to Exeter, taking Salisbury on his way, to see his friend and patron, the good Bishop Jewel. The story is so quaintly told by that genial old fisherman, Izaak Walton, that I am tempted to quote the passage verbatim :—

"At the bishop's parting with him, the bishop gave him good counsel and his benediction, but forgot to give him money; which when the bishop had considered, he sent a servant in all haste to call Richard back to him; and at Richard's return, the bishop said to him, 'Richard, I sent for you back to lend you a horse, which hath carried me many a mile, and I thank God with much ease;' and presently delivered into his hand a walking-staff, with which he professed he had travelled through many parts of Germany. And he said, 'Richard, I do not give, but lend you my horse; be sure you be honest, and bring my horse back to me at your return this way to Oxford. And I do now give you ten groats to bear your charges to Exeter; and here is ten groats more, which I charge you to deliver to your mother, and tell her I send her a bishop's benediction with it, and beg the continuance of her prayers for me. And if you bring my horse back to me, I will give you ten groats more, to carry you on foot to the college; and so, God bless you, good Richard.'"

That Russell entered on the work of the ministry with a due sense of the sacred office and his own responsibility, will no doubt be charitably questioned by many, who have only heard of his fame in the hunting-field. But, if an ever-earnest readiness to visit the sick and world-weary; to administer consolation to all who needed it; to relieve the wants of his poorer brethren, however poor himself; to preach God's Word with the fervour, if not the eloquence, of a Bourdaloue; to plead in many a neighbouring pulpit, whenever invited to do so, the cause of charitable institutions, the funds of which never failed to derive substantial aid from his advocacy during a period of fifty years—if such things be of good report, and carry any weight, no human being can say of him—though he would be the first to say it of himself—that his mission as a Christian minister had been altogether that of an unprofitable servant.

It was on the 14th July, 1877, that Mr. Russell, verging on his 82nd year, received a letter from the Rev. A. E. Seymour, the vicar of Barnstaple, inviting him to come over and help him with a charity sermon, adding, "Mr. Wallas (the late vicar) tells me you preached for the Blue-Coat School in this town fifty years ago, and thinks you would be willing to do so again next September. This I hope may be the case, and I know that many of my parishioners are hoping so too."

Mr. Wallas also informs him that "the receipts on that occasion were more than they have ever been since, except once, when the late Bishop Phillpotts preached; and then his lordship's collection only exceeded yours by a few shillings."

That gifted bishop, it will be remembered, was second to no man of his day in point of powerful reasoning and persuasive eloquence; he had, too, the advantage of being a bishop—a dignitary formerly so seldom seen in those parts that the country people, according to Grose, in their eagerness to catch sight of him, left their milk-pans on the fire till the cream was "smitched," or, perhaps, burned; and hence the proverb, "The bishop has put his foot in it."

The public, doubtless, no longer extend to the clergy addicted to field sports the same toleration they were wont to show them in former times. Those times have, indeed, undergone a change; but, with latitudinarianism, if not infidelity, rampant on one side, and Ritualism on the other, sapping the very foundations of our noble Protestant Church, and creating a widespread menacing cry for its disestablishment, it may well be doubted if either the cause of pure religion or the social welfare of the country is likely to be benefited by recent changes.

For instance, there are clergymen amongst us in the present day notoriously taking the pay of one Church and doing the work of another. Members they are of a secret society—Jesuits, it may be, in disguise—who, with "The Priest in Absolution" in one hand, and a manual "for the young" in the other, are inculcating the necessity of confession on children at the tender age of six or six and a half years; thus soiling the infant mind with the foulest suggestions, outraging the first instincts of English nature, and, as Archbishop Tait said, "conspiring" against the doctrine, discipline, and practice of our Reformed Church.

The hunting parson is, at least, no "conspirator;" and if he stands true to the colours under which he enlisted, conscientiously endeavouring to do his duty so far as light is given him to do it, who shall cast a stone at him for accepting the exhilarating and innocent recreation which Nature has given him a taste for, and which the charms of the country invite him to enjoy?

The truth is, the spirit of the Pharisee is too apt to warp not only our judgment but our charity; that of the writer, it may be, on the subject of enforced confession, and certainly that of the public on the hunting parson. It is a common fault with men, as Butler quaintly says, to

> "Compound for sins they are inclined to
> By damning those they have no mind to."

If hunting in itself be no sin, then it is an innocent pastime; and if so, why, if their sacred duties be duly fulfilled, should clergymen be denied its enjoyment? Is it not an act of tyranny and asceticism to say to them, "You are free to boat, shoot, fish, play cricket or lawn-tennis, and ride—but not with hounds; no, that is a recreation you shall not share with your fellow men?"

But the French proverb which says, "*Qui s'excuse s'accuse*," must not be forgotten; and Russell himself would have been the last to admit the need of apology on such a point. He would have said what an old country clergyman, who had been scurrilously attacked for his love of the chase, said before him: "I only wish my hours of recreation had all been spent as happily and as innocently as in the hunting field; but point out to me the moral turpitude of hunting, and I'll never follow a hound again."

To be planted as a curate on £60 a year at George Nympton, and to vegetate like a cabbage among a scanty population, engaged chiefly in agricultural labour; to pass his days without one out-of-door occupation beyond that of paying an occasional visit to a suffering cottager or a busy farmer; to endure the solitude of an Eremite, compared with the lively, social scene he had so recently quitted, was a state of existence so little in accordance with the stirring aspirations of Russell's mind, that the want of "something to do" became almost torture to him.

Against books requiring close study his whole nature rebelled; they had too long been his bane, both at school and at college; and rather than be forced to read, he would almost have endured the pains of purgatory.

The God of Nature would surely never have given him that innate love for a sylvan life which possessed him even on entering the world; nor would He have blessed him with those eagle wings which have enabled him so long to enjoy it, if he had been intended for a recluse or a mere book-worm; for, as well might the spots of the bearded pard be expunged, as that instinct blotted out from Russell's nature.

He had been but a short time in harness at George Nympton when he was required by his rector, who was also the incumbent of South Molton, to undertake the weekly duty of that parish besides that of his own. With this request he readily complied; and settling at South Molton, that being a convenient centre for his double work, he fulfilled the duties of both parishes for a considerable period; and this, too, with no little amount of additional labour, but without additional pay.

Nevertheless, had the sphere of his duty been quadrupled, the parochial work alone would still have been utterly insufficient to supply a man of Russell's powers with full occupation of body and mind. The early habits of his life, his wondrous energy, his muscular frame, the strength and endurance of which no fatigue seemed capable of subduing; and, above all, that innate fire—his love, or, to call it by its right name, his passion for the chase—combined irresistibly to suggest a stronger exercise than any he could find from the due fulfilment of parochial labour, however great that might be. So to hounds he turned—the summit to him of earthly enjoyment and manly recreation.

To hunt the otter, of all beasts of venerie the least known and most inscrutable, was his first effort; and, for that purpose, a scratch lot of five or six couple of hounds were soon gathered from his neighbouring friends.

If, in adopting that particular recreation, his object were to keep his muscles in strong play, and at the same time to delight his eye with the beauties of Nature, so profusely lavished on the meads, the moors, and the combes of that picturesque country, he could scarcely have made a better choice. But, in all likelihood, the low condition of his exchequer, coupled with that innate impulse which prompted him to long for the company of hounds at all seasons of the year, had far more to do with it than a craving for mere bodily exercise or a love of scenery.

The hounds, it has been said, were a "scratch lot," and Russell, even then a somewhat experienced amateur, must have felt as little proud of them as Jack Falstaff did of the ragged scarecrows before whom he marched so unwillingly into the town of Coventry. However, if they had only fulfilled the adage of "handsome is that handsome does," he certainly would have been the last man to find fault with any amount of mere outward defects in size, shape, or comeliness of form.

But not so; there was not a hound amongst them that would touch a trail; not one that would come to a mark and give him the slightest clue to the whereabouts of the hidden game; indeed, both his patience and energy were well-nigh exhausted by the continuous difficulty of

OTTER-HUNTING.

holding them on a stream. Wander away they would, into every brake and cover on his line of march; and if perchance a fox or a hare could be raked up, from that moment farewell to the rioters and the chance of aquatic sport for the rest of the day.

"I walked three thousand miles," said Russell (the country-people must have taken him for Van Wodenblock), "without finding an otter; and although I must have passed over scores, I might as well have searched for a moose-deer."

In failing, however, to make the acquaintance of that animal, his long tramps in quest of him did not, in one respect, prove altogether profitless; for then it was he acquired that rare knowledge of his country which ever since has remained, like an Ordnance map, imprinted on his memory. In after years, on many a starless night, with many a long mile between him and his kennels, through ravines dark as Erebus, through fords flooded by storms, over the pathless moor, by bog, fell, and precipice, that knowledge did him good service, bringing him always, like the instinct of the carrier pigeon, safely to his home.

In clinging to the course of the rivers—a point of the first necessity in drawing for an otter—the scenery that met Russell's eye on every side must have mitigated, to some little extent, the daily chagrin he could not help feeling at not being able to find the game to blood his hounds. The farmers, too, that followed him, not getting their sport, would be sure to express their incredulity in the very existence of the animal; and the assurance that "they had never seed no sich varmint up their bottoms" must have frequently grated on his ears during that long and profitless walk of three thousand miles.

Still, he was walking through an Arcadia. The meads, full of flowers, rivalling "the mosaic of a Swiss meadow;" the woods and slopes, wild as fancy ever painted them; the hill-tops, clad with heather, bracken, and golden furze; the combes, luxuriant with a variety of ferns of exquisite form and beauty, the queenly Osmunda being among the number; and, to crown all, even the bogs and brooks, mantling with the forget-me-not, which, by its soft, turquoise hue, might lead one to imagine their whole surface was studded with those precious stones.

Then there was the water-ousel, now dipping, and now running in search of its food, even while submerged, among the pebbles and sands of the silvery streams; and, more beautiful still, the lustrous kingfisher, glancing past him like a living emerald on lightning wings.

These were treats of Nature which proved a perpetual feast to Russell's eye; but the word "beaten" was not to be found in his vocabulary; like Robert Bruce, the oftener he was defeated, the stronger grew his will to conquer, and although, as Barbour relates, that monarch was so hotly pursued by John of Lorn, his inveterate foe, till the echoes of Scotland did actually

> ". . . . ring
> With the bloodhounds that bayed for her fugitive king;"

still the Bruce persevered, and did conquer in the end.

So did Russell; but in a far more peaceful way. The change in the tide of his affairs took place thus: Mr. John Morth Woolcombe, of Ashbury, near Hatherleigh, kept at that time a fine pack of hounds, averaging twenty-three inches at the shoulder—foxhounds, in fact, they were, as high bred as those of Meynell, although it was his pleasure to pursue with them the timid hare only.

Russell, happening to meet with a farmer who kept hounds in the neighbourhood of Hatherleigh, and hunted indiscriminately fox, hare, and otter, discovered from him that a hound called Racer, drafted from Mr. Woolcombe's pack, had fallen into his hands, and, moreover, that he was either too fast or too mute for his own old-fashioned cry.

"Now," thought Russell, "here's my opportunity; Racer must at least know what an otter is, so I'll buy him if I can."

"Will you sell the hound?" inquired he, in an off-hand way.

"Certainly," said the farmer, "with all my heart; but I must first ask Mr. Woolcombe's permission to do so."

That permission being readily granted, Russell paid the farmer a guinea, the price he asked for him; and, well pleased with his bargain, he brought the hound back with him to South Molton. It turned out, afterwards, however, that Racer had only once before tasted the scent of an otter; still he loved it dearly, and oft have I heard Russell declare he was the best otter-hound he ever saw.

Now Racer, as Russell soon found, combined in himself the two-fold qualities especially required in an otter-hound; for though mute before the otter was found, he was nevertheless a good trail-hound, and a sound, persevering marker; the very animal needed to guide and instruct the unscientific corps under Russell's command. So from that day the scratch lot began to understand what manner of beast it was they were required to hunt.

Their education may be thus described: As soon as Racer hits upon a trail, though he does not speak, his action indicates his love of it so strongly that the rest of the pack no longer stray from the stream; then, as the scent improves under the shade of some dark, overhanging alder, here and there a hound chimes in and backs him up; till at length, attracted by the eager and persistent mark of their pilot, tearing at the otter's door and announcing him "at home," one and all unite in a wild chorus; and thus by degrees, after a few such lessons, followed by an occasional find and kill, Russell has the satisfaction of seeing the whole lot changed into a working and useful pack of otter-hounds.

Hitherto, Russell had himself only seen one otter killed, and that was by Mr. Cooke, of Uplowman, near Tiverton; but, after Racer became his property, he scored the death of thirty-five right off the reel; a boon for which every son of Zebedee in that county must have been duly grateful.

During the six years he kept these otter-hounds in South Molton, none of which were ever kennelled, but found each a welcome home before the fire of an inhabitant, twenty couple at least passed through his hands, not one of which could ever be induced to touch the scent of an otter.

It is quite clear, however, that Russell did not at first know what age and experience afterwards taught him, namely, that the scent of the otter is not one to which hounds, of their own accord, will naturally stoop; but he might well have guessed it by the result of that fruitless leg-labour to which he patiently resigned himself for so long a time.

It is a curious fact that the veriest cur, the first time he crosses the line of a deer, will drop his nose and carry the scent as instinctively as a blind puppy will hunt for the teat of its dam. It requires, too, as every one knows, but little persuasion to induce hounds to enter at fox and hare; simply because those animals are their natural prey. But not so with the otter, the scent of which, until he is trained to it, appears to have little or no attraction for the nose of a young hound. Indeed, let a whole pack, however well trained, find an old otter in moderately strong water, and if left entirely to themselves, and man's hand and eye give them no aid, the chances of a kill, except by accident, will in every case be dead against the hounds.

It may fairly be inferred, therefore, from the unreadiness of hounds in first taking to the scent, as well as from the all but insuperable difficulty of killing the animal without supplementary aid, that Nature never intended the otter to be an object of prey for hounds; and that, in fact, the sport is to them an artificial one from beginning to end.

Nevertheless the otter is a really wild beast; his efforts to escape, when put down, are marvellously clever; the hounds become very fond of the scent, and the sport he shows, if given fair play, no pen can adequately describe. But it lasts only for a season of four short months, and it will be asked what, by way of recreation and congenial exercise, did Russell find to do during the other eight of the year.

The answer will, of course, be anticipated. He hunted whenever he had the chance of doing so. At that time, and for many years afterwards, a rare pack of hounds were kept in the neighbourhood by the Rev. John Froude, of Knowstone, a man better known, perhaps, in the western counties, for his utter disregard of episcopal, and, indeed, of all human authority, than even for the celebrity of his hounds. With him and his pack, then, Russell managed to hunt on every available occasion; enjoying to his heart's content both the sport and hospitality which Froude never failed to show him, and tiding over the winter season in a very happy way.

A fine, wild country was that in which the vicar of Knowstone took his pastime; but especially that portion extending towards East and West Anstey and Molland Down; a land of heath, bracken, and furze, with moors "immeasurably spread" in every direction.

Knowstone and South Molton, where Russell then lived, are, more or less, about ten miles apart; but as now, so then, whenever the hounds met, whether on his side of the country or on the other, neither the most inclement weather nor the longest distance to cover seemed ever to cause him a moment's hesitation.

In a letter Russell addressed to an old friend, he says:—

"My head-quarters at that time were at South Molton; and I hunted as many days in every week as my duties would permit with John Froude, the well-known vicar of Knowstone, with whom I was then on very intimate terms.

"His hounds were something out of the common; bred from the old staghounds—light in their colour, and sharp as needles—plenty of tongue, but would drive like furies. I have never seen a better or more killing pack in all my long life. He couldn't bear to see a hound put his nose on the ground and 'twiddle his tail.' 'Hang the brute,' he would say to the owner of the hounds, 'and get those that can wind their game when they are thrown off.'

"Froude was himself a first-rate sportsman; but always acted on the principle of 'kill un, if you can; you'll never see un again.'

"I saw him once shoot a hare sitting near a farmhouse where his hounds met on the following day; and where, of course, they did *not* find. He hunted on three days of the week, and shot on the others, when he could walk most men off their legs. I never saw him with a rod and line in his hand; but he was very expert with nets on land or in water. He was the most original man I ever met with. He had an old liver-coloured spaniel called Crack, a wide ranger, but under perfect command. He used to say he could hunt the parish with that dog from the top of the church tower. You could hear his view-halloa for miles; and his hounds absolutely flew to him when they heard it. Let me add, his hospitality knew no bounds."

This last tribute to Mr. Froude's memory will remind many a west-countryman of a story which, among the hundred and one related of him, described the reception he is said to have given to his Diocesan, the late Lord Bishop of Exeter. Week after week sundry newspapers had been publishing articles of the most scurrilous description, headed "Knowstone again;" the burden of which reflected on Froude's mode of life and the lawless acts perpetrated in that parish. These, of course, never failed to reach the bishop's eye; consequently the stout-hearted prelate, always a friend to be depended on when his clergy were, as he thought, unfairly assailed, summoned Mr. Froude to appear at the palace, and explain the grave charges thus publicly brought against him.

But neither did Froude obey the summons, nor would he give the bishop a chance of wigging him by attending his visitations; so, like Mahomet and the mountain, the bishop determined to go to him; a course which, short of legal proceedings, was the only one now open to him.

Accordingly, on a bitter winter's morning, the bishop, conveyed by a post-chaise from Tiverton, arrived at Knowstone vicarage, and having inquired if Mr. Froude were at home, was told he was, on hearing which he entered the house.

After a short delay in the cold guest-chamber, the bishop was shown into another apartment, where sat Mr. Froude before a comfortable fire, his head muffled in flannel and his voice apparently as hoarse as that of a carrion crow.

"I've come to see you, Mr. Froude," commenced the bishop, "to inquire if——"

"Oh, yes, my lord; 'tis cold work, sure enough, travelling over our moors; but do 'ee take a glass of hot brandy-and-water, 'twill keep off the shivers when nought else will."

Then, in spite of the bishop's protestations that he needed no alcohol, especially in the morning, Froude rang the bell and ordered a glass of brandy-and-water to be mixed forthwith, "hot and strong for the bishop."

Again his lordship positively declined the stimulant, and endeavoured to explain the object of his visit; but Froude, apparently not hearing a word he had uttered, cut him short by saying, "It's my only doctor, my lord, is a drop of brandy; and if I had but taken it when I got my chill I shouldn't now be as I be, deaf as a haddock, and nursing this fire like an old woman."

The bishop would hear no more; but making him a grave bow, took his leave, entered his carriage, and returned whence he came. In ten minutes from that time, so goes the story, Froude was seen to mount his horse and trot away in company with his hounds.

> "I cannot tell how the truth may be;
> I say the tale as 'twas said to me."

Russell, however, who knew Froude's sayings and doings better than any man living, and was wont, like Yorick, "to set the table on a roar" when throwing his tongue on that lively subject, maintained that if the bishop had invaded Froude's domain a dozen times the result would have been precisely the same; but that he only went once to Knowstone, and then, being admitted for a few minutes, beat a hasty retreat, and escaped from the house much faster than he entered it.

This is the story as Russell told it:—

"The bishop at length was determined to have an interview with Froude, and as his lordship was staying at the time with, I believe, that pattern of a country gentleman, Tom Carew, of Collipriest, he ordered a pair of horses from Cannon and started for Knowstone with that object in view.

"By some intuition, however, peculiar to himself, Froude suspected that such an event might occur, and at once set to work to frustrate the bishop's design. He stationed a signalman within hail of his house, on the only road leading to it from Tiverton, giving him orders, if he saw a chaise and pair travelling towards the vicarage, to hasten thither and sound the alarm.

"Accordingly, when the bishop did appear, Froude and his household were not only apprised of his approach, but duly prepared for his reception.

"'Can I see Mr. Froude?' inquired his lordship, in that mild, measured tone which he habitually adopted when he meant to carry his point. 'Be good enough to say the Bishop of Exeter wishes to have a few words with him.'"

"'Please to walk in, my lord,' replied the old housekeeper, Jane, who had gone to the door, and would have gone to the stake to serve her master. 'Mr. Froude is at home, but is up abed wi' some ailment or other.'"

"'Nothing serious, I hope?' said the bishop, taking a seat in the state apartment; and if so, I daresay he would not object to see *me* at his bedside.'

"Jane paused for a moment, and then, with some hesitation, replied, 'Perhaps not, my lord: leastwise, if you bean't afeered o' going there. 'Tis a faver o' some soart, but I can't mind what the doctor call'th it.'

"The bishop cocked his ear and looked uneasy. 'A fever, did you say? Rheumatic, perhaps, from exposure to wet?'

"'No, no; I've got that myself bad enough. 'Tis something a deal worse, I reckon.'

"'Not scarlet fever, I hope?'

The housekeeper shook her head despondingly. 'Worse than that, my lord.'

"'Typhus?' inquired the bishop, no longer able to hide his look of alarm.

"'Iss, that's it; seem'th to me that's what the doctor ca'd it. 'Tis a whisht job, fai.'

"The bishop clutched his hat, and with little ceremony took his departure; and although he announced his intention of repeating his visit at a more convenient season, he never again set foot in the parish of Knowstone.

"When the bishop had fairly disappeared," Russell adds, "Froude put on his long gaiters and went out hunting for the rest of the day."

"I told 'ee so, Jack; I know'd he'd come," he said to Russell the first time he met him after that event. "But there, he's never likely to come again; the air of Knowstone's too keen for him, I reckon."

Though an athlete in intellect, the bishop, according to Russell, was no match for Froude in those minor tactics, the success of which depended on manœuvre and finesse; in that line he could have beaten Machiavelli himself. His lordship, it is said, met Froude one day with a greyhound, commonly known in Devonshire as "a long-dog," walking by his side: "And pray, Mr. Froude," said the bishop, with a courteous, but restrained air, "what manner of dog may you call that?"

"Oh! that's what we call a lang-dog, my lord; and if yeu was on'y to shak' yeur appern to un, he'd go like a dart."

The idea of that dignified and ceremonious prelate shaking his apron, like an old woman, to frighten the dog, is so ludicrous that, if it did not beget even in his eye a twinkle of mirth, he must have struggled hard to restrain it.

Russell's anecdotes of Froude would fill a volume; but to produce a tithe of them in these pages would be to give the latter undue prominence in the present memoir. Besides, however pointed anecdotes may be if told by a racy tongue like Russell's, still, when written, they are very apt to meet the reader's eye with a lifeless and blunted effect.

There can be little doubt that the friendship and example of a man like the vicar of Knowstone did not only influence Russell at the very outset of his professional career, but, in all likelihood, biassed the whole course of his after life. To a young man, socially inclined and fond of hunting, the attraction of Froude's company must have been irresistible; for Froude was witty, original, hospitable; and, moreover, exercised a kind of mysterious power, such as men of strong will are known to possess, over those with whom he associated. Above all, he had a crack pack of hounds, and was himself, as Russell described him, a "first-rate sportsman."

This rare quality, had he possessed no other fascination, would have been alone sufficient to charm Russell's heart; ay, and to lead him, as it did from that day forth, into a willing and life-long captivity.

# CHAPTER V.

THE TEIGNBRIDGE CRICKET CLUB AND THE PARTY AT STOVER—MR. GEORGE TEMPLER AND THE "LET-'EM-ALONES"—THE "BOLD DRAGOON," "NUNKY," AND THE REV. HENRY TAYLOR.

> Whate'er the stranger's caste or creed,
> Pundit or Papist, saint or sinner;
> He found a stable for his steed,
> And welcome for himself, and dinner.
>
> WINTHROP M. PRAED.

During the next six years of his life, that is, from 1819 to 1825, Russell still continued to reside at South Molton; doing his work as a curate to the satisfaction of his parishioners; and, when off duty, rarely missing a day in the winter season, either with the hounds of his attractive neighbour, Mr. Froude, of Knowstone, or with the far-famed pack of Mr. Templer, of Stover; where, come when he would, he was at all times sure to find a hearty welcome and the best of company.

Those six years may fairly be termed the period of his final apprenticeship in woodcraft; for, soon afterwards we find him in the responsible position of an M.F.H., playing, it is true, a somewhat uphill game, but still adhering with unflinching tenacity to that sylvan groove which

Nature apparently had formed him to fill, and from which he never deflected throughout the long course of an eventful life.

During the summer season, however, another out-of-door recreation, besides that of otter-hunting, appears to have provided him, so long as he indulged in it, with strong exercise and a pleasant pastime. It was the game of cricket; which, although established at Lord's by the Marylebone Club so far back as 1787, had taken many a year to travel into Devonshire, where it is doubtful if it became generally played before 1823 or 1824. The up-and-down character of the country, in which it would be difficult in scores of parishes to find a perfectly level field, might have been some reason for its long-deferred introduction into that county. Be that as it may, there are no records to show that the noble game of cricket became an institution in Devon before the 18th of May, 1824, when a club was formally established at Teignbridge, that locality being admirably adapted for the purpose, the play-ground being level as a die, and conveniently near to the houses of several of its most prominent members.

Russell attended the first meeting, held in a "linhay" or cowshed, on that occasion; played in the first game; and, with two of his brothers, was constituted an honorary member of the club on its natal day. But whatever his qualifications might have been, it cannot be said that he afterwards became an ardent cricketer; nor is it related of him by his contemporaries that he ever distinguished himself, either as a good "field," batsman, or bowler. His thoughts, in fact, were still on hounds intent; the ruling passion had sole possession of him, and he could no more have devoted his energy to cricket than to a game of marbles.

The Rev. Henry Taylor, of West Ogwell, the Rev. John Templer and his elder brother, Mr. George Templer, of Stover, were members; the former having been chosen as president, and the latter as vice-president of the newly-formed Club. Mr. Templer, a gentleman of brilliant intellect and most charming manner, had for some time previously established at Stover a pack of dwarf fox-hounds, averaging nineteen inches at the shoulders, with which he hunted, when he had the luck to find him, the real wild article; but, when a blank was apprehended, a bagman, which, always at hand, was turned down in view of the hounds.

The system was a novel one, hitherto unpractised in this or any other country; but the sport shown and the hard riding it gave rise to, owing to the habit of saving the fox alive, when the hounds had fairly run up to him, will be remembered in the county so long as Heytor

Rock looks down on any one survivor of Templer's friends. At least a score of foxes were kept within two spacious yards expressly for this purpose; and as they were attached, each one to its separate coop, by a long chain revolving on a swivel, they were able to take plenty of exercise and keep themselves in good wind; the gallop of the animals, like that of a horse in a circus, being sometimes accelerated by a light tandem-whip handled by a groom. Of the stoutness of one, yclept the "Bold Dragoon," I have heard both Templer and Taylor relate some stirring tales; he had been turned out thirty-six times, had generally led them a long dance, and never failed to enjoy a fresh rabbit for supper on safely returning to his kennel home.

When Mr. Templer parted with his pack, in 1826, a lot of the larger hounds went to the Rev. H. F. Yeatman, of Stock House, Dorsetshire; while the lesser, including the far-famed "Let-'em-alones" (the bag-fox pack), were dispersed throughout the country; Sir Henry Carew, Mr. Hammett Drake, Mr. Worth, of Worth, Mr. Hole, of Georgeham, and others, having purchased the whole of them in separate lots. From these precious relics, as they were speedily discovered to be, many couples were subsequently secured and brought together by the united efforts of Russell, and his coadjutor, Mr. Arthur Harris, of Hayne; and formed the nucleus of that famous pack which showed such unexampled sport over the Tetcott and Pencarrow countries in 1828-30; a wild moorland district extending from Torrington to Bodmin, in Cornwall, unquestionably the finest hunting-ground in the West of England.

Thirty odd years have drifted away on the stream of time since the genial and big-hearted George Templer was carried to his last ancestral home at Teigngrace; but it will interest the reader to know something more of the man who is acknowledged to have been Russell's chief Gamaliel, and whose hunting-horn, as Mr. Harris tells us, "passed so worthily to his apt and favourite pupil."

Templer's hospitality at Stover literally knew no bounds. The company, too, he selected for his guests were for the most part men of standing in the county—Worthies of Devon—the bare fact of their being sportsmen, as well as gentlemen, being the "open sesame" to Templer's heart.

"A Party at Stover in 1823," written in elegant verse by the gifted host, includes, for instance, the names of no less than four guests who were subsequently Masters of Foxhounds in his own or the adjoining county of Cornwall: namely, those of Sir William Salusbury Trelawny; Mr. John King, of Fowelscombe; Mr.

John Crocker Bulteel, of Flete, Russell's first antagonist at Plympton School; and that of John Russell, then, however, a Master of Otter-hounds only.

Sitting at Templer's ample board, it may well be imagined how Russell, if no wine-bibber, still drank in and enjoyed, to his heart's content, those racy draughts of hunting lore, of which his host possessed so copious a supply; and which he (Russell) profited by so largely in after years. He must have felt, as he would himself have said, "up to his hocks in clover" among such company.

Templer's power over fox-hounds, governed more by kindness than the lash, delighted his eyes; so unique was the system of discipline and control with which they were managed, even in the presence of a fox. "His mode of tuition," writes Mr. Harris, "was so perfect that each hound comprehended every inflexion of his voice; every note of his horn was intelligible to them, and conveyed a full meaning; and to the wave of his hand an instant obedience was given that required neither rate nor sterner discipline to urge. He was ably seconded by his friends and assistants, the late Mr. Harry Taylor and Mr. Russell; and perhaps there never was exhibited a greater perfection of hunting, of scientific control over hounds, and of skill in eliciting their utmost powers of chase and hunting, than was afforded by the establishment of Stover, under the superintendence of this memorable triumvirate."

When a bagman was about to be turned out it was always done in view of the hounds, Templer standing among them with his hunting-watch open in hand; nor would a hound attempt to stir till fair law had been allowed, and the last word of the signal, "One, two, away!" bid them to the chase. A hound, called "Guardsman," had become so very knowing at the work that, instead of looking after the fox, he kept his eye fixed on the watch; and, the moment he saw the case closed, away he went, like an arrow from a bow.

The business then was to save the fox alive; and, whether he were a wild fox or a bagman, such was the hard riding and such the obedience of the hounds to a rate, that, nine times out of ten, the animal was picked up before them, without a hair of his skin being broken. Blood was a finale to which, at home, they were never treated, and yet a harder-driving lot never entered a cover. But as Nimrod, after his visit at Stover, tells us, "To show that Mr. Templer's hounds can kill foxes when suffered to do so, it may not be amiss to mention that whilst they were at North Molton, for the purpose of hunting alternate days with Mr. Fellowes's or Sir Arthur Chichester's hounds, at the Chulmleigh Club, they killed three brace of foxes in four days."

And those foxes, be it observed, were the wild moorland tartars, bred in the rough country surrounding Exmoor.

Under a tutor, then, so well qualified to instruct him in the countless mysteries of the "noble science," it would, indeed, have been a wonder if Russell, so fashioned by Nature for the chase, had not fulfilled to the utmost the expectations with which he was then credited by so able and experienced a master. That he did not disappoint him, the world will bear strong witness in the pupil's favour.

Nimrod, who was fortunate in meeting both the Rev. Henry Taylor and Russell at Stover, has left us the following brief sketch of those two men:—

"There is one gentleman who is a constant attendant on Mr. Templer's hounds, a very fine horseman over a country, and, report says, quite the clipper of the West. This is the Rev. Henry Taylor. There is another gentleman of the same cloth, the Rev. John Russell (but much better known by the name of 'Jack Russell'), who, though he resides about thirty miles from him, hunts a good deal with Mr. Templer, and who also stands high among the Devonshire bruisers. This gentleman finds hunting so conducive to his health, that with stag-hounds, fox-hounds, harriers, and otter-hounds, he contrives to enjoy it all the year round. The last-mentioned pack are kept by himself; and he has killed the almost incredible number of twenty-five otters in the last two summers, for which he should receive the thanks of the fish! Each of these gentlemen spent the evening with us at Mr. Templer's, and added much to its conviviality and pleasure."

Where all were welcome, it would be almost invidious to single out one as the most favoured and constant guest of the Stover party; but, in truth, Henry Taylor of Ogwell—the boy known at Eton as Ninth Harry—was that man. But for him, on his famous horse Nunky, the career of the "Bold Dragoon" would have been cut short very early in the day, and his dark hide converted into "a hundred tatters of brown;" for a finer horseman or a nobler man never followed a hound; and he it was who almost invariably contrived to save the life of that gallant fox.

On one occasion, however, both he and Nunky nearly came to serious grief, and narrowly escaped with their lives. The anecdote was first told me by Mr. George Templer, and afterwards confirmed by Taylor himself; whose natural modesty and true nobility of soul, though I had the honour of knowing him intimately for nearly a quarter of a century, would never permit him to tell me a tale in which he himself figured as the hero.

The "Bold Dragoon" had been turned out in the Vale of Teigngrace; and crossing the River Teign, then flooded by heavy rains, was leading the pack at a rattling pace in the direction of Ugbrook Park, when the whole field were brought to a sudden check at sight of the "brimming river."

The ford, known to a few, was now invisible, and the only bridge, more than a mile away, seemed too far to be available. What then was to be done? The fate of the "Bold Dragoon" was a certainty, if there were no one up to rate the hounds; and his Colossus mare was scarcely more valued by Templer than that fox.

"Go for Jew's bridge," shouted a cautious member of the hunt; "that's our only chance for catching the hounds:" and away went the field helter-skelter in that direction; every man of them except Taylor.

Seeing a flight of rails close to the river bank, and concluding they were placed there to prevent cattle from crossing the ford, Taylor rode his horse straight at them, thinking to land him, perhaps, up to his girths on dropping into the stream. But, alas! the spot proved to be one of the deepest pools in the Teign river: the horse and rider disappeared; but the latter, having been an expert swimmer at Eton, soon came to the surface, and, striking out vigorously, gained the opposite bank in safety. But now, great was his dismay on looking round, to find that Nunky was nowhere to be seen; not a wave nor a gurgle indicated his whereabouts below; and, for some seconds, Taylor felt assured the horse had been stunned, and had gone down like a stone to the bottom.

Happily he was wrong; as the hoofs first, and then the legs of the animal, gradually appeared above water; and then, as the body grounded about twenty yards below on the gravelly ford, which Taylor had failed to hit, he discovered that his horse's fore-legs had been caught by the reins, and that every time he struck out he jerked his own head under water.

To plunge again into the whirling stream, to unclasp his knife, cut the reins, and take a pull at Nunky's head, was the work of a second, when the brave beast jumped on his legs, and after a few sobs to clear out his pipes, Taylor vaulted into the saddle and dashed off in pursuit of the hounds.

A fever he had caught at Eton had utterly destroyed the hair of his head, and consequently he always wore a sandy-coloured wig, made by that eminent artist, Mr. Piper, of Exeter. His wig and hat, however, were carried to sea, while he was discovered scudding away under bare poles,

"Taking hedges for billows and mountains for seas;"

nor, like the moss-trooper of old, did he slacken his rein or "stint to ride," till he had picked up the fox and bagged him alive.

I drew the story out of the dear old fellow over a bottle of port wine in his sanctum at South Poole, when he added, "It's quite true, but Templer didn't tell you all. On crossing the Newton road I met an old woman, and tossing her a shilling she handed me her blue flannel apron which I wrapped round my head, and thus turbaned, rode like a grand Turk to the end of the run."

Such was the man and such the horse of whose deed Templer wrote in a strain of the truest admiration :—

"Fearless and first Ninth Harry urged his course,
Charging the fences with resistless force ;
Poor Nunky pays for all, a friend indeed
So good a Nunky proves in time of need."

That uncle was Mr. Edward Cooke, who, sometime Under-Secretary of State for Ireland during the administration of Lord Castlereagh, gave him the horse.

But to return to the Teignbridge Cricket Club: that Russell took no active interest in the game may be inferred from the fact that, notwithstanding the high popularity to which the Club soon attained in the county, he ceased to be a member of it early in the day. The ground, it is true, was at a long distance from his home at South Molton, some thirty-five or forty miles away; but had he really loved the game, that distance would certainly not have been an impediment to which he would have given a moment's thought.

The Club, however, had already done him good service; it had brought him into friendly association not only with the Stover party, but with many influential men connected with that side of the county. At the death of one of its best players, and certainly one of its most valued members, the Rev. Henry Taylor, his bat, carrying like Curius Dentatus the marks of many a hard-fought tussle on its battered front, was presented to the Club by his late widow, and being elevated to a niche of honour in the banqueting-room, received from the pen of a loving friend the following inscription:—

Hail, honoured relic of the manly fame
By Taylor won at every noble game!
Some gentle stream may haply mourn the tree*
That decked its margin, ere it fell for thee;
But deeper far Teignbridge laments the day,
When that stout arm was turned again to clay:
Relic, alas! thy gladsome work is done,
Death is the bowler, and the game is won:
But rest thou here, still eloquent to tell
The grief of those who loved the man so well.

E. W. L. Davies.

* It may not be generally known that cricket-bats are made from the willow tree.

The hunting men, however, with whom Russell associated at Teignbridge, brilliant riders and first-class sportsmen as a few of them were, constituted but a small portion of the party who met at Stover to enjoy Mr. Templer's hospitality, and hunt with his hounds. The following gentlemen, fellow-sportsmen with Russell, the remembrance of whom will long be cherished in the county of Devon, are notably mentioned in the spirited verses to which allusion has already been made.

First on the list comes Mr. John King, of Fowelscombe, "John King of the West," an able sportsman, who, according to Russell, knew the habits of a fox better than most men of his day. After hunting a portion of Mr. Pode's country in Devon, Mr. King became Master of the Hambledon Hounds, and subsequently, while following Mr. Trelawny's pack, died in the saddle on Dartmoor.

2. Mr. John Crocker Bulteel, of Flete, the originator of the Lyneham Pack, afterwards so famous under the mastership of Mr. Trelawny. Besides being a keen sportsman, Mr. Bulteel's genius was one of the highest order, and the sallies of wit, which, like the sparkling brooks of his native country, flowed so pleasantly from his tongue, must have made the very rafters of Stover ring with merriment. In such company whether in the field or at "table-board,"

good-fellowship and sport must have reigned supreme.

3. Mr. Thomas Bulteel, the "spruce little cousin" of Mr. J. C. Bulteel, a light-weight and a bold rider, whom, when hounds were running hard, no timber could stop, no fence dismay.

4. Mr. Paul Ourry Treby, of Goodamoor, the well-known "fox-hunter, rough and ready," a classic scholar, and a rare specimen of a high-minded English gentleman.

5. Mr. Salusbury Trelawny, afterwards Sir William S. Trelawny, a lineal descendant of Jonathan Trelawny, Bishop of Bristol, who, with six other prelates, was sent to the Tower by King James the Second; an act that gave rise to the patriotic song still sung by Cornishmen with unabated enthusiasm, a verse of which runs thus:

> "And have they fixed the where and when?
> And shall Trelawny die?
> Then twenty thousand Cornishmen
> Shall know the reason why!"

Of Sir William and a hound of his, called Whirligig, Mr. Arthur Harris, of Hayne, records the following interesting anecdote:—

"According to tradition Whirligig was an extraordinary hound in every way, and it is said that he could kill a fox single-handed. Certain it is that both the hound and his master performed feats that old men still love to chronicle.

On one occasion, the story goes, Salusbury Trelawny had brought his fox, late in the day and nearly at nightfall, to a point on the Tamar below Newbridge. The river was swollen and rapid, and it was judged impossible for a fox to have swum such a distance in so rapid a stream. Salusbury Trelawny thought otherwise, so did Whirligig, and neither were of a temper to be diverted from their purpose. Getting into a small boat, he rowed over to the other side, sitting in the stern and holding the bridle of his hunter, Cattern or Lufra, lightly in hand, while the mare and the hound—both animals attached in a singular degree to their chivalrous master—crossed together, swimming side by side. Not a hound followed. Whirligig recovered the line on the other side, killed the half-drowned fox, and master, hound, and horse, with the head and brush, returned the way they came. Brave 'Old Sarum!' he was indeed a glorious fellow: he and Newton Fellowes were samples of the '*genus homo*' not easily to be found in a modern day."

In addition to the names already mentioned, nine other guests are severally described as forming the

> " . . . . party assembled at Stover
> To hunt in the morning, and feast when 'twas over."

They were the Rev. Edward Clarke, of St. Dominick, Mr. George Leach, the Rev. John

Templer, Mr. William and Erving Clark, of Buckland Tout-Saints, Mr. Charles Gandy, Mr. Henry Twysden, R.N., Mr. John Lyne Templer, of Highland House, and Captain J. Avern, R.N.

Alas! to Death's grim Ferryman all, including the subject of this memoir, have been summoned to pay their last copper!

# CHAPTER VI.

He Falls in Love—Rides by Night to Bath—His Grotesque Mount in Milsom Street—Is Married, and removes to Iddesleigh—Keeps Foxhounds, and forms an Alliance with Mr. C. A. Harris—Difficulties with Fox-killers.

> Without the smile from partial beauty won,
> Oh! what were man? a world without a sun!
>
> Campbell.

Towards the end of 1825, or the beginning of 1826, an event affecting the happiness of Russell's life, at home and abroad, bid fair, at least, for a time, to imperil the devotion which, up to this period, he had so exclusively shown to the sylvan Queen, who beyond all doubt hitherto had reigned in his heart without a rival.

But strong and enduring as the bonds were in which the goddess retained her willing captive, the time had now arrived when they were destined to prove but as green withs compared with those of Venus, whose power both the gods and men have alike shown to be irresistible.

About this time he met with a lady whose attractions at once arrested the current of his thoughts, and brought him on bended knee to sue for her hand. That lady was Miss Penelope Incledon Bury, the daughter of Admiral and Mrs. Bury, of Dennington House, near Barnstaple. Both the father and mother being pure North-Devoners, and claiming descent from two good old county families, they were proud of the "haveage" to which they belonged. Nor could they have taken exception to Russell's pedigree; he himself being a descendant of the Russells of Kingston-Russell; for, at the time of the Sampford Courtenay riots in the West, Lord Russell, then at Exeter, appointed one of his own relatives to preach against "the old religion;" and from him came the Russells who have remained in the county ever since.

Mrs. Bury, the mother of Penelope, was of the knightly family of Chichester, of Hall, whose pedigree is chronicled by John Prince, the worthy Vicar of Berry Pomeroy.

If Russell, then, had an eye to a "lass wi' a lang pedigree"—a point he would have considered of the first importance in selecting a horse or a hound—he could scarcely have made a better choice. But it is obvious that other and broader views must have influenced his judgment in this matter; for a more sensible, warm-hearted, generous woman than Penelope Bury proved herself to be, never breathed the breath of life. Russell must have stood an inch higher in stature when he found himself first favourite for so fair a prize—the only real prize in life he may, with truth, be said to have ever won.

But the event should not be anticipated. When Mr. George Templer, of Stover, parted with his big pack to the Rev. H. F. Yeatman, in the early part of 1826, Russell and Templer paid him a visit at Stock House, near Sherborne; when, under his inauguration, the Blackmoor Vale country was first established. To entertain his friends, whether indoors or out of doors—a felicitous gift he possessed beyond ordinary mortals—Mr. Yeatman ordered out his own famous pack of harriers (which, by-the-bye, were dwarf fox-hounds, as perfect in shape as they were in work), and showed them a capital day's sport; when the hare was sinking, Russell, to save her, put his horse at a chained gate, rode over it, and picked up the hare in front of the hounds.

Nearly fifty years after that event, Mr. Digby of Sherborne Castle, finding himself in company with Russell at, I believe, Lord Poltimore's house in Dorsetshire, asked him if he remembered the first time they met in the hunting-field?

"Perfectly well," replied Russell; "it was with dear old Yeatman's hounds in 1826; the first time Templer and I stayed with him at Stock House."

"Quite true," replied Mr. Digby; "you rode over a chained gate, and took up the hare before me. I could have shot you on the spot."

"You'd have spoiled some sport if you had," said Russell not a little amused that the incident, and youthful jealousy it had given rise to, should be remembered after the lapse of so many years.

That very night, after the dinner and day's sport had been duly discussed, Russell mounted a hack, one he had brought with him from South Molton, and, starting from Stock, he shaped his course, as he best could, directly for Bath, hoping to reach that city, a distance of some fifty odd miles, before the inns and stables were all closed for the night. At Warminster, however, he found it expedient to leave his own horse behind him and hire a fresh one, the landlord of the principal inn being quite ready to supply him with "a rare goer," which he averred "would carry him like an infant in a cradle, and cover the ground in less than two hours."

"Bring him out, then," said Russell, "as quickly as you can; that will suit me exactly."

The night was now pitch dark; not a moon nor a star in the sky; not a ray of light, except that from a dim horn-lantern, enabling Russell to distinguish the head from the tail of the horse on which he was about to mount. However, he was soon in the saddle; the beast, too, was a willing one, being probably, like John Gilpin's horse,

> ". . . . right glad to miss
> The lumb'ring of the wheels;"

but never before nor since did Russell undergo such a bumping as on the ribs of that Warminster hack.

On his arrival at Bath, long after midnight, happily for him one hostelry still remained open, the White Lion Inn; where, finding he could obtain a bed for himself and a stall for his horse, he rested for the night. But when he quitted the animal and committed him to the charge of the ostler, such was the darkness still prevailing that Russell knew no more about the shape, appearance, and colour of the beast than he did about the Greek horse that entered Troy. He might have known, however, that the heroes inside that wooden steed must have had a rough time of it if its movements were not easier than those of his Warminster hack.

"Feed him well," said Russell to the ostler, as he groped his way out of the yard; "and don't forget to bring him in the morning to No. 9, Milsom Street, exactly at eleven o'clock."

The Pump Room books of that day, if in existence, would still show the names and numbers of the visitors who were then occupying No. 9 in that fashionable locality; they were no other than Admiral, Mrs., and Miss Penelope Bury, from Dennington House, North Devon.

Here, then, was the guiding star which had led Russell to abandon both friends and hounds at Stock; and in spite of the gloom, had lighted his path with a hopeful ray to the city of waters, at which we now find him safely arrived. He had promised Miss Bury to ride with her in the morning, and of course took care to be in attendance at No. 9 in good time before the horses were ordered and the lady prepared to start. Other cavaliers, however, had been invited to join the party; notably, the Rev. Alexander Baillie, a fine, handsome young fellow, as agreeable as he was good-looking, and a perfect beau; also the long-lamented John Bayly, a finished horseman, and one of the best men across country in all England; besides one or two more, mounted on steeds well-bred and with skins glossy as satin itself.

Miss Bury, too, was now in the saddle; and, but for a short delay, occasioned by the non-arrival of Russell's horse, the whole cavalcade were prepared to start at the appointed time. At length the ostler made his appearance, hurrying forward, as he best could, an animal

Russell at Bath in 1826.

that seemed only fit for a dog-kennel; he was black as ink, had no hair on mane or tail, and scarcely an ounce of flesh on his bones; for, literally,

> "His strutting ribs on both sides show'd
> Like furrows he himself had plow'd;
> For underneath the skirt of pannel,
> 'Twixt every two there was a channel."

Above all, an old-fashioned post-boy's saddle, brass-mounted and secured by a huge crupper to his rat-tail, formed a conspicuous feature on the garran's back; and that, coupled with his poster-like appearance, was quite enough to stir up first a titter, then a roar of laughter, as it quickly did, among the lookers-on.

Never, perhaps, was lover placed in a more trying predicament; the shafts of ridicule being the most fatal of all weapons to a man bidding for promotion, if he is made the unhappy butt at which they are aimed. Many a hero, with courage enough to head a Balaclava charge and face the deadliest foe, would have shuddered to mount that beast under existing circumstances, and would certainly have darted off in search of another charger less picturesque in his points, and more befitting the light brigade assembled in Milsom Street on that eventful morn. Comparing their steeds with his own, he might well have thought that the companionship of such a Rosinante would not only compromise his own dignity, but outrage the feelings of his gay and well-mounted comrades.

But Russell had no such apprehension; he stood his ground and joined heartily in the laugh; told them of the landlord's craft at Warminster, and his own inability to detect it, owing to the Stygian darkness that prevailed at the time and throughout his journey. He then sprang into the saddle; and by him at least, if not by one other of the party, the quaint figure and accoutrements of his horse were speedily forgotten; nor for one moment did they appear to trouble his thoughts during the rest of the day—a day he loved to record as one among the happiest, if not *the* happiest, of his long life.

But if, on this memorable visit to Bath, there were other gallants in the field better mounted and better equipped than the Devonshire parson, certain it is that he, like Ulysses of old, held his own against all comers; for, on the 30th of May, 1826, the fair Penelope honoured him with her hand, and converted him thenceforth into a happy Benedict. Soon after this auspicious event, he retired from the charge of George Nympton and South Molton parishes; and, after devoting but a brief period to the usual hymeneal holiday and its attendant mysteries, he removed with his handsome bride to Iddesleigh, near Hatherleigh; and, his father being the rector, he accepted the curacy of that parish under him.

There is a story current, however, that before he finally quitted South Molton, he and Mrs. Russell attended divine service at that church, and occupied, of course, a pew together. Now at that time there lived at Whitechapel Farm, near South Molton, a celebrated character called John Sanger, an eccentric, hard-riding yeoman, who, although weighing eighteen stone and mounted on a thirteen-hand Exmoor pony, had more than once beaten over the moor Mr. Newton Fellowes, the great Squire of Eggesford, whose hunters were notably well bred and the talk of all the country. Sanger belonged to Bishop's Nympton parish; but, on that Sunday, when Russell and his bride made their appearance at South Molton Church, he occupied a seat at a little distance off, but exactly fronting their pew.

Immediately on coming out of church he marched up to Mrs. Russell, and with hat in hand, and a profound bow, he said:

"Good morning to you, ma'am; I have never seen in all my life such a fine woman as you are. But you have spoiled my devotions; for I couldn't take my eyes off you all church time."

This, beyond all doubt, was no mere compliment; but the honest expression of a plain, out-spoken man.

It was but a short time after his marriage with Miss Bury that Russell continued to keep otter-hounds, for on removing to Iddesleigh, the proceeds of which living his father had assigned to him, he found himself in the centre of a country so gloriously wild, and so adapted to fox-hunting, that he determined at once to elevate his standard and follow that sport in preference to the other. Accordingly, in the autumn of 1826, when the woodlands were changing colour and draft-hounds their kennels, Russell, gathering together about ten or twelve couple from various sources, but chiefly from the relics of the famous Stover pack, entered on his first campaign in the wilds of Hatherleigh, "hunting," as he says, "anything he could find around his own garden;" for the bounds of his maiden country, if such it could be called, were at first woefully confined to a very limited area.

The Rev. W. H. Karslake, of Dolton, appears to have been the only gentleman who, at that time, kept hounds within a short distance of Iddesleigh; but as they were harriers, it occurred to Russell that the enjoyment of the nobler sport might well be secured in so inviting a field, not only without prejudice to that gentleman, but with the concurrence, and, as he hoped, the goodwill of the two neighbouring Masters of Foxhounds, the Hon. Newton Fellowes and the Rev. Peter Glubb. The latter had for many years kept and hunted a very killing pack near Little Torrington; while the former, who lived at Eggesford, occupied, with his grand pack of foxhounds, a rough and extensive country, over which, by virtue of his manorial possessions, he claimed, if he did not exercise, the almost feudal rights of a baron of the fifteenth century. For though,

> "Kind, like a man, was he; like a man, too, would have his way."

The kennels of both these packs were within ten miles of Iddesleigh, and nearly equidistant from that place; consequently, in so circumscribed a country, over which he might almost have flown a paper kite, the prospect of pursuing the wild animal with success would indeed have been a hopeless one. It would also have involved him in endless strife, for he must inevitably have encroached on the conventional rights of those gentlemen, and aroused their jealousy and ill-will at every turn. Iddesleigh, if he did so, he was well aware would be looked upon as the centre of a civil war, and he as a kind of Rob Roy—a marauder and freebooter, who, by violating a law strict as that of the Medes and Persians, would be entitled to no quarter under such outrageous circumstances.

To obtain, then, an enlargement of his too narrow bounds—just a few outlying covers get-at-able by him, but rarely drawn by them—Russell, rather than incur such odium, appealed point blank to Mr. Newton Fellowes and Mr. Glubb, both of whom readily and kindly concurred in granting him the favour he asked; namely, a slice of their respective countries on either side of Iddesleigh. By that cession, which, with his little pack, proved to be a sufficiently ample one, he found, as he described it, "flinging room both for himself and hounds."

But notwithstanding the unexampled sport he was able to show with his first scratch lot, some of which were mute and some too free of tongue, many given to riot, to skirting and other hereditary faults, he was not long in discovering that he had still an uphill game to play in attempting to establish an independent dynasty in that country.

The sport of legitimate fox-hunting being utterly ignored by a majority of the natives, it had long been, and still was, their practice to kill a fox whenever and however they could catch him, fulfilling to the letter the sentiments of the Highland chieftain—

"Who ever reck'd, where, how, or when,
The prowling fox was trapp'd or slain?"

In fact, to such an extent did this practice prevail, that for the first season or two, owing to the scarcity of foxes, Russell was compelled to adopt the primitive plan of hunting both fox and hare with the same hounds; so that when the real wild article was not to be found, the other was always at hand to give his hounds a spin and keep his field in good humour.

He had not been long at Iddesleigh when, one day as he was drawing for a fox, at some distance from home, his ear caught the sound of a church bell, rung in a jingling fashion, and with more than usual clamour. A stranger might well have supposed it to be a signal of alarm intended to warn the country-side that a fire had broken out on some neighbour's premises, and that the need of help was urgent and pressing. But no such thing; as Russell's prophetic spirit too well divined, it was the signal that a fox had been tracked to ground, or balled into a brake; and the bell summoned every man who possessed a pickaxe, a gun, or a terrier, to hasten to the spot and lend a hand in destroying the noxious animal.

Russell's letter is now before me, describing his first adventure with a party bent on murdering a fox in his new country:

"During the winter of the first year I was at Iddesleigh, the snow at the time lying deep on the ground, a native—Bartholomew *alias* Bat Anstey—came to me and said, 'Hatherley bell is a-ringing, sir.'

"'Ringing for what?' I enquired, with a strong misgiving as to the cause of it.

"'Well, sir, they've a-traced a fox in somewhere; and they've a-sot the bell a-going to collect the people to shoot un.'

"'Come, Bat, speak out like a man,' I replied, 'and tell me where 'tis.'

"'In Middlecot earths, sir; just over the Okement.'

"I was soon on the spot with about ten couple of my little hounds, and found, standing around the earths, about a hundred fellows—the scum of the country—headed, I am almost ashamed to say, by two gentlemen, Mr. Veale, of Passaford, and his brother-in-law, Mr. Morris, of Fishleigh, the father of Colonel W. Morris, of the 'Light Brigade'—that brilliant swordsman to whose memory a monument is erected on Hatherleigh Moor.

"I remonstrated with these gentlemen, and told them plainly that if they would leave the earths, and preserve foxes for me, I would show them more sport with my little pack in one day than they would see in a whole year by destroying the gallant animal in so un-English a way.

"Impressed, apparently, by what I had said, both gentlemen instantly bade me a 'good morning,' turned on their heels and left the place; while a few shillings, distributed among the crowd by way of compensation for the disappointment I had caused them, induced them to disperse and leave me almost sole occupant of the 'situation.'

"Then, after waiting half an hour or so near the spot, I turned my head towards home; but, before I arrived there, I met a man open-mouthed, bawling out, 'They've a-traced a fox into Brimblecombe; for I hear Dowland bell a-going.'

"So off I went to Dowland in post haste; found out where the fox was lying, turned him out of a furze bush, ran him one hour and forty minutes—a blaze of scent all the way—and took him up alive before the hounds on the very earths I had so lately quitted; where, unfortunately for him, a couple of scoundrels had remained on the watch, and had consequently headed him short back from that stronghold."

But Russell had not yet finished with the fox-killers; for, as he says, "The very next day after the run from Brimblecombe, a man came to Iddesleigh on purpose to inform me that the bell was going at Beaford, and that a fox had been traced into a brake near that hamlet. The brake, in reality, though not far from Iddesleigh, was in Mr. Glubb's country; but, feeling sure that the necessity of the case would justify the encroachment, I let out the hounds at once, and hurried to the spot with all speed.

"On arriving at the brake I found only one man near it; and he, placed there as sentinel, was guarding it from disturbance with a watchful eye. I asked him to tell me where the fox was; but he gave me a very impertinent answer, saying 'he knawed better than that; and wasn't a-going to do no such thing.'

"I kept my temper, however, as well as I could; and pulling out half-a-crown, I said, 'There, my man, I'd have given you that if you had told me where he was.'

"The fellow's eye positively sparkled at sight of the silver. 'Let me have it, then, he replied, 'and I will show you where he is to a yard.'

"On giving him the money, he pointed to a tree on the opposite side of the valley, and said, 'There, do you see that tree t'other side? Take the hounds to it, and they'll soon find him.'

"'I've drawn the brake inside that hedge already,' I said, 'and he isn't there.'

"'No,' he replied, but he's on the comb of the hedge, close to that tree.'

"And so he was. I ran him an hour, and lost him near where he was found. Then, just as I was calling the hounds away to go home, down came a crowd of men, women, and children, the first chiefly from the village inn, to see this fox murdered. Many of them had brought their loaded guns, were full of beer, and 'eager for the fray.' And when they discovered that I had disturbed *their fox*, as they were pleased to designate him, their language was anything but choice.

"A strapping young fellow, one of the principal farmers in the parish came up to me and said, 'Who are you, sir, to come here and spoil our sport?'

"'You would have spoiled mine,' I replied, 'if you could.'

"'You have no business here,' he said defiantly.

"'As much as you have,' I replied; 'for the owner has given me leave to hunt over this estate, and I mean doing so, too, whenever I please. So get a horse, come out with me, and I'll show you some fine sport, if you'll only give up shooting foxes.'

"'We'll shoot them whenever we can; that I'll promise you,' he said, in an angry tone.

"At that moment one of the hounds began to howl. I looked round, saw she was in pain, and asked, in a threatening manner, 'Who kicked that hound?'

"No one spoke for half a minute, when a little boy said, pointing to another, 'That boy kicked her.'

"'Did he?' I exclaimed; 'then 'tis lucky for him that he *is a little boy*.'

"'Why?' said the farmer with whom I had previously been talking.

"'Because,' I replied, 'if a *man* had kicked her I would have horsewhipped him on the spot.'

"'You would find that a difficult job, if you tried it,' was his curt answer.

"I jumped off my horse, threw down my whip, and said, 'Who's the man to prevent me?'

"Not a word was spoken. I stood my ground, and one by one the crowd retired, the young farmer amongst the number; and from that day forward I secured for myself and successors not only the goodwill and co-operation, but the friendship, of some of the best fox-preservers that the county of Devon, or any other county, has ever seen."

The names of a few are still to be found in the parish of Beaford: viz., Hearn, Snell, Arnold, Leverton; and especially a well-to-do farmer at Dolton, named Wadland, who, though harriers were kept in his parish, preferred hunting with fox-hounds; and many a time, as Russell relates, has he seen him and a white-smith, called Heard, of Beaford, crossing and recrossing the Torridge on foot and in the depth of winter, following his hounds. Fox-hunters both were to the backbone.

After that event there can be little doubt that the farmers, to their great credit, from one end of the country to the other, finding the kind of man they had to deal with, and the rare sport he was able to show, by degrees gave up the malpractice to which they had been so long addicted; and before two years were over, so far from persecuting the fox, many a poor farmer would rather have lost the best sheep in his flock than seen the gallant animal killed in any fashion except by hounds.

The influence, indeed, that Russell very soon acquired, not only among the farmers, but the great cover-owners of that country, was quite marvellous; it was not attributable to territorial or monetary qualifications; for as all the world knew, he certainly was no Carabbas, nor did the tide of his exchequer ever rise above low-water mark; but it was entirely due to his manly power as a sportsman, to his acute knowledge of the fox's habits, his mode of getting at him and driving him through the strongest covers, to the fascination of his thrilling cheer, and, above all, to the charm and heartiness of his manners. In truth, the feeling of the farmers towards him amounted almost to a devotion, and he was treated with a kind of hero-worship, as if he were a man formed in a different mould from other men.

The following anecdote, kindly contributed by the Rev. H. Bourchier Wrey, who vouches for its authenticity, affords a strong illustration how a word from a man of Russell's influence might have had such effect on a common-sense juryman as to enable mercy to triumph over the strict letter of a law which, from its undue severity, became abrogated not long after the event here recorded.

Tom Square was a man of peculiar habits—off by night and abed by day; earth-stopping in the season, and when that business was over, discovering the whereabouts of litters, and whether the young vagabonds had afterwards strayed: these were the exploits for which Tom was renowned. His nocturnal habits, however, led eventually to serious results: the sharp moor air, acting keenly on a probably empty stomach, tempted him to look with hungry eyes on some well-to-do Exmoor hoggetts, which, from time to time, the owners found to be absent without leave.

In a word, he took to sheep-stealing; and as that crime was known to be increasing in the neighbourhood, the farmers combined to set a watch and, if possible, detect the culprits. So our poor friend Tom, with others, "got into trouble." He was suspected, watched, caught red-handed, and, although many believed his assertion that "'Twas the very fust time he had ever doo'd zich a thing," yet was he proceeded against according to law; he was arraigned, tried, found guilty, sentenced, and the extreme penalty carried out—in fact, poor Tom Square was hanged.

Shortly after this sad event, Russell happened to fall in with James R., a neighbouring farmer, who, as the former had been told, had served on the jury in the above case. "Why, Jem," said Russell, accosting him in a tone of strong remonstrance, "how came this about? You were on the jury which tried Tom Square! —there surely was something to be said for the poor fellow. I've been told it was the first time he had ever done so. You know what a quiet man he was, always ready to do a good turn for a neighbour. 'Twas a pity, Jem, that you should have given your voice against him."

"Bless us, Mistre Rissell, yeu doan't zay zo. My senses! If us had on'y but knaw'd *they* was yeur honour's thoughts, us wid ha' put it right, fai.' But there, my Lord Jidge said he did ouft to be hanged—and zo us hanged un. But, bless 'ee, if us had on'y knaw'd yeur honour cared about un, us wid ha' put it right in quick time."

Again, a case of libel was about to be tried at Exeter between Russell and a gentleman called Nott. A special jury being sworn, one of them, Captain Adney, thus addressed his brother jurymen: "Now, gentlemen, pray understand me! I've a pair of new buckskin breeches on" (he always wore them and top-boots), "and I've made up my mind to sit here till my skin comes through them to the bare boards, before I give a verdict against Jack Russell." In five minutes afterwards the case was compromised, to the relief and entire satisfaction of Captain Adney.

Some years afterwards I was present myself when Russell received the following letter from a farmer on the North Molton side of his country; it ran thus:

"Sir John Rissell,

"Yeur honour will plaize to cum up to Ben Twitching wi' th' dogs: us be ate out o' they voxes. Mistiss kipth on a-telling up and zeth us shan't ha' a Geuse to kill, cum Chrismus. But I've a zaid I'd gi' her a new gown to mak' up for't; zo her han't a vexed zo mich zince. But do 'ee cum & gi' us a bit o' sport, Sir.

"Yeur honour's humbl Sarvent,

"T. T."

To give a catalogue of all the farmers' names who hunted with Russell and became eventually the staunchest fox-preservers, would now be a long and difficult task; for so many were they that the list would at least fill a column or two of the *Times*. A few, however, must not be omitted; such good men and true for instance, as Mr. Peter Tanton, of Wrays

Farm, whose brake at Wrays never lacked a litter of foxes. He was the owner of a celebrated grey mare by "Crickneck," her dam being a grey Exmoor by "Katerfelto"—this last horse, the sire of such wondrous stock, and the hero of that attractive story written by Mr. Whyte-Melville, is said to have been captured after his long run on Exmoor; and then bought, according to a tradition still prevalent in the region of Hatherleigh, by the Rev. John Russell, sen., the rector of Iddesleigh, and Russell's father, in whose possession the horse died. Then there was Mr. John Brendon, of Red Windows, near Chillaton, a fine rider, with consummate nerve and good hands. The Eastcotts of Broadwoodwidger and Norton; Brown of Hollacombe, Parson of Panson, Seccombe of Seccombe, a family that have held their own at Seccombe from a period antecedent to the Norman Conquest: Cory of Staddon, Oliver Palmer of Tinhay, Tickel of Bratton-Clovelly, and that rare specimen of a yeoman, Smale of Thorn.

But the encouragement Russell met with from the cover-owners around him was, in some respects, equally warm and gratifying; for, besides the cession of the country made to him by Mr. Newton Fellowes and Mr. Glubb, another large landed proprietor, Mr. John Morth Woolcombe, of Ashbury, undertook to preserve the wild districts of Broadbury for him; while he himself, although hunting three days a week with his own hounds, rarely failed to join Russell's little pack, whenever they met within reach of Ashbury. Many others, too, supported him in like manner, promising to preserve foxes, and inviting him with much heartiness to draw their covers whenever it suited his purpose to do so.

But, as a general rule, the support they gave him was limited chiefly to such concessions; material aid, in the form of a subscription, was neither asked for nor given; and, although large fields attended his meets, the sinews of war for hounds, horses, and keepers were at first, with one exception, provided by himself alone. That exception was Mr. C. Arthur Harris, of Hayne, a young enthusiastic squire, devoted to hunting, and himself a Master of Hounds. He had made Russell's acquaintance in 1826, at the Chulmleigh Club, which flourished for so many years under the able auspices of Mr. Newton Fellowes, Mr. J. M. Woolcombe, "the Lord of Ashbury," Mr. L. Buck, Mr. J. Dicker Fortescue, and other Devonshire Worthies, both of the Northern and Southern divisions of the county; but of that club more anon.

One day's hunting together was alone sufficent to convince Harris that Russell's knowledge of the craft and management of hounds was of no ordinary stamp or quality; and shortly afterwards, out of sheer admiration for his "talents," which a few more days had confirmed, he proposed throwing in his lot with him and bearing a liberal share, but not an equal one, in the maintenance of the united packs.

They struck hands at once; the offer being accepted by Russell subject to the following reservation, namely, that the hounds should belong to him, and that he alone should hunt and control them, terms to which the younger and less experienced sportsman very sensibly agreed. Accordingly, on a given day in 1827, the two packs met at Five Oaks, near Okehampton, in all about seventy couple, which Russell, knowing to a handful of meal the value of every hound, quickly drafted down to thirty-five couple. With this lot he proposed hunting fox alone, giving the country two days a week, with an occasional bye-day according to circumstances.

It should be mentioned, however, that previous to this arrangement, sundry interchanges of hounds, and especially of puppies, had taken place between him and Mr. Harris; all above twenty inches going to Russell, and those under that standard to the Hayne kennels. It was at this period that a hound in Russell's pack, called "Daphne," by Meynell's "Dreadnought," from

Meynell's "Princess," attracted the special admiration of all who witnessed her marvellous sagacity and power of nose. She was perfect in every way: in drawing, in driving, and in line-hunting. With a wave of the hand from Russell, she would draw a linhay, a pig-sty, or any conceivable place in which a beaten fox would try to conceal itself.

It is related of her that, after a hard chase in the Hatherleigh country, the hounds had brought their fox into a farmyard, where they threw up, and failed to carry it a yard farther. "Daphne," however, flinging to the front, held the line into a vacant cow-house; then on to the manger, half filled with hay, where she just whimpered, then clambering over the rack into the loft, or "tallet," forced, as it were, the running, and out bolted the fox, ran the ridge of a thatched outhouse, jumped down into a pig-sty, and there the hounds had him in a moment. "Mr. Woolcombe, of Ashbury, nearly rubbed his nose off with delight."

The combination of the two packs had taken place but a short time, when, towards the end of the season of 1827, an episode occurred which, but for an immediate explanation on the part of Russell, might have caused a rupture of the newly-formed alliance, and brought it there and then to an untimely end. A bye-day had been arranged near Five Oaks, in the Bratton-

RUSSELL FINDS A HARE, FIRST.

Clovelly country for the purpose not only of enjoying a day's sport, but of closely testing the merits of the united pack. True to his time, Mr. Harris, accompanied by two friends who were staying with him, namely, Mr. John Glanville and Mr. William Coryton, of Pentillie, made his appearance at the appointed rendezvous; but there they found no hounds, no Russell, nor a human being to greet their arrival.

After waiting for some time, not without sundry growls and misgivings, Harris, unwilling to lose the chance of sport and disappoint his friends—who had been invited purposely to witness the work of the combined forces, and Russell's skill in handling them—pulled out his watch and proposed allowing another half-hour before they gave him up and returned whence they came. In the midst of this quandary the music of a pack of hounds in full cry suddenly burst on their ears; and at the same time, a countryman coming up, Harris inquired if he had seen the hounds, and whose they were then running so merrily.

"Passon Rissell's, sir, in coose," responded the man; "they'm a driving hard, sure enow; and he home to the tails o' mun."

Utterly unable to account for such an extraordinary proceeding on the part of Russell, the three gentlemen determined to go in pursuit and ask him to explain his apparent want of courtesy in throwing off so "wide of the meet," and disappointing them of their day's sport. On coming to a turn of the road near Inwardleigh Moor, there they spied Russell, cool as a cucumber, sitting at his ease on the back of Billy, his famous pony-hunter, and quietly watching the hounds.

"What on earth are you about?" inquired Harris, in a somewhat hasty and impatient tone.

"Very sorry to have kept you waiting, Arthur," responded Russell, good-humouredly, "but the truth is, I fed rather late last night, and the hounds being scarcely fit to trim a good fox at once, I thought I'd find a hare first, and let them clear their pipes a bit before they tackled the stouter animal. They'll come to the road in a minute, and I'll stop them then."

So he did. The hounds were then trotted off to a small spinney at the back of Five Oaks, where they found at once; and away they went, straight as a bee-line, over the Inwardleigh Moor, carrying a fine head over Bowerland Moor towards Bridestowe, and on to Sourton and Prewley Moor; killing him between that and Lidford, on Dartmoor. Time, one hour and forty-five minutes.

It is superfluous to add that, under the influence of that glorious run, the cloud of the morning vanished like a summer mist, and never more darkened a day of that brief but happy alliance.

## CHAPTER VII.

THE ARTIFICIAL FOX-EARTH—ACCESSION OF COUNTRY—THE BODMIN MEETINGS—LONG DISTANCES TO COVER—SIR TATTON SYKES—THE IVY BRIDGE HUNT WEEK—RIDES HOME.

> O, said he, you will never live to my age, without you keep yourself in breath with exercise, and in heart with joyfulness; too much thinking doth consume the spirits; and oft it falls out, that, while one thinks too much of his doing, he leaves to do the effect of his thinking.
>
> SIR PHILIP SIDNEY.

Russell had been married one year, within a day, when, on the 29th of May, 1827, his wife presented him with his first-born son, whom they named John Bury—a precious though a short-lived offering, for the child died, and was buried in Iddesleigh Churchyard on the following 31st of May. On the 23rd of August, however, in that year, 1828, just three months afterwards, a second son was born to them at Dennington House, and received the names of Richard Bury Russell—a gentleman who for some time was Colonel of the North Devon Militia Artillery, a J.P. for that county, and died in 1883.

On turning over some manuscripts relating to those early days and the versatile power of his little pack, I find, in Russell's handwriting the following letter, which, for the uncommon day's sport it records, is entitled to a prominent place in this memoir:—

"One evening soon after the hounds had been fed, who should ride to our door at Iddesleigh but Billy Morris, a great chum of mine, then a small boy living with his father and mother at Fishley, but afterwards a distinguished swordsman, and one of the glorious Six Hundred in the Balaclava Charge.

"'I've a holiday to-morrow, Mr. Russell,' he said, 'and I've come to ask if you will kindly bring out your hounds, and show me a day's sport.'

"'With all my heart,' I replied; 'but I have promised your father's tenant at Norleigh to kill a hare for him; so come and meet me there at ten o'clock.'

"'I'll be there to a minute,' he said, thanking me warmly, and then galloping off on his pony, 'big with hope.'

"It was a wretched morning—a regular downpour of rain—and no one came to the meet but dear little Billy and Lord Clinton's steward from Heanton. Well, the hounds found a hare, and killed her; found another, and she went as straight as a line to Gribbleford Bridge, on which we also killed her.

"'Now' said Billy, 'just throw them into uncle's covers; there's a fox there, I know.'

"'Not on any account,' I replied, 'till I have his permission to do so.'

"'But I'm sure you may,' he continued; 'for he told me so last night.'

"I begged him, however, to ride up to Passaford, half a mile off, and bring me word 'yea or nay,' from his uncle, and promised that I would wait an hour for his return. I did wait a full hour, when suddenly the hounds dashed in over the road-fence, and in an instant a fox was on his legs. Ran him up close to the house, but I saw nothing of Billy; then breaking away, he put his head straight for Dartmoor; but the hounds raced up to him before he reached Sourton. I viewed him ahead, and saw him crawl into a large furze-bush on the open moor; rode up to it, and, before the hounds arrived, had him in my arms. But there was no house, and therefore no bag, within a couple of miles; so I threw him down, and they ate him—no one up but myself. I then went back to Norleigh; but, before I arrived there, a farmer came up and asked me to kill a hare for him, which I did; the hounds, however, tore her so much that he begged me to try again. I did so, and found a tough old lady, that gave me as good a run as the dog-fox had done, though not so straight; and I killed her also—two brace of hares and a fox—a very satisfactory day's work, which was talked about at every farmer's ordinary, far and near, and established my little pack on a firm footing from that day forth."

But to return to his coadjutor, Mr. Harris, of Hayne. Owing to the hitherto malpractice of the natives for so long a time, and the consequent scarcity of foxes throughout the land, he quickly saw that unless some plan were adopted by which he could at once protect the stock and secure a find, even two days a week would be too much for the country; especially as Russell, unlike the man whom one jack-snipe supplied with sport for a whole season, almost invariably killed his fox whenever he found him. In the year 1828, for instance, Russell found thirty-two foxes, — killed twenty-eight, and earthed a brace; besides killing seventy-three brace of hares with the same scratch pack, of which hares the hounds certainly ate their share, namely, thirty-six brace.

Foxes, however, and foxes only, were the sole object of the new alliance; and with a view to cultivate and increase their number, besides feeing keepers and propitiating the farmers' wives with attractive and useful presents—a handsome red shawl to one and a family Bible to another—Mr. Harris set to work to construct artificial earths in three of the chief covers on the Hayne Estate; the plan for which had been given him by Mr. Paul Ourry Treby, of Goodamoor, one of the best friends to fox-hunting the Dartmoor country ever knew.

The following rough sketch will probably enable the reader to understand the plan on which the earth was formed. It consisted simply of a narrow walled drain; which, being just large enough to admit a small terrier, was constructed on the slope of a hill in the shape of the letter Y.

In the lower or main entrance was an iron plate worked by a spring, but fixed by a pad-lock, and covered with earth, over which plate the foxes travelled habitually.

In the centre was a wide circular chamber, from which the upper passages branched off; and the top of that chamber being covered with a close-fitting lid, the food for the cubs was popped in through it. These were fed twice in the week until full-grown, and afterwards every Saturday.

When a fox was wanted, the spring plate was unpadlocked; and the upper entrances being stopped, each with a strong gorse faggot, the moment he entered, the plate tripped up behind him, and there he was safe and ready for the coming event.

It was usually a two o'clock affair; and when a glass or two of old sherry—that spur in the head which is said to be worth two on the heel—had been handed about in front of the mansion, Blatchford, the keeper, at a given signal, ungorsed the upper entrances just before the hounds came up; then put in a terrier at the lower end, and away.

It never failed; but it was a curious fact that foxes bolted from the Newton Wood earth, at one end of the park, almost invariably made for the wilds of Dartmoor, while those found in the Townleigh earth, on the other side of the park, broke away in quite a different direction. It puzzled even Russell to account for the why and the wherefore of this understanding between the fox families, but so it was.

The secret was well kept for years; but the certainty of having a fox on foot directly after the sherry had been imbibed, gave rise to many strange reports on the subject: some said it was a bagman from Leadenhall Market: others fancied—the natives notably—that there was some "whistness," or witchcraft, in the business; it might be, as they thought, the work of Dick Down, the old huntsman who was eaten by the Hayne hounds, and whose ghost was known to haunt the covers round the park. But Mr. John Crocker Bulteel, in his humorous mood, gave another version of the matter, and amused the county with a story which Blatchford, he said, had told him, when he brought down a hound to Flete from the Hayne kennels. On asking Blatchford how the world went with him, he replied: "Well enough, sir, thank 'ee, on the whole; but, Lor, my stummick be almost a wored out by lying so long, wi' the fox in a bag, on that cold ground up to Newton Wood, a-waiting for the squire's holley, and for Parson Rissell to bring up they hounds, and then to let un goo. I've scarce no stummick left, yeur honour; 'tis fairly stived up wi' th' cold."

The foxes, however, were no bagmen, but the real old Hectors of the moor, as they so often proved themselves to be by going straight away for their native and far-distant homes. Vixens and game were scarce in those days, and to satisfy the cravings of nature, it was marvellous how far a fox would travel in search of the one and the other. The cubs fostered in the artificial earth on arriving at maturity soon brought immigrants to the colony from a distant land, and with one of these before him, whether found in the drain or a neighbouring cover, it was no child's-play for Russell and his hounds to pull him down ere he reached his own diggings in some inaccessible tor on rugged Dartmoor.

Oh! it would stir a man's heart to the core to hear Russell describe some of those Broadbury runs, which the brush of a Carter, or the pen even of a Whyte-Melville, would have been powerless to paint with a like effect. But to have seen and enjoyed them, as he and his friends did, must have been a foretaste to them of the Elysian fields.

"It was said by Voltaire, that Marlborough had never besieged a fortress which he had not taken, never fought a battle which he had not won, never conducted a negotiation which he had not brought to a prosperous close." So wrote Lord Stanhope; and every one who has read his charming history of Queen Anne's reign will remember that the Duke of Marlborough's achievements—himself beyond all doubt, one of the first military chiefs of that or any age—could never have been so brilliant and so uniformly successful but for the support he obtained from "the Grand Alliance."

In like manner, if it be permitted to compare great things with small—the war of powerful nations with the sylvan campaign which Russell was waging among the remote and peaceful Britons of the far West—it is equally certain that he, too, proved himself a great general in his way; killing or accounting for his fox almost every time he found him; and conquering all classes, not less by the sport he showed than by his genial fellowship, manly bearing, and consummate tact. Nor should the support he met with from his alliance with Mr. Arthur Harris, of Hayne, remain unacknowledged; for beyond all question, the active and liberal co-operation of that gentleman did him invaluable service in his first start as a Master of Hounds.

Although not yet in possession of that property, his father and mother being still alive, the young squire brought all the influence of his paternal acres to bear not only, as we have seen, on the cultivation of foxes, but on the still further extension of the country; promising Russell he would not rest, nor would he let his friends rest, till he could draw every cover, if no bigger than a blanket, from Torrington to Bodmin.

In helping Russell to promote these objects, which he did with unflagging zeal and energy, Mr. Harris had the good fortune to be materially supported by a kind maiden aunt, yclept Penelope; and so zealous was she in the cause of fox-hunting that, in her eighty-eighth year, she remained for some hours in her pony-carriage watching Mr. Henry Deacon, the present able Master of the H.H., drawing the Hayne covers, and finding his fox at length in Arraycot Wood.

Among the best of the hounds selected by Russell from the Hayne kennels, and afterwards drafted by him, was a litter of five, bred from the Belvoir Rosamond by a noted hound of

Russell's, called Mercury; they were not only pictures to look at in point of shape and beauty, but hard drivers and never idle. Unfortunately, however, they were very small hounds, and did not nearly come up to the standard which Russell, with the prospect before him of seeing his country largely extended, was anxious to raise to twenty-two inches; so, matchless as they were, both in work and form, the Rosamond lot were sent to Mr. Tout, of Burrington; while others, for a like reason, went to Col. Lloyd Watkins, of Pennoyre, Mr. George Coham, of Coham, the Rev. E. Clarke, of St. Dominick, and lastly, to the Rev. Pomeroy Gilbert, of Bodmin Priory; a gentleman, in Russell's own words, "blessed with a big heart, given to hospitality, and withal a most accomplished sportsman."

To many a remonstrance against drafting such a valuable lot, Russell would simply quote, if not the very words, at least the opinion of a well-known authority on such matters: "A little hound will go well in some countries: a large hound, if fed to go, will go well in all;" and he would add emphatically, "that's my opinion, too."

But the sport he had shown, and continued to show, with his little pack had already made his name famous throughout the western counties; insomuch that many large landed proprietors, whose covers pertained neither to Mr.

Glubb's hunt, nor to that of Mr. Newton Fellowes, came forward and invited him not only to draw them when he pleased, but to consider them for the future as part and parcel of his own country. Among those may be mentioned Mr. J. M. Woolcombe, of Ashbury, Mr. Savile, of Oaklands, Mr. Tremayne, of Sydenham, and Mr. Harris Arundell, of Lifton Park.

But, in addition to these valuable acquisitions, the trustees of Sir William Molesworth, then a minor, were good enough still further to enlarge his borders by giving Russell permission to draw the Tetcott and Pencarrow covers. Again, the Duke of Northumberland's covers at Werrington, the Duke of Bedford's at Endsleigh, those of Mr. Baring Gould, Colonel Fortescue, of Buckland Filleigh, Mr. Luxmoore, Mr. Buckingham, and of Lord Clinton, were all placed at his disposal, while at the same time a general promise was given that foxes, for the future, would receive fair play.

When the season, then, of 1828 had fairly set in, Russell must have felt as if the morn of a golden age was dawning upon him, so full of promise, so bright and encouraging was the prospect that now lay before him. Like the Colossus of Rhodes, he had one foot on Broadbury and the other planted on the Bodmin moors; with not one, but many great rivers between them; and a country abounding in wild open moors, fairly undulated, and holding a grand scent, over which a hound and a horse could travel together at tip-top pace, while every passage of a run might be seen by the rider; a country, in fact, such as Meynell and Warde never saw in their happiest dreams.

Like the "Old Berkeley" of former days, which, when hunted by Mr. Harvey Combe and Mr. Majoribanks, with the famous Harry Oldaker for their huntsman, extended from Barnett to Cirencester, this grand moorland country stretched east and west, literally from Torrington to Bodmin, a distance of upwards of seventy miles, including the vast intervening space, north and south, between Exmoor and Dartmoor. Then, for the convenience of the hounds in so wide a range, they occupied, according to their meets, kennels at Iddesleigh, Hayne, Bodmin, and Pencarrow; Iddesleigh, of course, being their head-quarters at all other times.

It would be a long task, and in most cases a downright infliction on the reader, however patient under the recital of mahogany-runs that reader might be, if even a tithe of the brilliant and continuous sport shown by Russell from 1828 to 1832 were recorded in this memoir.

Nevertheless, in order to represent the man in his true colours, and show that, as a huntsman, he was equally good all round, a few only of his most remarkable runs—brilliant with a burning scent, line-hunting with moderate, or, again, with a cold and catching scent—have been selected for that purpose.

Late in the autumn of 1828, the fixture being Broadbury Castle, Russell and his little ones met with a greeting such as few have received and he could never forget—grips of welcome on every side from the large field assembled to hunt with him in that wild country. Conspicuous among the Worthies of Devon and Cornwall were J. M. Woolcombe, of Ashbury; "Gallant Tom Phillipps," of Landue; the late lamented baronet Sir Walter Carew; W. Coryton, of Pentillie; F. and J. Glanville, of Catchfrench; Arthur Harris, of Hayne; Captain M. Louis; Paul O. Treby, of Goodamoor; H. Bourchier Wrey, a gentleman always well mounted, and from his spurs to his hat neat as a new pin; L. Buck, of Moreton; Whyte, of Pilton; Erving Clarke, of Buckland Tout Saints; W. Gurney, of Bratton-Clovelly; and Moore-Stevens, of Cross.

Russell, as it happened, was short of horses on that occasion; but as luck and good fellowship would have it, he was gloriously mounted by a friend in need, Mr. Arthur Harris, who put him on Reuben Apsley by Gainsborough, a chestnut horse, perfect as a fencer and a rare goer in deep ground. Found and away at once; over the moor at a trimming pace to Hindabarrow, where they threw up. Russell, however, in spite of advice to the contrary, caught hold of his hounds, and taking them back to a road where he had seen a hound hesitate for a moment, hit off his fox; held the line for a mile or more steadily along the high road, then quitting it, dashed over the moor and raced up to him in Germanswick Wood, bringing him away in view, and running into him on Brockscombe Moor. Time, forty minutes.

Returning homewards, a fox jumped out of a hedgerow capped with gorse, and away they went at score, over Beaworthy Hollow and Soper's Moor, across Wagaford Water, running from scent to view and rolling him over on the open moor in fifty-two minutes, without the ghost of a check from find to finish.

Heavy and deep were the moorlands, while the boundary fences were big enough to stop a red-deer. Russell, in each run, went straight away with his leading hounds, taking the fences as they came, and maintaining the lead from first to last; though Phillipps on Foster, a noted hunter by Gainsborough, Morth Woolcombe on Crown Prince, Treby on Spectre, L.

Buck on Alpha, Captain Louis on Harlequin, Coryton on Raven, Harris on Rosabel, and Mr. H. Bourchier Wrey on Bodkin, struggled hard to catch him; but in vain. He rode like a man, and handled his hounds, according to the opinion of all present, as no one else in Devon could then have done.

When congratulated on the place he had kept, he jocularly replied, "No wonder, Arthur; it was your horse; but they were my own spurs."

Then, to begin the New Year auspiciously, on the 1st of January, 1829, Russell displayed a rare acquaintance with the tactics of a dodging fox; and a perseverance in pursuing him worthy of a sleuth-hound. Found in Harper Wood, and went away to Abbot's Hill, skirting covers and running a line of inclosures down to the Torridge, which they crossed and re-crossed with slow hunting and an indifferent scent; Russell very patient, but now and again hazarding a wide cast to get, if possible, nearer to his fox. At length, the scent mending, he cheered on his hounds, and catching an occasional view, as the fox dodged over his foiled line, he clapped them on from time to time, forced him into fresh ground, crossed the river again, and at last pulled him down gallantly, after a long and trying chase of two hours and fifteen minutes.

Mrs. Russell was out on the above occasion, and held, as usual, a forward place throughout the run; the patience of her husband and the perseverance of the hounds giving her the greatest delight.

Cornwall, like its sister county, is famed, as all the world knows, for its hospitality; and now it was that certain Cornish gentlemen threw open their halls, their covers, and their kennels, to welcome Russell across the border and provide him and his field with a fortnight's hunting twice in the year—and such hunting, over those wild moors, the Roughtor and Brownwilly wastes—the grassy, scent-holding lands of Tetcott and Pencarrow—as made the country ring with the sport from Tavistock to the Land's End.

"Many a tale," writes Mr. Harris, "is even yet told in the settle of the wayside inn, of the runs that happened during that hunting period of unwonted brilliancy. No farmer within the adjoining or distant parishes, who had a horse or a pony, failed to be present; labour was comparatively suspended; and even the women—'care creature'—put on their Sunday bonnets and shawls to go and see Mr. Russell find a fox. The houses in the neighbourhood were full of guests, and these hunting meetings possessed rather the character of triumphant ovations than the appearance of ordinary fixtures. Petitions were made by the farmers to arrange the meets so as not to interfere with Tavistock market; and a sale of stock was not exactly put off, but the advertisement of it was once delayed until after the Russell fortnight."

These were the Bodmin Meetings, one of the chief promoters of which was that excellent sportsman, the Rev. Pomeroy Gilbert, of Bodmin Priory; for he it was who secured Russell as his guest, whose kennels and stables were placed entirely at his disposal, and whose influence, had Russell needed it, would have been amply sufficient to insure for him a hearty reception throughout that land. At Pencarrow, too, though Sir William Molesworth was not yet of age, friends assembled from afar, till the house was filled to the rafters; stalls for two horses being allotted to each guest; and the kennels, when required, to the use of Russell's hounds.

The country houses, in fact, vied with each other in the warmth and extent of their hospitalities, insomuch that the old-fashioned sign of the wayside inn might have been aptly hung over their own doors: "Good entertainment here for man and horse."

A memorable day was the 16th of February, 1829, when Russell found three foxes together in Deviock Wood, near Bodmin, and killed all three before the sun set on Brownwilly tors. A brace broke cover at once, going away, like a loving pair, side by side; while the third stole off without being viewed, and put his head straight for the moor.

Breaking on their very brushes, the pack stuck to the former, pelting after them like a storm of hail; when, after a short burst, the foxes separated, and so did the hounds; Russell sticking to one division and screaming to his field to stop the other. Stop them, indeed! the moor was before them, the scent breast-high, and the best horse that ever was foaled would fail to head them now in their desperate onward course.

Mr. Harris on Rosabel, an Irish mare by Poteen, did his best; so did Colonel Raleigh Gilbert and many others; but they never came up even to a tail-hound.

And now occurred an incident which, but for the clever animal under him, might have terminated with serious, if not fatal results, both to Rosabel and her rider. Coming best pace to a high boundary fence, built with stone and coped with turf, the mare faced it gallantly in her stride, bucked upon top, and then, with a vigorous spring, fairly cleared a couple of bullocks standing for shelter under the moor-wall. Had either of the beasts shifted its position and turned moorwards, a collision must have occurred, which would probably have brought the day's sport to a tragic end.

Another very remarkable feat of equitation was performed by the same gentleman about this time. On returning, after a day's fox-hunting, to Hayne *viâ* Tinhay Bridge, his progress was momentarily arrested by discovering that the bridge, consisting of five arches, was under repair; four of which were only partially finished, while the space intended for the centre arch was left entirely open, the river running rapidly and visibly some fourteen feet below. Mr. Harris, happily, was on Skylark, a Foxbury mare bred by Mr. Brendon, of Cazantick, and a perfect hunter. To the horror of the adjoining cottagers, many of whom were watching him from their doors, Mr. Harris rode over the hurdles that fenced off the bridge; then, giving the mare her head, she felt cautiously for a sure footing amid the broken masonry, and, collecting herself, jumped to the top of the first arch, then on to the second, paused a moment on the brink of the centre arch, as if measuring the exact width of the chasm, then rose coolly and collectedly and cleared it at a bound. The two remaining arches were easily topped; then came the hurdles, and away.

Gaylass, Woodbine, Guilty, Comedy, Desperate, Madcap, Singer, Daphne, and Mercury are running for blood, and will not be denied. And though Harris and Colonel Raleigh Gilbert, the future hero of many a brilliant campaign in

India, and afterwards so famous at home both in "silk and in scarlet," are riding like madmen to stop them, their efforts are utterly vain. Nay, had Jove's winged messenger been there, the god himself could never have stopped those nine merciless hounds, as on they sped, like very demons, in pursuit of their prey.

In thirty-five minutes the fox—that gay Lothario—bright as a new guinea when he first broke cover, but now beaten and begrimed with soil, bites the dust, and is torn, as Mr. Whyte-Melville has it, into

"A hundred tatters of brown."

But what of Russell? On bringing back the hounds to Helland Wood there they found him, sticking to his fox, like the Old Man of the Sea to Sinbad the Sailor; and driving him like wildfire, through that great cover, as if it was no bigger than a willow-spinney.

"A fresh hat in the ring," thought Russell, as he greeted the nine hounds thrown in at head: "Now then, Arthur, we shall have him in no time;" and they killed him in an hour and twenty minutes.

On counting the hounds it was found that three of them were missing; and anon came tidings that a third fox had slipped away, and that those hounds had been seen by a turf-cutter near the Jamaica Inn, streaming away towards Brownwilly. Jemmy Reynolds, kennel-man to

Mr. Pomeroy Gilbert, was then despatched after them; and, on approaching a tor of that wild moor, he heard the three hounds beneath it, marking among the cavernous rocks that lay at its base. In went his terriers; and Jemmy, soon handling his fox, brought him home that night, in great triumph, to the Priory kennels.

A friend who was present on that occasion, writes thus: "I never knew of a pack finding three foxes at once—with scent breast-high—and accounting for all three of them, as Russell's did on that day."

Perhaps there is no more remarkable feature in Russell's long career than the hardihood of frame and power of endurance he has exhibited—and that, too, without showing fatigue—in riding long distances to cover, hunting his hounds all day, and returning home at night, from points frequently far more distant than even the morning meets. In all the annals of the chase few men, if any, taking the outside of a horse as their conveyance, have equalled him in this respect.

The late Sir Tatton Sykes, a man of Herculean strength and courage, comes nearest to him in the long road distances he was wont to accomplish in the saddle alone. But it will be remembered that Sir Tatton rode only thoroughbred hacks, animals that travelled like oil, and from their fine condition, did their ten miles an hour with ease to themselves and luxury to their rider.

His kennel at Eddlesthorpe was at least fifteen miles from his mansion at Sledmere, and he was constantly in the habit of riding thither on hunting mornings before his hounds left for a meet yet many miles farther. It is related of him that, "if asked to go a hundred miles to ride a race, he puts a clean shirt in his pocket, his racing jacket under his waistcoat, a pair of overalls above his leathers, and, jumping upon a thoroughbred tit, arrives there the next day by the time of starting; and, when the race is over, canters his thoroughbred home again."

Far different was Russell's case from Sir Tatton's. Subject always to a short stud and indifferent hacks, which not unfrequently were Exmoor ponies, sometimes half-broken and wild as the red-deer, Russell fought his way over the roughest roads in England, starting often before daylight, and returning still oftener long after nightfall, guided by instinct or the stars of heaven to his far-distant home.

It may well be imagined, therefore, that in the matter of hacks and cross-country roads, Sir Tatton's performances, however long in the saddle, were scarcely more than pleasant exercise compared with those of Russell's. Still, Sir Tatton was a wonder; and in Yorkshire, for many a future day, anecdotes of his kindly but quaint habits, and especially of his manly prowess, not only as a sportsman, but as an accomplished athlete, will be cherished even as household words.

Once, on paying his annual visit to London, whither he had ridden, as usual, every yard of the way from Sledmere, he called in at Tom Spring's, in Holborn, and, speaking in the shrill tone which characterized his voice, he begged to be served with a tankard of their oldest and strongest ale. Besides himself and the barmaid, the only other person in the room was a square-set, broad-shouldered man, evidently a member of the pugilistic fraternity. On seeing the tankard brought in, the man said, in a mimicking way, "Here, Betsy, bring that ale to me, and take a jug of mild beer to that old woman."

Sir Tatton turned up his cuffs and buttoned his coat—a process which brought the prize-fighter to his legs in one moment; and at it they went, there and then.

In less than ten minutes the ruffian was knocked into a coal-scuttle; and, having discovered his error, refused to continue the unequal fight any longer.

"You may now drink the ale, my man," said Sir Tatton; "and then go home and tell your wife you have been well thrashed by an old woman."

This is exactly what Russell might have done in the heyday of his Oxford life.

But now, a few examples will suffice to show how severely long were the distances to cover which Russell habitually performed, both with foxhounds and staghounds, from the first hour of his mastership down to the last year of his life. More than once has he gone, in the grey of the morning, on horseback, from Iddesleigh to Four-hole Cross on the Bodmin moors—over fifty miles—hunted as long as there was light to see a hound, then, singing "Dulce, dulce domum," turned his horse's head and ridden, through the gloom of night, back to his home.

Milestones were never heeded by him when the object was to meet hounds; indeed, along the wild tracts and by-roads over which his course usually lay, no such landmarks could have been seen on the longest summer-day.

During the stag-hunting period of 1877, Russell, in accordance with his custom for the last sixty years, on every occasion but one, rode to Cloutsham Ball and Hawkcombe Head, hunted all day, and returned to his residence at Tordown by eleven o'clock p.m.; the distance to either meet being about twenty-five miles, more or less, and the road in many parts little better than a mere bridle-path. Long habit, which is second nature, added to a physical frame apparently insensible of fatigue, could alone enable a man in his eighty-second year to do such distances in the saddle, not only without suffering, but with a rare appetite for the next day's sport.

But a week's work performed in the spring of 1874, when he was only in his seventy-ninth year, has, I believe, no parallel in the records of such feats. He was invited by Admiral and Mrs. Parker to stay a week with them at Delamore, their seat near Ivybridge, on the southern side of Dartmoor, to meet Mr. Mark Rolle, whose hounds were about to hunt that country, by invitation from Mr. Trelawny, on alternate days in conjunction with his own.

Russell would unhesitatingly have said "Nolo Episcopari," if even the Palatinate of Durham had been offered to him; but to enjoy, at the same time, the hospitality of Delamore and the treat of a week's hunting with the crack packs of his two friends was more than he could resist; so he responded to Mrs. Parker's bidding with a grateful acceptance.

Accordingly, on Monday, the 23rd of March, he was off betimes, riding part way and doing the rest by rail—a distance altogether of more than eighty miles. Arrived in time for the meet, and hunted all day with Mr. Rolle's hounds.

Tuesday, met Mr. Rolle at Ivybridge.

Wednesday, Mr. Trelawny, Newnham Park.

Thursday, Mr. Rolle, Brent Station.

Friday, Mr. Rolle, Delamore.

Saturday, Mr. Trelawny, Hanger Down.

Unfortunately, the weather during the week was not favourable to scent; consequently, with no lack of foxes, the sport did not prove exactly the dainty dish Mr. Trelawny's hospitality would have set before his friends. Having earthed their fox within a mile or so of Ivybridge on that sixth day, Russell looked at his watch, and, finding it was just two o'clock, he took his hat off to Mrs. Parker, bid her and the field good-bye, and then, homeward bound, steered his course northwards directly over the moor.

Between his home and Hanger Down, whence he started, the distance is roughly estimated at seventy miles; and as he pricked on merrily, and never quitted his saddle, with the exception of changing his horse midway, till he reached his own stable door at eleven p.m., it cannot be less. He then dined heartily, slept well, and the next day, to crown the week's work, performed three full services in his parish with his wonted animation, earnestness, and effect. "Before he had taken anything to eat, however," writes Admiral Parker, "he sat down and filled a sheet of note-paper to my eldest daughter, saying he had tasted nothing, not even a biscuit, since he left our breakfast-table that morning at ten, and that he felt neither hungry, thirsty, nor tired after his day's work. The distance from Hanger Down to Dennington," the Admiral adds, "cannot be less than seventy miles."

But besides Russell, there were a few others in that country, kindred spirits and friends of his, whom no road-work could daunt when the meet was a good one ; gentlemen who, hunting either with Russell, Mr. Tom Hext, of Restormel, or the Landue hounds, were in the habit of riding incredible distances to cover, and returning afterwards to their homes at night, because they could find no comfortable sleeping quarters in the neighbourhood of such popular meets as Tetcott, Broadbury Castle, Chapman's Well, or Dosmary Pool.

Mr. Trelawny, of Coldrennick, who hunted the Dartmoor country for thirty years with such signal success, was notably one of these ; but again, like Sir Tatton Sykes, the hacks he rode—Lalagé, Melmoth, and Landsend—were simply perfect.

Another was Mr. C. A. Harris, who, to meet hounds near Beaford, started from Pentillie Castle at six a.m., and, after a blazing run and a kill in Castle Hill Park, sixty-five miles from Pentillie, returned thither to dinner at half after six, the distance in road-riding alone being about one hundred and fifteen miles. It was done with a couple of hacks, "Meg Merrilies" and "Ladybird," the last by "Anacreon" from Mr. H. Bourchier Wrey's "Ellen," by "Rainbow," doing her eighteen miles an hour each way. The country-folk, at first sight, must have taken him for Dick Turpin himself; and, if they did not raise the hue-and-cry,

> "Stop thief! stop thief! a highwayman!"

they must have been sharp enough to discover that the mare Mr. Harris rode was a bright bay, and not the veritable "Black Bess," of matchless speed and historic renown.

# CHAPTER VIII.

Has no Regular Whip—His Three Horses—Termination of the Alliance and Contraction of his Country—Mr. J. Morth Woolcombe—The Pencarrow Run—Mrs. Smith, of Porlock—The Four Vixen Cubs.

> When the country is deepest, I give you my word
> 'Tis a pride and a pleasure to put him along;
> O'er fallow and pasture he sweeps like a bird,
> And there's nothing too wide, nor too high, nor too strong.
>
> Whyte-Melville.

The formation of Russell's new and "independent dynasty," and the grand sport he was able to show with his little pack, gathered though it was from all points of the compass, has been roughly sketched in the foregoing chapters; and now, it will be asked, by what active and competent whip was he supported, or what other efficient aid did he receive to enable him to bring about such satisfactory results? The question is easily answered: so strongly was he animated by the spirit of "self-help," so well did he know the country and the habits of the wild animal he hunted, that, with the exception of casual and very uncertain assistance from his field, and the occasional service of a raw lad—a Jack-of-all-work called Sam—he literally did the work single-handed, and depended on no one but himself.

To ride a long distance to cover in the morning, to hunt a pack of foxhounds all day, and at night to jog slowly home with them to their perhaps far-distant kennel, is usually held to be work enough and to spare for any ordinary man; but if, in addition to these duties, he has to depend mainly on himself to keep them together when they divide, to stop them on riot, and, in fact, to do the work of a whip, or even two whips, besides his own, he need, like Alcides, have a double share of strength, activity, and endurance to do it all, and do it efficiently.

Nevertheless, this task, the ordinary work of at least two men, imposed as it was upon Russell by that old complaint of his—tightness of the chest—was not only no toil to him, but a real labour of love—one he would have ridden "bare ridge" to perform, nay, sacrificed his last crust to enjoy.

Beckford, the Blackstone of hunting law and practice, informs us that "no pack of foxhounds is complete without two whippers-in," and moreover, adds this testimony to the advantage gained by the help of a good whip: "I think I should have better sport and kill more foxes with a moderate huntsman and an excellent whipper-in, than with the best of huntsmen without such an assistant." Again, "No one knows better than you do how essential a good adjutant is to a regiment; believe me, a good whipper-in is not less so to a pack of fox-hounds." Then, with reference to the duty of a whipper-in, he continues, "While the huntsman is riding to his head-hounds, the whipper-in, if he has genius, may show it in various ways; he may clap forward to any great earth that may by chance be open; he may sink the wind to halloa, or mob a fox when the scent fails; he may keep him off his foil; he may stop the tail-hounds and get them forward, and has it frequently in his power to assist the hounds without doing them any hurt, provided he has sense to distinguish where he is wanted most. Besides, the most essential part of fox-hunting, the making and keeping the pack steady, depends entirely upon him, as a huntsman should seldom rate, and never flog a hound."

Notwithstanding the importance, then, attached by Beckford to the business of a whip, and the high qualifications which should be found in a man acting in that capacity, Russell managed for some time to do well without one, depending, as we have seen, solely on himself and the rough boy already referred to. But, though rough in appearance, Sam had his wits about him, and very soon profited by the lessons in which his master spared no pains to instruct him. For instance, Sam, with a view to his education, was occasionally permitted to join the well-appointed pack of the Hon. Newton-Fellowes, and at such times was especially charged to keep his eye on Stephen, first whipper-in to the latter, and carefully to note his tactics.

Then, the pastime of the day over, Russell would summon the lad to his dining-room, put him through his facings, and minutely test the result of his day's schooling by asking him such questions as the following:—

"Now, Sam, you saw the second whip riding after and rating those riotous puppies, Fleecer and Frantic, when he was a lanyard or more behind them; was he right or wrong in doing so, and what would you have done?"

"Got to their head, sir, and then rated them."

"Quite right, Sam; but, bear in mind, if you want to punish a hound, you should hit him first and rate him afterwards."

"Supposing a change takes place in cover, and the hounds divide, which lot should you stop?"

"That depends on the huntsman, sir: if he holds to one lot, I should stop the other, and get them forward as fast as I could."

"That's right, Sam; and don't forget to do the same by the tail-hounds. Good boy; you may go now."

Thus schooled, theoretically as well as practically, Sam, blessed with some genius and strong common sense, became in the course of a few years as useful and clever a whip as ever followed a hound; so that, with his help and the use of his own significant horn, Russell, not caring a button for show, but only for the sport, could well afford to dispense with the needless encumbrance of a more costly staff.

Some years afterwards John Beale, huntsman to Sir Walter Carew, and subsequently to the Tiverton Hounds, did wonders single-handed with the latter pack. He had the rare knack, when a fox was up, of getting to their head and keeping his horn going merrily alongside the leading hounds, a signal so well understood by the rest of the pack, that he rarely left a hound behind him in breaking away from the deepest covers. Many condemned him as being a tinker in his trade, making more noise than was either necessary or agreeable; nevertheless, the system worked admirably—that lively blast and sharp wild cheer of his gathered up the deep-drawing hounds as no whip in the world could have done it, and brought them, out and together, on the very back of their fox; for nobody knew better than he did that "a fox well found is a fox half killed."

Thus, without the help of a regular whip, "old John Beale" killed his foxes, and did it handsomely, showing such sport as, so long as that generation lasts, will not readily be forgotten in the Tiverton country.

Russell's plan was very much the same—his horn was half the battle to him; but, educated as he had been in the high-class school of Mr. George Templer and Mr. John Codrington, his style, as might be expected, was that of a gentleman; for although quite as energetic as John Beale, and with an eye like a hawk to his head-hounds, no one was ever heard to object either to the lively shake of his horn, or to the soul-stirring echoes of his musical cheer. On the contrary, as a farmer was once heard to say, "It fairly mak'th a man's heart jump in his waistcoat to hear Passon Rissell find his fox; 'twixt he and the hounds, 'tis like a band of music striking up for a dance."

The history and character of the pack hunted by Russell during his residence at Iddesleigh having been thus briefly recorded, the reader will now expect to learn something of his stud, what his powers as a horseman were, and how he acquitted himself as a rider to hounds.

To describe him as having been a brilliant performer across country, or to compare him, for instance with such men as Mr. Assheton Smith, Mr. Lindo, or Lord Alvanley, would be wholly beside the mark; for, in the first place, Devonshire, with its picturesque scenery, deep woodlands, hollow combes, and banks averaging ten or twelve feet in height, is a very different country to ride over from the undulating pastures and flyable fences of the Midland counties. In the next place, his financial means, to which allusion has already been made, always acting as a drag on his wheel, not only limited his choice, but constrained him to the disadvantage of a short stud, and to the absolute necessity of husbanding its resources, whenever an opportunity enabled him to do so.

Thus it may with truth be said that in moments of the purest enjoyment, when scent served and hounds were running breast-high, the thought of easing his horse and saving its legs was never absent from his mind; that was the one care that sat behind his saddle—the spectre that haunted him when the game was at its height—the one unpalatable drop in the bumper of enjoyment he was drinking to the dregs; for the thought of to-morrow would obtrude itself, would make him constantly dismount and lead his horse over high banks, when, if his stud had been less limited, he certainly would have taken the quicker, and, to himself, the far easier mode of getting at his hounds.

Russell, therefore, could neither be called a bruiser, nor even a hard man, in the common acceptation of that term; but his judgment as a horseman could never be impugned; he had fair hands, a quick eye, a heart in the right place, and so firm and yet easy a seat in the saddle, that no one who looked at him when mounted but would say, "That's a workman, every inch of him."

Nevertheless, despite the drawback mentioned, and all other difficulties, Russell very rarely failed to be close to his hounds; nor, though he lamented his "cumbrous weight"—some twelve stone odd—did the three brave horses that carried him so safely and well for many a hard season appear to be overtaxed by the work, or show any signs of unnatural decay. They were called Billy, Cottager, and Monkey.

The last, a chestnut horse, although somewhat uncertain in his temper, became a hunter of great renown in the country, doing his work admirably, and coming home gay as a lark after the longest day. The second was an entire horse, very clever at his fences, but very vicious; he would turn round and bite like a bull-dog if the rider gave him the ghost of a chance. Even in his gallop he would occasionally take a grab at the point of Russell's foot; and, had he caught it, would have torn the boot ruthlessly from his leg. Twice he seized him by the coat, but fortunately without doing more damage than merely rending the garment. Once indeed he very nearly brought an old friend of Russell's, Dr. George Owen, to serious grief. They were riding in chase side by side—the hounds running hard—when Cottager, in a sudden paroxysm of temper, made a fierce grab at Owen's horse; but, luckily, instead of catching him with his teeth, he only caught the saddle-cloth and one skirt of the rider's coat. These he tore from the back of both, leaving the worthy doctor—the "Owen swift and Owen strong" of that country—in the ludicrous predicament of Bailie Nicol Jarvie, when cut down by the dirk of the Highland gillie.

On another occasion, Russell, when riding Cottager and hunting with a new draft from the Hambledon Hounds, found a fox near Beaford Moor, and pressed him in cover so sharply that he turned short and broke away, unknown to him, down wind. Losing sight of the pack, and fancying he viewed a tail-hound at the extreme end of the moor, he rode up, and there found an Irish packman, Peter Dougan by name, standing on a bank, and blown by the chase; but still staring after it with bated breath and longing eyes.

"Have you seen the hounds, my man?" inquired Russell, eagerly.

"Iss, your honour; they're jist ahead, running like a peal of bells."

"Then jump up behind me, pack and all," said Russell, charmed with the man's enthusiasm and evident love of hunting; "jump up, and you shall see a bit more of the sport."

"Bedad, then," said Peter, "that I'll do;" and as Russell adjusted Cottager to the bank, Peter and his pack took their place behind the cantle, notwithstanding the broad meanings displayed by the horse at being thus loaded. He then turned to kick furiously, and never stopped kicking till he had fairly floored Peter and his pack.

Not long after this adventure, when Russell was riding the chestnut horse Monkey, Peter again met him, and said he had a great favour to ask him, and that was, that he would allow him to ride that horse over a five-barred gate, with his hands tied behind his back, his face to the horse's tail, and without saddle or bridle. "And," said Peter, entreatingly, "I'll give ye me pack, sir, af ye'll let me do it; and, by me sowl, 'tis worth five pounds."

Russell, in a state of wonderment, inquired why he was so anxious to perform such a feat, pointing out the danger of attempting it in such a fashion.

"Faix, your honour," replied Peter, "I should like to tell 'em what I've done in England when I get back to the ould country."

Monkey with hounds, and in a good temper, would jump any ordinary five-barred gate; but otherwise wouldn't rise at a fender. "Had I granted his request," said Russell, "the horse would have broken Peter's neck to a dead certainty."

For years afterwards the Irishman, on his annual journeys to England, never failed to include in his pack a few silk pocket-handkerchiefs of the blue bird's-eye pattern, which he brought especially for Russell's use; and it was with no little difficulty that he could be persuaded to take payment for those articles, so devoted an admirer was he of Russell and his hounds. And so well known to the hawking fraternity in Ireland was Russell's name, that not five years ago—forty years after Peter Dougan's date—the former overtook two Irishmen near South Molton, and having packs on their backs, he inquired whence they came: "From Ireland, your honour," was the reply; "we landed at Ilfracombe last night."

"Have you any handkerchiefs of this pattern?" asked Russell, showing them a bird's-eye blue one.

"No, your honour; they are very scarce now."

"Well," he replied, "I bought them from a countryman of yours, Pat Dougan by name."

"'Tis Peter Dougan you mane; and you are Mr. Russell, ef you had them from him.

Ah! poor Peter; he dearly loved hunting, and was always talking about your riverence; he's been dead many, many years."

On parting company the packmen volunteered to bring him the handkerchiefs he required; a promise which, after due time, they did not fail to fulfil.

Now for Billy, the stand-by of Russell's stable, and, as he was wont to declare, the best horse he ever crossed in his life. Billy was a bay pony, fourteen hands high—"big as a mountain and long as to-day and to-morrow." He was by a two-year-old grass colt by Twilight, a grandson of Eclipse, out of an Exmoor pony; and was bred by Mr. Wreford, of Clannaborough, so well known to Devonshire men as one of the most successful breeders of blood stock in the West of England.

Of the stout and enduring qualities of Billy it is enough to say that Russell never knew him beaten; nor, as a proof of it, did he ever fail to come home merrily, however long the day, and pick up his corn to the last grain in the manger. His staying powers in chase, his bank-fencing, and mode of getting through heavy ground, under the weight he carried and the pace he maintained, were truly marvellous. "Russell," writes Mr. Harris, "mounted me once on Billy, and little did I anticipate the great treat in store for me. The meet was at Broadbury Castle;

and thinking him a pony I at first rode him quietly; but when the hounds began to run, Billy pulled at his snaffle, and letting him go he went with a will right up to the head, as if he had said to himself, 'That's my place, and I mean to keep it.' And so he did; no bank could stop him; no pace choke him off; he could stay all day, and go a cracker through dirt up to the very last. In fact, he was in every respect a steed worthy of his renowned ancestor; and I much doubt if Wreford ever bred a gamer or a better animal."

Russell, it is almost surperfluous to say, valued him as the apple of his eye; nay, if he had suffered himself to be tempted by gold, he might at any time have filled his pockets with the price of Billy. But to all offers Russell cried, Avaunt! and death alone divided the twain.

Nor was that altogether strictly the case; for, when the event took place after a faithful servitude of more than ten years, Billy's glossy hide, being removed by skilful hands, was sent to a tanner's, and afterwards formed the covering of a most comfortable armchair. The legs and hoofs, the latter beautifully polished and fitted with invisible castors, were all Billy's; and well might Russell, reclining in the once familiar seat, and perhaps dozing after a long day's work, be led by fancy's dream to believe that Billy was again under him, sharing the sport together as of yore, and bearing him on eagle wings to the front of the chase.

Such a dream would surely be far less unnatural and far happier than the endless inconsequential visions in which men, dipped in Lethe's stream, are so apt to indulge.

But, though Russell would ofttimes allude with tearful regret to the memory of Billy, he conferred the same honour on Cottager and Monkey; and there they all stood in the dining-room at Tordown as if the gods in a moment of compassion had transformed the trio into easy armchairs, determined that Russell and his friends, like Baucis and Philemon, should not be parted even by death.

Such was his mode of cherishing the remembrance of the faithful brute companions that had served him so well in life; and on their part they were still, as it were, doing him grateful service by administering to the comfort of himself and guests, and reminding them of many a bygone day of thrilling sport and innocent recreation.

Frederick the Great, we are told, expressed a wish even in his will to be buried with his favourite dogs, and especially near the horse that had carried him so often to victory; but Russell's fancy for conserving the relics of his mute friends and enjoying their company, still present in the form of armchairs, conveys a far pleasanter notion than that of the old warrior, whose last words were, "I shall be near him very soon." Notwithstanding his will, however, his faithful pets did not "bear him company," for his body received the burial of a Christian, and lies under the pulpit in Potsdam Church.

Many a pleasantry would Russell pass when inviting a guest to take a seat on one of his old friend's backs. "There," he would say, "give old Cottager a turn; he'll carry you as easily as a feather-bed; and he never bites now." Or, "Try Billy; if he can't go through dirt as he once could, he's up to any weight and won't give you a fall."

These, however, are later reminiscences of Tordown, the Alpine home to which he removed on quitting Iddesleigh in 1832, and to which he once more recently returned; hoping, as he then expressed it, to remain there till "the golden bowl be broken, and the spirit shall return unto God who gave it." But the sketch given of the horses has carried both writer and reader over the scent, and a backward cast—never a favourite one of Russell's—is now necessary to recover the line.

Russell had now entered on the third season of his mastership, and so far had literally basked in the sunshine of success; but in the autumn of 1829, without being an augur, he was not slow to observe that over the Tetcott and Broadbury districts loomed ominous clouds, which portended a break-up of the present arrangements, as well as probably an extensive change in the landmarks of his country. Nor was he kept long in suspense; for on Friday the 13th of November his pack met at Five Oaks for the last time under the old *régime*. A glorious finale, however, crowned the event; he killed a brace of foxes, the first in fifty minutes and the next at the end of a long dodging run, in which by the manner he handled his hounds Russell's woodcraft was eminently displayed.

The circumstances that led to the change were complicated. In the first place the country was much too large for the means at command; for, owing to the ardent support of the yeomen-farmers, far and wide, foxes had largely increased throughout the land; consequently the damage fund and the expense of feeing the keepers, etc., rising proportionately, the sum total amounted soon to a serious charge on an exchequer too often inconveniently straitened and never over-flowing. This, perhaps, may be considered the root of the matter. But there was also a general suspicion among Russell's friends that jealousy had a finger in the pie; and that that feeling, intensified by the impression that the country was insufficiently hunted, prompted a small party, including the Molesworth Trustees, to come forward and suggest the need of another pack of hounds, and therefore the curtailment of Russell's country.

So the Landue pack, under the command of as gallant a rider as ever crossed a country, Mr. Phillipps, late of the 7th Hussars, better known as Tom Phillipps, was forthwith started, and the Tetcott, Hayne, and Broadbury covers wrested from Russell, and handed over to him. He then took formal possession of the country, "the limits of which," writes Russell, "appear to me to be illimitable; for they claimed all the covers from Hatherleigh—three miles from my kennels at Iddesleigh—to Wade Bridge, ten miles below Bodmin."

Phillipps, however, met one morning at Gribbleford Bridge, only two miles from Hatherleigh, found four brace of foxes in the cover—a dog, vixen, and three brace of cubs —but made a mull of it, called off his hounds in disgust and went home, a distance of thirty miles at least to his kennel. After some time it was communicated to Russell that Phillipps would never draw those covers again; so, as the country was a choice one, comprising the fine moorland district of Broadbury, the wildest in the West of England, Russell bethought him how he could best recover his footing and bring about the desirable end of securing it for his own.

A turn in his favour by the wheel of fortune soon gave him a suitable opportunity. Mr. J. Morth Woolcombe happening to join him one morning, "they found," in Russell's words, "a right real Dartmoor Hector, and away he went for his native moorland, straight as a bee-line; but he never set foot on it, for we ran into him about a mile short of his haunts. Just before we killed him, he crossed some enclosures, and the hounds coming back to us, I held up my hands and said, 'Stand still, gentlemen, pray! the fox is in this field.' It was not two acres and it was plough.

"'Nonsense!' cried Woolcombe; 'we should see him if he were.'

"'He is here, I tell you, if I know my hounds.' And in a moment they seized him within a few yards of his horse's feet.

"'His delight was unbounded; he begged me as a particular favour to go home by way of Ashbury, invited the whole field into the hall, drew cork after cork of champagne, toasted the little Iddesleigh pack and their master, and promised similar hospitality whenever they killed a fox within reach of his domain.

"He kept his word too up to a certain time, when, for some reason I never could fathom, he sent his brother Robert over to Iddesleigh to negotiate for the purchase of my whole pack. I was not at home; but when I returned to dinner Mrs. Russell said, 'Robert Woolcombe has been here all the morning, waiting to see you.'

"'And did he say what he wanted?' I inquired.

"'His brother is anxious to buy your hounds, and sent him over to treat for them; they think that, as a clergyman, you ought not to keep them.'

"'They are very kind neighbours,' I said, 'and I fully appreciate their good feeling; *but* at the same time I hope I do them no wrong if I altogether mistrust their motives.'

"'Robert is coming again to-morrow,' continued Mrs. Russell, 'and is bent on seeing you.'

"Before the morrow arrived, however, being forewarned as to the object of his visit, I was fully prepared with my answer.

"The next day he accordingly came; and as he took me by the hand, I said, 'Well Robert, and pray what's your pleasure?'

"'I came to buy your hounds,' he responded, bluntly; 'what's your price?'

"'Three hundred guineas,' I replied, 'for all but five couple, which I shall keep.'

"'A bargain,' he said; "I'll take them. But what are you going to do with the five couple?'

"'Keep them as a nucleus for another pack.'

"'Oh, that will never do,' he said; 'we want the country; the hounds are no use to us without it.'

"'Then you shall have neither, Bob,' was my decisive reply.

"And so ended the negotiation. We then parted, and I went on hunting the country and killing the wild animal as heretofore."

It was a real grief to Russell for many a day afterwards to discover, as he very soon did, that foxes in the Broadbury country became scarcer and scarcer yearly, and that at length Mr. Woolcombe went so far as to wage open war against the whole race by ordering his keepers and tenants to trap, shoot, and destroy every fox they found bred or travelling over his estate. And so rigorously was this mandate executed, that a paragraph appeared in the papers announcing the number of vixens and cubs he had destroyed, and calculating that he had rid the country of no less than two hundred and fifty foxes, great, small, and forthcoming. Nay, large placards were printed at Okehampton and posted in the neighbourhood, setting forth the above gross statement, and justifying the slaughter as one of meritorious service to the whole community.

But although at the time it was denounced as a most unneighbourly proceeding on the part of Mr. Woolcombe, there are good grounds now for believing that he was, in truth, influenced by conscientious scruples only, rather than by any ill-will to Russell ; for in speaking of him apart from his profession, he was wont to express his unbounded admiration of his manly power and pre-eminent ability in all that pertained to the science of woodcraft.

Great indeed was the indignation, especially of the hunting community, at this wholesale massacre of the foxes. One Jack White, a horse-dealer, is said to have upbraided Mr. Woolcombe, who was a very tall man, to his very face.

"Let me tell you, sir," said Jack, "that you're six feet four of the very worse stuff as I ever seed wrapped up in one bundle. Gude morning, sir."

It was not without good reason, therefore, that Mr. Phillipps, either from a mistrust in the friendship of the cover-owners, or from a manly feeling that he would be doing Russell an ill-service by continuing to hunt that country, declined, after the day at Gribbleford Bridge, to bring his hounds again to that locality, and thenceforth devoted himself exclusively to the region round about Tetcott and Pencarrow. One thing is certain, that in every transaction with respect to Russell and the Broadbury country, Mr. Phillipp's conduct was always straightforward and altogether unimpeachable.

Early in the spring of 1831, the young baronet, Sir William Molesworth, then in his twenty-first year, having invited a large party of gentlemen to meet Phillipps and the Landue hounds at Pencarrow for a fortnight's hunting, the house was filled to the rafters. Two stalls were allotted to each guest, and hacks *ad libitum* found room in the stables of the neighbouring tenants. The few survivors of that meeting—and now, alas, they are very few—will never forget the 16th of February in that fortnight, when a fox was found at Polbrock, near the riverside, every hound breaking away almost on his back, bringing him over the paling into Pencarrow Park, and by the Roman mounds away to Helland Wood; thence tearing on with a burning scent over the virgin soil of the vast rough enclosures, they carried a grand head, and, dashing five or six couple abreast over the big boundary fence, broke out on the moor and on to the Launceston and Bodmin road, where they dropped into slow hunting and then threw up.

The road was of granite, hard as iron and dry as brickdust; but a hound called Memory, with nose well down, held on, faintly feathering here and there, yet still on—the rest of the hounds, with heads up, being hopelessly at fault. Phillipps, growing impatient and grasping his horn, was turning to cast them towards the

The Finish of the Pencarrow Run.

Torrs northwards, when Russell, keeping his eye on Memory, held up his hand and exclaimed, "Do, pray, give her time. There!—she has it, I tell you, and will fling her tongue in half a minute if you'll let her alone."

But Phillipps *would* make his cast, while Russell and Mr. Pomeroy Gilbert remained stationary, intent only upon Memory, as she still persevered steadily on the road. At length, a patch of wet soil giving her a chance, she dropped her stern, and at the same time throwing her tongue, dashed over the heather-bank on to Temple Moor and away. Russell's scream was too thrilling, too rapturous, to describe. Away, away, over that grand waste of heather—a thorough wilderness; not a vestige of man; not a solitary patch of gorse; not even a twig to shelter a wild animal for leagues.

Racing him to the boundary fence of the moor above Trebartha the hounds caught a view, and instantly as if by a stroke of magic they and the fox vanished from the scene. It seemed to the foremost riders, Mr. Charles Trelawny on Oswestry, Mr. Phillipps on Foster, Mr. Harris, Mr. Coryton, and Mr. Tom Hext, who was the first to view him, that the earth had opened her jaws and swallowed them alive; and such was the case; the shaft of an old mine lay open, and they had fallen

"Into utter darkness, deep engulphed."

The fox, indeed, with the activity of a wild beast, had clambered on to a broken beam; but three of the leading hounds were swimming about in the dark water at the bottom of the mine, some seven fathoms deep; while the rest of the pack had stopped short of the abyss and scrambled out.

"Gone to ground with a vengeance," exclaimed Phillipps, with bitter emphasis, dreading the loss of his hounds.

In a few minutes some miners appeared on the ground; but not a man of them would go down, not daring to face the dangers of the decayed framework in the precipitous shaft. Not so, however, "Jack Russell," who, with a knotted rope in one hand and his hunting-whip in the other, lowered himself, amid a shower of loose stones and earth, to the beam on which the fox was crouching. Then running the thong through the keeper of his whip, and fixing the noose round the animal's neck, he shouted aloud, "Haul away, I've got him!" and in half a minute he and the fox were landed again on *terra firma*.

"Save him, Phillipps; he is a gallant fellow and deserves his life," said Russell, begging hard for a reprieve.

But Phillipps sternly said, "No," and tossed him to the hounds.

Then to save the three brave brutes now struggling in the pit from a longer immersion,

Russell was again prepared to go to the rescue, had not Colonel (afterwards Sir Walter Raleigh Gilbert) persuaded a miner, by the bribe of a capful of silver, to go down; and secured by a rope round his waist, to bring up the hounds, one by one, safely "to bank."

It was a grand run throughout: sixteen miles as the crow flies—measured on the map—and the last seven over the wild open moor without the shadow of a fence or check from first to last.

Russell to the end of his life spoke of it as one of the finest things he had ever witnessed; but the cream of the run, the finishing touch—that brilliant passage over the Bodmin Moor—was due to him and him alone.

Of the many queer incidents that befell him in those early days, the one he met with at Porlock is by no means the least amusing; and as it illustrates the feeling of a strong partisan in favour of him and his hounds, it shall be told as nearly as possible in his own words.

"In the spring of 1830 I took my little pack down to Porlock to enjoy a week's hunting in the open and extensive commons in that locality; and rare sport we had day after day both with fox and hare. I was accompanied by the Rev. J. Pomeroy Gilbert, there to be joined by the Rev. H. Farr Yeatman, two of the best and most accomplished sportsmen I ever met, to whose names let me add that of George Templer, of Stover; such a trio they were as the world has rarely seen together in the hunting-field.

"On our return from the hills one evening, Mrs. Smith, our hostess at the Ship Hotel, where we were staying thus accosted me—

"'If you plaise, Mr. Rissell, that old scamp, Squire Tamlyn, as they call 'en, hath a been down here to forbid you from hunting over his property. Now hearken to me, sir, and us'll tackle 'en, as all sich varmint ouft to be tackled. Ask 'en to come here and dine with 'ee to-morrow, and when he'th a sot down comfortable afore the fire, give the t'other gentlemen a wink to leave the room, and I'll come in quietly behind 'en, seize his both arms, and then do you wallop 'en over the face and eyes till he sings out for mercy. I'll never let 'en go, mind, till you've a finished with 'en; and that I'll promise ye.'

"At this point I ventured to remonstrate with her, urging, first, that it would be a gross breach of hospitality, and then that a summons for the assault would be sure to follow.

"'But,' exclaimed the woman, 'the magistrates shan't get a word out of me to convict you, sir, if he doth get a summons; and what's more, I'll tell 'em two or three such pretty stories about 'en, as he won't like to hear; and there the matter 'll end.'

"The next day," says Russell, "with the view of propitiating Mr. Tamlyn, I wrote him a very polite note inviting him to dine with us; but he declined the honour, much to the disgust of Mrs. Smith, who consoled herself with these words, 'Well, never mind, I'll give it to 'en myself the first time I set eyes on the mean old scamp.'

"And," continued Russell, "I have reason to believe that she absolutely kept her word; for she was a veritable termagant—a tigress in petticoats."

One result of the week's sport being somewhat remarkable, it may interest the reader to have it in Russell's words: "The very day Tamlyn went to Porlock to forbid my hunting, I found a fox in the heath on Lucat Common, his property. Thinking it was a vixen, I rode up to the bush out of which she jumped, and, behold! curled up in a warm nest were four live cubs. I tied my handkerchief to a bush hard by, and rode after the pack as fast as my horse could carry me. But it was a blaze of scent all the way; and in thirty minutes, to my great annoyance, they ran into and killed poor little Vicky. I then returned to her kennel, took up the cubs—all four vixens—and sent them by Bat Anstey to Iddesleigh, fifty miles away. An earth was made for them under Halsdon, Mr. Furse's residence;

and in and around that earth they remained, being ear-marked, and thriving well, till the following October, when suddenly they disappeared, and I never had the good luck to find one of them again with hounds.

"*Six years afterwards*, I met the late Mr. Newton, of Bridestowe, in Barnstaple, and he asked me if I had ever ear-marked—describing the mark—any foxes and lost sight of them.

"'Yes,' I said; 'four cubs, all vixens.' 'Then,' he replied, 'I found them last March in some brakes near Broadwood-Widger, twenty-five miles below Halsdon; had good runs with each, and killed all four.'"

# CHAPTER IX.

Removes to Swymbridge—His Kindness to the Gipsies—St. Hubert's Hall—The Vine Draft—The Chulmleigh Club—The Bishop of Exeter and the Charges against Russell—Bishop revokes the Curate's License—Mr. Trelawny on the Chulmleigh Meetings.

> His house was known to all the vagrant train,
> He chid their wanderings, but relieved their pain;
> Careless their merits or their faults to scan,
> His pity gave ere charity began.
>
> Goldsmith.

Mr. Russell had resided just six years at Iddesleigh, when, in 1832, the prospect of preferment being held out to him, he was induced to remove to Tordown, in the parish of Swymbridge; a lone country-house overhanging a picturesque combe, and approached by a steep by-road leading from that village to Exmoor. To Mrs. Russell, especially, the change proved a most welcome one, inasmuch as it now brought her back to the scenes of her early youth, again to dwell among her own people; Dennington House, the seat of Admiral and Mrs. Bury, being situated on the opposite side of the valley in the same parish.

In 1833, soon after he had planted his garden and taken full possession of Tordown, the Perpetual Curacy of Swymbridge and Landkey became vacant, and the benefice being in the gift of Whittington Landon, then Dean of Exeter, Russell was appointed to it in that year.

Appropriate enough was the title of "Perpetual Curacy" to such a benefice; for the whole annual income derived by the incumbent amounted to less than £180, out of which sum he was not only required to provide and pay a curate for the annexed parish of Landkey, but to meet perpetual calls from a large population of poor parishioners, who naturally in the first place looked to him for help in their numerous emergencies. To have called it a "living" would have been simply a comedy; for, when these and various other liabilities incidental to Church property had been deducted, the residue might be reckoned as *nil*, or even as something less than that, for the incumbent to live on.

Rightly, too, was it thus named in another sense; for *there* Russell was planted for forty-five years—and so far he may fairly be considered the Perpetual Curate of Swymbridge. During that period, however, the parish has undergone various and important changes for the better; its annexation with Landkey, for instance, has been severed; new schools have been established and endowed; while, at a distant hamlet called "Traveller's Rest," a commodious chapel has been built, the cost of which depended on means mainly raised by Russell's exertions.

"When I was inducted," Russell writes, "to this incumbency, in 1833, there was only one service here every Sunday—morning and evening alternately with Landkey, whereas now, I am thankful to say, we have four services every Sunday in Swymbridge alone." To this it may be added that the fine old church of that parish, described by Mr. Pearson, A.R.A., of Harley Street, as "one of the most interesting churches he ever saw," has been admirably restored by that gentleman at a cost of nearly £3,000.

Russell's great influence among the yeomen and tenant-farmers of North Devon, and the genial spirit with which he managed them, as a Master of Hounds, has been already referred to in a former chapter; a kind word from him doing more to secure their goodwill, and promote the cause of fox-hunting, than the Bank of England notes of less popular men. But, if little has hitherto been said on the subject of that inner circle—his own parish—over which he has presided for so many years, it must not thence be inferred that he lacked at home the honour he found abroad; for no man has been more venerated, nay, loved, by the poor among whom he has ministered than Mr. Russell. And with good reason, too; for, in season, or out of season, no one of them in distress ever appealed to him in vain.

Nor did the wandering tribes of gipsies that were wont to sojourn a while on the waste spots in his parish—that race of Ishmael of whom it is said, "his hand shall be against every man, and every man's hand against him," form an exception to that rule.

Instead of persecuting them as trespassers and plunderers, by impounding their donkeys, compelling them to strike their tents at a moment's notice, driving them and their children from pillar to post, and treating them more like wolves than human beings, he never failed to protect and befriend them whenever he thought they were unmercifully or even unfairly used. It was one of the old gipsy regulations of the Kirk Yetholme tribe, Sir Walter Scott tells us, to respect, in their depredations, the property of their benefactors; so these North Devon gipsies, in return for Russell's kindness, were always scrupulously careful to give him no cause to complain of their presence, or regret his own forbearance; and whatever their shortcomings may have been with respect to other property, his, at least, never suffered from their depredations in any way. Often has he been heard to say, "to the best of his belief he never lost a head of poultry, nor even an egg, by the hands of the gipsies."

But their appreciation of his kindness was more than negatively shown; they took active steps and a signal opportunity of proving their devotion to Russell by coming forward, of their own accord, to protect his dwelling-house, when they had reason to believe it was threatened by burglars. A desperate gang had infested the neighbourhood for some time, the houses of the clergy having been made the chief object of their depredations, far and near. At length it was whispered about that Russell's, which had so far escaped, would be the next to suffer, the gipsies not being the last to hear the rumour.

The alarm, however, after some time passed off; and one day, as Russell was riding near Stonecross, on his way to Exmoor, he met Seth, the stalwart son of the King of the Gipsies, and thus accosted him: "Is it true, Seth, that you and your men, hearing that my house was likely to be attacked, have been keeping watch over it for many nights together?"

"Quite true, sir; and let me tell you, if we had caught them on your premises, they would never have gone home alive."

But, long before that event happened, Russell had secured the goodwill of the Romanies for ever, by a somewhat risky transaction on his part. He was riding down to Haccombe on a visit to Sir Walter Carew, and passing by Partridge Walls, near Eggesford, was hailed by a blacksmith, who, coming out of his forge, begged his advice under the following circumstances: "If you please, Mr. Russell," he said, "here's a gipsy who wants to buy my black mare; but he has no money in his pocket, and wants me to trust him. Now, I can't afford to part with her and lose the money; so what had I better do?"

The gipsy was standing by at the time; and, as Russell fixed his gaze upon the open and manly face of the swarthy young fellow, he felt convinced by its expression that his purpose was an honest one, and strong in that conviction, he asked him his name, putting a further question or two to him before he gave the blacksmith an answer.

On hearing his name, Russell said "Then you are the man who was encamped last year with your wife near Iddesleigh, soon after your marriage?"

"No, sir; that was my brother."

"If I pass my word for the money, will you pay it?"

"Yes, sir, I will," he replied unhesitatingly.

"Then," said Russell, turning to the blacksmith, "you may look to me for the money; if he don't pay you, I will."

The blacksmith appeared satisfied; but still anxious to clench the nail properly, he warned Russell that he certainly should come upon him if the gipsy failed to keep his word.

Russell becomes surety for the Gipsy.

About a week afterwards, Russell was again passing the blacksmith's forge, and, reining up his horse, he inquired if the money had been paid by the gipsy.

"Yes, sir," he replied; "every penny of it."

In becoming "surety for a stranger," and that stranger a gipsy and a horse-dealer, it is only too wonderful that he did not "smart for it;" but it was just the reverse: he gained by that and other acts of kindness to his race, the goodwill and gratitude of the whole "vagrant train." Nor was their gratitude a matter of sentiment only, for the King of the Gipsies, a very old man, falling ill, and feeling that his earthly hours were drawing to a close, expressed a last wish that a charm he had long worn and prized greatly—it was a silver Spanish coin, Temp. Car. III. Rex Hispaniæ—should be handed over to Mr. Russell, in token of the sympathy he had ever shown to him and his tribe. He left him also, as a legacy, his royal rat-catcher's belt; and on his death-bed sent him a message begging he might be buried in Swymbridge Churchyard by Mr. Russell himself.

The patriarch's chief legatee could scarcely do less than comply with so simple a request; and accordingly in that God's-acre, where "the rude forefathers of the hamlet sleep," he now lies; and there, to his memory, his people have erected a substantial monument, acknowledging the receipt and marking the last resting-place of his borrowed earth. He was buried on a Saturday afternoon, Russell exacting a promise from his son Seth, that he and his camp would not move on the Sabbath-day. But, on the following Monday, Russell, having occasion to travel moorwards, found them on a waste place near Stonecross, four miles from the encampment they had occupied on the Saturday.

"How's this?" said he, hailing the young gipsy, who stepped out to meet him; "you promised me not to move till this morning; and you must have come here yesterday. I thought I could trust you, Seth."

"So you can, sir; but we couldn't help it. Mr. ——" (a neighbouring magistrate) "sent a constable to order us off directly, or he said we should all be locked up in jail."

While they were yet speaking, a handsome young gipsy woman, apparently in the bloom of health and vigour, came forth from one of the tents, and, with a prophetic air, said, "Good morning, Mr. Russell; the next person you bury will be myself." And on that day week, as the Swymbridge register will testify, he buried her. She was the old king's daughter.

Now, Russell was neither a superstitious nor a very credulous man—the Vicar of Wakefield and he in that respect could scarcely be more dissimilar; but, from that day, he was tainted, if not impressed, with the belief that something of the Cassandra foresight—the power of looking into futurity, that abyss of impenetrable darkness—is possessed by the gipsy race; at all events, prevalent as such an idea has been among men of the strongest minds—and their name is legion—it may be doubted if many, or any, could give better grounds for their phantasy than Russell.

Testimonials, in the form of silver goblets, salvers, and such-like presents, are far from being always a proof that the recipients have really deserved them; nor, though Russell has had in his day a fair share of such honours, would they now be referred to if one of a very unusual and remarkable character had not been conferred on him some time before he had fairly settled at Tordown.

Mr. C. A. Harris, of Hayne, animated by a strong and unqualified admiration of Russell's powers, both as a huntsman and a man, conceived the notion of doing him honour by a plan of singularly novel and unique design. It happened that, after a sharp burst with a fox in that country, Russell ran him to ground in an old quarry near Hayne, the excavation of which had been long discontinued. Whether he killed him or not, deponent sayeth not; but it is on record that from that date Mr. Harris determined to convert the quarry into a rustic temple in honour of Russell and his friends.

The quarry, overhung by old trees and situated on a dry rocky bank, was first hollowed out and paved with blocks of Dartmoor granite; an entire British village, including two or three kistvaens, being utilized for that purpose. Then, round the circular enclosure were formed, out of the same relics, twenty-two stalls, over each of which the carved head of a fox and an heraldic banner with a motto appropriate to each occupant were displayed, the name and residence of the knight being added thereto.

A *fête* of inauguration, including all the chief families of the district, took place at the time, and from that day St. Hubert's Hall has been the rendezvous of many a picnic party, attracted thither no less by the picturesque scenery than by the singular honour done to fox-hunting.

It was only a short time before Russell had made up his mind to quit Iddesleigh, the fame of his little pack having exceeded all expectation, that a break occurred in his hunting life, which created a general sensation, not only among his own devoted followers, but among others who only knew of his intense delight in the company of hounds. He parted with the whole lot, lending them, at least for a time, to Mr. T. Hext, of Restormel Castle, a gentleman in whose hands he well knew they would suffer no harm.

The pressure of a few friends, who probably believed they were doing him good service, had at length prevailed, and he was forced, as it were, at the point of the bayonet, to adopt their well-meant advice. But it was a trial and a wound to his feelings, the keenness of which Time, that soother of all sores, was ineffectual to heal.

For two long years this interregnum—a period of constrained inactivity and bondage, to one of his muscular habits—weighed like an incubus on his spirits, and clogged the wheels of his life with the daily want of something he missed, and of something more to do. The tedium, in fact, had become almost unbearable, when one day, as he was leisurely inspecting the blossom on his apple trees and calculating their autumn crop—reckoning his chickens before they were hatched—a surprise awaited him for which he was little prepared.

Six and a half couple of strong young hounds, a draft from the Vine, had been sent to him from Mr. Harry Fellowes, with an intimation that "they had all passed the distemper, and that no better blood had ever tackled a Devonshire fox." "There they stood," said Russell, "alone in my kennel—the greatest beauties my eye had ever rested on—looking up in my face so winningly, as much as to say, 'Only give us a trial, and we'll not disappoint you,' that I mentally determined to keep the lot and go to work again."

But the same friends were still at hand to counteract the temptation; and so great was the pressure put upon him, that again he consented with a heavy heart to abandon his design, and send the six and a half couple after the rest down to Restormel.

Accordingly, they were actually taken out of kennel to be so forwarded, when Mrs. Russell, witnessing her husband's dejection at parting with them, interposed and said, "Then they shan't go, John, if you don't like it. I don't see why you shouldn't have your amusement as well as other people." So back they went into Russell's kennel, and from that day he continued to keep hounds till 1871, when he parted with his last pack to Mr. Henry Villebois, of Marham Hall, Norfolk, a gentleman well known to the world as an old master of hounds and a distinguished sportsman.

It is related of the late eminent Bishop of Exeter, Henry Phillpotts, that soon after his appointment to that diocese in 1831, he was travelling on a visitation tour through the north of Devon, and seeing a pack of hounds in full cry, and a large number of gentlemen in black coats crossing the road in close pursuit, he turned to his chaplain, and said in a solemn tone, "Alas! this neighbourhood must have been visited by some fearful epidemic. I never saw so many men in mourning before."

The chaplain knew the country better than the bishop, and said nothing; while he identified the mourners, one after the other, as brethren of his own cloth, and personal friends. But not long did that keen and far-sighted prelate remain unacquainted with the habits of his clergy in this respect; and although for years he did all in his power to discountenance and suppress the practice, the love of hunting was too strong even for him; it still flourished like a plant indigenous to the soil—deep-rooted and ineradicable.

Russell, as might be expected, became the especial object of his fatherly solicitude; he held what is called "a chapter living," and besides, he was known by the bishop to be an able and popular preacher, and as such, it was only natural that his diocesan should be doubly anxious lest the effects of his ministerial eloquence should be weakened by his prominent and avowed association with the hunting-field. "As *you live*," would the bishop say, "so will men believe; and if the shepherd go astray, well may the flock."

But Russell, unable to see, if he endeavoured conscientiously to fulfil his duty, that he was either going himself or leading his flock astray by indulging in his favourite recreation, withstood the bishop's monitions with a firm but respectful attitude. After a time, however, his lordship, a man of inflexible purpose, on receiving a serious charge against him, and believing it to be well founded, pounced upon Russell with the swoop of an eagle, and summoned him and his accuser forthwith to the palace at Exeter.

The charge was this, that he (Russell) had refused to bury a child on the day named by its parents, because it was his hunting-day.

Both parties being assembled before him, with Mr. Secretary Barnes seated at a side-table taking notes on the bishop's behalf, his lordship recited the charge, and said gravely, "Is that true, Mr. Russell?"

"Will your lordship permit me to ring the bell?"

"Certainly," replied the bishop.

The bell was then rung, and a servant making his appearance, Russell said, "Be so good as to send in that woman who is now waiting in the hall."

As she entered the room, Russell turned to the bishop and said, "That is the mother of the child, my lord. I requested her to accompany the clerk of the parish (Wm. Chapple) to the palace to-day, paid her fare, and here she is. But, otherwise, I have not said one word to her on the subject of the present inquiry. Your lordship can put any question you please to her."

The bishop then asked her if the charge were true.

"Nit a word o't, my lord," she answered, unhesitatingly.

He then requested her to state what had taken place on the occasion, and given rise to such a report.

She replied that her husband had asked Mr. Russell to bury the child on a Wednesday or Thursday, on whichever day was most convenient to him; that he chose the latter, and buried the child on that day.

"And pray," said the bishop, "were you at all inconvenienced by keeping the body a day longer?"

"Not a bit o't, my lord; us might have kep' un till these day—'twas but a poor atomy thing;" meaning it was quite a skeleton.

The bishop, finding in this charge no *primâ facie* case made out against Russell, proceeded at once to investigate other charges brought by the same accuser; who, as it turned out, had been grossly misinformed on each and all; and as they, too, shared the like fate, falling to the ground without a tittle of evidence to support them, but, on the contrary, with much to disprove them, his lordship turned sharply on him and said: "I am quite shocked to think, sir, that you should have brought so many charges against Mr. Russell, and been unable to substantiate even one of them."

Much disappointed apparently at the result of the inquiry, and still unwilling to relax his grasp upon Russell, the bishop thus addressed him—

"But the fact still remains, I grieve to say, that you, the incumbent of Swymbridge, keep hounds, and that your curate" (who was also present) "hunts with you. Will you give up your hounds?"

"No, my lord; I decline doing so."

He then turned to the curate and said, "Your license, sir, I revoke; and I only regret that the law does not enable me to deal with the *graver* offender in a far more summary way."

"I am very happy to find you can't, my lord," said Russell, "and still happier to know that I have done nothing in contravention of the law, and that it protects me. May I ask then, my lord, if you revoke Mr. Sleeman's license, who is to take the duty at Landkey next Sunday?"

"Mr. Sleeman may do it."

"And who the following Sunday?" inquired Russell.

"Mr. Sleeman again," responded the bishop, "if by that time you have not secured another curate."

"I shall take no steps to do so, my lord; and, moreover, shall be very cautious as to whom I admit into my church," replied Russell, significantly.

It may be added that, immediately on hearing the result of that conference, the parishioners of Landkey sent up their churchwarden with a "Round Robin" in Sleeman's favour; and from that day he remained the curate of Landkey till he married and removed to Whitchurch, a family living near Tavistock, to which he succeeded on the death of his father.

"But, my lord," continued Russell, "there are many other clergymen in your diocese who keep hounds"—here a groan from the bishop—"why am I singled out among so many?"

"Name them," said the bishop impatiently.

"That I decline doing," replied Russell, firmly. Whereupon the whole party, to their great relief, were dismissed from the episcopal presence.

Mr. Ralph Barnes, however, overtaking Russell at the palace gate, stopped him by saying, "You told the bishop there were other clergymen in the diocese who keep hounds; you are bound to name them, sir."

"Well," said Russell, "as I believe that one of them, at least, would not object to my doing so, I give you the name of the Rev. John Froude, of Knowstone."

That gentleman, as the reader is aware, had already given the bishop more than one backfall, which neither he nor his secretary would be likely to forget; he had proved himself, in fact, more than a match for both; and his lordship was far too clever a strategist to renew an attack which, if unsuccessful, his good sense told him would only weaken his episcopal authority.

It is no figure of speech to say that, at that period, there were probably a score of clergymen who had packs of their own in the diocese of Exeter; three of whom kept fox-hounds only, while the others hunted nominally the hare.

So the bishop, in commencing, as he very soon did, an energetic crusade against them, had a host to deal with; every one of whom, not being a curate, would be likely to cry "no surrender"—nay, to defend their right of re-creation in that fashion to the last shot in their locker.

There is a story of one—the vicar of St. B.—an old friend of Russell's on whom soft words and angry monitions were expended alike in vain; both being equally powerless to bring him either to the bishop's palace or his visitation courts. At length, his patience being exhausted, his lordship issued a formal citation commanding him, at his peril, to attend his next triennial visitation at T——, on a given day.

This step on the part of the bishop, it should be premised, took place at the time when he was engaged in the great Gorham trial; a case which the Judicial Committee of the Privy Council decided against him by an overwhelming majority, Knight Bruce being the only legal member of the committee who did not agree with that decision. So marked a judgment in favour of Mr. Gorham, who had been the object of a long and harassing law-suit without, as was then believed, due and reasonable cause, gave rise, of course, to strong comments on the part of the Liberal press; which, adding fuel to the fire, brought down a certain amount of obloquy on the bishop's name.

Just at the time when the result of this trial was in every man's mouth, the visitation at T—— took place. On the appointed day, the bishop having delivered his charge, the apparitor then proceeded to summon the clergy severally by name; and as each came forward to answer the roll-call, a pause and dead silence ensued when the name of the vicar of St. B. was twice called without any response.

"Is the churchwarden of St. B. present?" inquired the bishop in a solemn voice.

On which a fine old-fashioned yeoman, of portly figure and ruddy countenance, stalked up in his top-boots, and stroking his head deferentially announced himself as the churchwarden of St. B.

"I am very sorry to hear," said the bishop, addressing him, "the sad things that reach me respecting your vicar——"

"My lord," said the yeoman, interrupting him, "don't believe a word of them. I hear strange tales about your lordship, but I don't believe a word of them, not I."

Another story is told of the bishop and a clergyman in his diocese, who, if not Russell himself, must have been some one very like him: "I am told, my lord," said the latter, "that you object to my hunting."

"Dear me," said his lordship, with a perfectly courteous smile, "who could have told you so? What I object to is that you should ever do anything else."

Sarcasm could scarcely go farther.

I will now give a few extracts from the letters of an old friend, Mr. Trelawny, of Coldrenick, who writes thus respecting Russell and his hounds:—

"The rising generation—the gormandising, battue-shooter, and similar people—should learn something of the heroes of old, who, alas! are dying out and leaving few behind them to fill up the gaps. Where now are your Osbaldestones, Kintores, Rosses, and such-like men?

"Even in fox-hunting, the number slain is everything; and owing to the number of foxes bred, how seldom do we see a run of ten miles from point to point, much less the fifteen or twenty of olden times; I have long thought the *number* spoils the *sport*.

"When, let me ask, will Lord —— see such a fortnight as was once seen at Chulmleigh; when with Carew's and Russell's hounds, in twelve consecutive hunting-days, the shortest runs were twelve miles from point to point, as the crow flies?

"But, in those days, five and twenty brace killed by a four-day-a-week pack was voted enough. Now, forsooth, if 'my lord' cannot count sixty brace of noses on his kennel door, he is miserable."

Then, the nightly meetings after the day's sport was over, Mr. Trelawny describes with a few happy and graphic touches:—

"It would not be easy, nowadays, to muster at a fox-hunting dinner such men as the two Russells, father and son; Sir John Rogers (uncle to the present Lord Blachford), George Leach, George Templer, and the late John Bulteel. The pointed and playful sallies of wit, with which the two latter enlivened the meetings, combined with the racy anecdotes and classical combats of Mr. Russell, sen., and Sir John Rogers, who kept the ball going with unceasing gaiety, was indeed a treat never to be forgotten.

"I remember that once, at Chulmleigh, we had no less than six M.F.H.'s present at one dinner-party, viz., Newton Fellowes, who sat next to me, John Bulteel, John King, Templer, Sir Walter Carew, and Jack Russell. The first stuck to his port like a man, flooring his two bottles in true orthodox style; while the others drank punch—Henley Rogers (the Admiral) and Sir John mixing the 'materials;' Sir John of gin, most patronized, and the Admiral of rum."

Again, Mr. Trelawny adds: "Whenever I have sat at the same dinner-table with Jack Russell he has been the life of the party."

The sale of horses by auction, which took place after dinner, while the symposium was at its height, was often considerable, and added no little to the amusement and sociality of the Chulmleigh meetings. It was competent for any one to put up his friend's horse without even consulting him; the rule being that the owner should be allowed *one* bid *only* to protect himself. Consequently, many a man, bidding carelessly, too often found himself in the possession of a steed or steeds he had not the remotest intention of buying; the owner declining to interfere by a bid of his own with the last bidder.

A shilling being dropped into a wine-glass and the horse named, the bidding was then started by the auctioneer to the club—an office ably, and often wittily, fulfilled by Mr. John Dicker Fortescue, at Chulmleigh, and, at a later date, by Mr. John King, of Fowelscombe, at the South Molton meetings.

But Russell, never a good sitter round the wassail-bowl, very rarely took part either as a buyer or seller in these auctions; for, at the hour of their commencement, generally a late one, he would, as a rule, steal away to rest, enforcing, as he did so, his old maxim on those who pressed him to stay: "Hunting, I tell you, is worth any sacrifice; and if you sit up and get a headache, you can't thoroughly enjoy it. So, by your leave, good-night, gentlemen."

# CHAPTER X.

His Power in Distinguishing Hounds after once Hearing their Names—Parts with his Pack—Starts Again—Kennel Management—Firing, etc.—Four Days' Work—Mr. Houlditch as Whip—Kindness to a Curate—A Scene between them at Lanacre Bridge on the Moor.

> Here's a health to all hunters of every degree,
> Whether clippers, or craners, or hill-top abiders;
> The man that hates hunting, he won't do for me,
> And ought to be pumped on by gentlemen riders.
>
> Old Song.

The old saying that the "dog will have his day," is a proverb by no means inapplicable to the Chulmleigh Club; for, after flourishing with much vigour and success for more than twenty years, symptoms of decay set in, and at length became too apparent, when Mr. Templer, Sir John Rogers, Mr. Bulteel, and other prominent members ceased, one by one, to attend its meetings.

The dog had had his day; but still, fox-hunting in the North of Devon not only suffered no check on the ultimate dissolution of that club, but, on the contrary, exhibited year after year a strong and increasing vitality, striking deep roots into the genial soil, and thriving steadily and vigorously under the fostering care of John Russell and Newton Fellowes.

The latter gentleman, indeed, besides maintaining a noble pack of hounds on a grand scale, and doing all in his power to promote the cause of fox-hunting, not less by territorial influence than by his own kind-heartedness and hospitality, did more to improve the breed of horses than any man in the West of England; Czar Peter, Escape, Colossus, Anacreon, and Mufti forming a part of his stud, the last being an invaluable hunter, bred by the Duke of Bedford.

Partial, however, as Mr. Fellowes was to thoroughbred stock, it was a favourite theory of his that to breed a useful Devonshire hunter—a weight-carrier, with powerful quarters, and airy forehand—the produce of a thoroughbred mare by a strong but light-actioned pack-horse was a far better cross than the one so commonly adopted by the farmers of that country, namely, a cross from a pack-dam by a thoroughbred sire. But on this point his own practice, it must be remembered, was little in accordance with the above theory; as, indeed, might be expected from so great a lover of blood-stock as the Squire of Eggesford.

So much for Russell's neighbour; now for himself. The big, raking hounds in which Mr. Fellowes so delighted, and which swept the moor with so grand a head, were in Russell's estimation too big for the high banks and close covers of that country. Still, their power of driving on a half-scent, their indomitable perseverance, and, above all, their tambourine, sonorous tongues, which made the deep combes of Devon ring again with applause, fairly charmed Russell's heart. He could thus tell to a yard how they were turning in cover; and, barring their unwieldy size, so far as his means would permit, he did all he could to fashion his own pack after that model. But, of course, it was an unequal game between the pocket of the feudal lord on one side, and that of the perpetual curate of Swymbridge on the other! And although the latter contrived, by hook or by crook, to get together after a time quite as killing a pack of hounds as any in England, they were the gleanings only of many kennels, and consequently, in point of uniformity and grand appearance, were as unlike those of his neighbour as a Satyr might be to Hyperion.

Still, "handsome is that handsome does," and year after year the sport Russell continued to show, equalled at least, if it did not surpass, that of any pack in the country. With him, in those days, so long as a hound was a good worker, it mattered little what his looks were. "Let me go into a strange kennel," he would say, "give me the pick of the pack and I'll take first and foremost the plain-looking ones; there is sure to be good stuff in them, or they wouldn't be there. The same may be said with regard to the fair sex; when you see a plain woman married, depend upon it, she has been chosen for qualities which amply compensate for the absence of mere beauty. Nature, you know, is just, and ever loves a fair balance."

To ordinary observers, unaccustomed to hounds, one hound is so like another that, unless the colour were distinct, they would, in ten minutes after their names were given, be unable to say, "This is Dulcimer and that Dardan." Nay, the great majority of men, who go on hunting for season after season with the same pack, would be hopelessly at fault if called on to point out a single hound by his right name, often as he may have led the pack and they heard his name. The features of a flock of sheep—Southdown, for instance—are all alike to men who are no shepherds; nevertheless, to those whose care they are, the visage of each sheep is as well known as that of every hound in his pack to a kennel-huntsman.

Russell, however, had a marvellous power, amounting almost to an instinct, in this respect; the gift of nature it was, beyond a doubt, cultivated by long and familiar association with hounds—a gift which enabled him, after he had once seen a pack leisurely drawn from one court into another, to distinguish them, and for the most part call them by their right names when he met them in the field on the following day.

Will Long, huntsman to the Badminton hounds under three Dukes of Beaufort, was so impressed by this faculty of Russell's that it quite astonished him. "I have been mixed up with hounds all my life," said the veteran, "but I never met any man like Mr. Russell. Why, he was a couple of hours on our flags one day, and the next, when we were out hunting, he didn't want me to tell him the name of this hound or that; he knew them almost as well as I did."

A curate of Russell's, in the absence of the higher authority, was once consulted by a gentleman, who had been recommended by his physician to keep a pack of harriers.

"But," said he, "as I shall never remember their names, nor know one hound from another, if I get a whole pack at once, I have determined to buy a couple at a time, and make their acquaintance before I take in any more."

And this method of learning their names he absolutely adopted.

During his long residence at Tordown, Russell more than once parted with the greater part of his pack, retaining only a few couples as a nucleus for a fresh and stronger lot. On one occasion some twenty couples had been drafted for foreign service, and it is a fact that the gentleman who became their master, and hunted them himself for the whole season, knew the name of but one of them—a hound called "Primrose"—at the end of it, her colour being different from that of the other hounds. Neither did he trouble his head to inquire the history of a single hound.

"Tyrell told me," wrote Mr. Russell to an old friend, "that he gave him (the aforesaid gentleman) a setter and a pointer in the month of August, and that he could not, in the following Christmas week, tell him the names of either, nor which was the pointer and which the setter, though he had shot over them for four months."

Again, among the lot he took was a hound called "Abelard," to whose classical name in connection with the ill-fated "Eloise"—that most exquisite poem—his reading had never soared. Never, too, having noticed the name in any list of hounds, he was sorely perplexed, and came to the conclusion that some mistake must have occurred, and that the hound's real name was "Happy-Lord." "'Tis a merry little hound, you know, and that's why, I suppose, Russell gave him that queer name," he said, as he drew the hound with the point of his whip, and distinctly called him "Happy-Lord."

There is a story told of a fine old-fashioned Devonshire squire, a friend of Russell's, long since passed away, that having a fancy for hounds' names terminating with "maid," he gave orders to his huntsman to call the first three bitches that came up from walk as follows:—"Barmaid," "Dairymaid," and "Ganymaid."

Nor is that a solitary instance of the confusion created by the sex of Jove's cupbearer; for Russell relates that Dr. Troyte, of Huntsham, having received a dog-hound, so called, from Mr. Newton Fellowes, old Will Dinnicombe, his huntsman, refused point-blank to call the hound by that name; declaring to his master that "nobody, as he knowed, but Squire Fellowes wi'd a ca'd a dog-hound Ganymaid; and ef yeu plaise, maister, us'll call un Ganyboy; 'tis more fitty like." Will had his way, and from that day the hound went by the latter name.

Hounds, as we all know, are governed by their likes and dislikes, their fancies and prejudices, very much in the fashion of human beings; but with this difference—the honest brutes do not disguise their feelings, as the animals gifted with reason are too apt to do. Sir John Eardley-Wilmot in his very interesting "Reminiscences of the late Mr. Assheton Smith," represents that eminent sportsman as having possessed a "fascination" over hounds; while they, on their part, always evinced the strongest attachment towards him.

"I recollect," relates one of his friends, "his once having out five couples of drafts, whom he had never seen before. Sharp, his kennel-huntsman at that time, gave him the names written down; he then called each hound separately, and gave him a piece of bread, and then returned the list to the huntsman, saying, 'I know them now;' and so they did him. On other occasions, when the fixture was 'Oare Hill,' and the hounds were awaiting his arrival, Dick Burton used to say, 'Master is coming, I perceive by the hounds;' and this long before he made his appearance. When he came within three hundred yards, no huntsman or whip in the world could have stopped the pack from bounding to meet him. In the morning, when let loose from the kennel, they would rush to his study window, or to the hall door, and stand there till he came out."

Mr. Musters, too, that paragon of gentlemen huntsmen, although he seldom visited his kennel, and saw little of his pack except in the hunting field, was the very idol of his hounds; nor, associated as he was with the sport they enjoyed, was such an attachment to be wondered at, for he led them in the chase, and where their instinct failed, his judgment stepped in and cheered them to victory.

And for that very reason, no man in the world was ever more loved by hounds than Russell himself. "It isn't the man," as he rightly maintained, "who feeds the hounds whom they most like; but the man who opens their prison door, lets them out of kennel, and says, 'There, go forth and enjoy your liberty;' and then helps them in their work."

On one occasion, owing to the inveterate opposition he met with from a great landed proprietor, whose tenants and keepers were ordered to kill foxes over the whole extent of his wide domain—a difference in politics being the chief gravamen—Russell once more came to the conclusion that, for the sake of peace, he would give up his hounds, and again he parted with a large draft.

Soon after this event he met Sir John Duntze, who, hearing what had taken place, seemed loth to believe the unwelcome news. "You can't live without hounds, Russell—I know you can't," said the incredulous baronet. "Now," I'll make you an offer; I'll give you five pounds, if you'll give me one for every year that you don't keep hounds."

And Sir John was right; for the following season saw Russell reinforced with a strong draft from the Hambledon, which, with old Milliner and a few hounds of the Mercury blood set him going again with renewed vigour.

Russell catches a Fawn.

That Milliner was a hound after Russell's own heart. A light whimper from her—for she'd occasionally speak on a drag—had a world of meaning in it for his ears.

"We shall find in this cover," he would say; "that's a tongue that never told a lie."

Then came the double-tongue, and the fox was on his legs that instant.

His best friend at this time, both as a fox-preserver and a liberal supporter of his hounds, was Sir Arthur Chichester, of Youlston, who, although still with his regiment, the 7th Dragoons, not only gave Russell the benefit of his territorial influence, but aided him handsomely with the sinews of war. Sir Arthur, in early youth, had been well entered by his father, who kept hounds at Youlston, and who, when Mr. Templer's packs were broken up, was lucky enough to secure a fair share of the "Let-'em-alones" for his own kennel—the best of which, however, fell soon afterwards into Russell's hands.

The present baronet had succeeded to his title and retired from the army for some time, when Russell, paying him a visit on a beautiful summer's morning, found him in the park busily engaged in riding down the deer, which he had made up his mind to get rid of and kill, one by one, as they were wanted for his own and his friend's use. His mode of operation being somewhat unique and original, Russell's interest was much attracted by the exciting scene. By the help of a second and even a third horse, Sir Arthur was able to ride down the stoutest buck; and then with a lance, after the manner of pursuing the boar in India, he contrived to spear it with marvellous adroitness and precision.

"I'll give you that fawn, Russell, if you can catch it," said the baronet, pointing out a lively little fellow, galloping beside its dam.

In a moment Russell's horse was in full swing; and in less than ten minutes he had captured his panting little prize, alive and unhurt. He carried it to Tordown in his arms; and happening to have a hound-bitch, called Cloudy, whose puppies had been destroyed on that very day, he put the fawn to her, and after a brief but cautious introduction, had the satisfaction of seeing the pair nestling together on the most intimate terms. This fawn, brought up among the hounds, and subject like them to kennel discipline, waxed after a time into a fine, healthy, and bold animal; so bold, that it would knock the hounds off the benches without ceremony, in order to get at and cuddle by the side of its foster-mother. But alas! like most pets, it came to an untimely end; the hounds had been taken out of kennel, and the poor fawn, in rushing after Cloudy and attempting to jump through a gate, dashed its brains out against the bars and died on the spot. Will Rawle—Russell's henchman, kennel-man, and faithful servant for forty years—was inconsolable, declaring he would rather have lost his Christmas pig than that fawn.

Perhaps at no period of Russell's life was his pack stronger, or more efficient, than about the year 1840; but as, with the exception of a few hounds bred by himself from the old Stover strain, it consisted mainly of drafts from other kennels, the lot as a whole were, of course, unlevel and ill-matched, and on that account would scarcely have passed muster at a flag-scrutiny even in those days; still, if taken individually, every hound had a character of his own, and bore the tower-stamp impressed on his face, and, we may be very sure, was fairly entitled to his daily meal. Deeds, and not looks, were the prime consideration; for, as in the celebrated Tom Hodgson's case, "no Modishes and Merkins were kept, because they were too handsome to hang, and too bad to give away; but almost every hound looked like his master, as if he knew how to kill a fox."

It is almost needless to add that, notwithstanding the care of the kennel-man already referred to, the condition of his hounds was closely and constantly supervised by Russell himself; nor is it too much to say that, the constitution of each individual hound being so well-known to him, he could tell to a scruple the proportion of broth, or flesh, which should be given to one and not to another. That, in fact, was the great secret of their killing and enduring powers; they were always up to the mark, and consequently far superior in condition to the wild animal they were called upon to hunt.

"I was in the kennel with him on one occasion," records an old curate, "when, pointing to a hound with a long face and a high crown, called Gainer, he said, 'That hound has been injured in the stifle, but he's so good on the line that I can't afford to draft him; fire is the only remedy, and the sooner it's done the better.'"

"So, suiting the action to the word, he ordered Will Rawle to couple up the hound and lead him to a post in the courtyard. On that post, about four feet from the ground, was a strong iron ring, through which the chain-couple was passed, and the hound hauled up till he stood almost erect on his hind legs, with his head close to the post, around which the couple was then secured. The iron being quickly heated, Russell caught the hound by the hind foot, straightened the leg, and performed the operation with the most artistic skill in something less than one minute. The scoring was perfect, and he went through the whole of it without a particle of help from Will or myself.

"A day or two afterwards," continues the same informant, "we were jogging together to a meet at Yard Down Gate," the pack following leisurely along, some almost under the stirrup, and a few at the tail of Russell's horse. He was chatting merrily, as usual, but, at the same time, his eye never ceased travelling from one hound to another, as if he were studying the condition and fitness of every hound in the pack for the day's work before them. Suddenly he stopped his horse, dismounted, and handing the rein to me, said, 'Lavender's not quite right; hold my horse an instant while I look her over.'

"He then examined her eyes, and before I could understand what he was about to do, pulled a lancet from his pocket and bled her on the spot. A man we met soon afterwards was then sent back with her to Tordown.

"Again, the meet being on this occasion at the Mervin's Arms, Russell, on looking over a young black-and-white hound called Waverley, recently sent to him from a distance, discovered him to be unbranded.

"'This won't do,' he said, 'we shall probably run to-day from Whityfield to the deep covers of Henstridge, above Berry-Narbor, and if we loose that hound we shall never see him again.' He then jumped off his horse, took the hound between his knees, and drawing a small scissors from his pocket-book, he instantly and most cleverly cut out a great R in the hair of Waverley's ribs. 'There,' he said, 'no matter where he turns up now, he'll be sent back to my kennel for fifty miles round.'

"True enough, we found in Whityfield, Leveller, Gameboy, and Falstaff breaking almost on his back, as the fox, a white-tagged old Hector, put his head straight for Henstridge, where, after a sharp burst, he saved his brush by going to ground. Found No. 2 at Arlington; ran to Youlston, Cocksley, Pigslake Wood, crossed the river, and killed him by moonlight in a cottage above Goodleigh. The whole village, with the parson at their head—one of that good old sort yclept Harding, of Upcot—turning out to greet Russell and welcome his field."

"But Russell, too, as well as his hounds, must have been in fine form at that time, or the hardihood even of his frame could never have stood the strain imposed on it by the four following days' work, which, by an old letter of his, is thus recorded: "I left this house (Tordown) on one eventful morning, rode to Iddesleigh (twenty miles), whither I had sent the hounds the evening before, found a fox and killed him during one of the most awful storms of thunder, lightning, and rain I ever saw.

Scent breast high from first to last. I then rode to Ash, Mr. Mallet's place, dined there, and danced afterwards till one o'clock; went to bed and rose again at three; pulled on my top-boots and rode down to Bodmin, just fifty miles, and met Tom Hext's hounds about five miles from that town. Found a good fox and killed him; dined with my old friend Pomeroy Gilbert, and again did not get to bed—much against my rule—till the little hours. Rested the next day, if walking several miles to a country fair could be called resting; then off next morning at three; rode back to Iddesleigh, took out the hounds, found a fox in Dowland, and killed him close to the Schoolmaster Inn in Chawleigh parish, twelve miles as the crow flies. I then turned my horse's head for Tordown, and was sitting down to dinner at my own table, and all the hounds home, at six o'clock, the distance being fully twenty miles from the said Schoolmaster Inn to this house."

Owing to a succession of bad harvests throughout the land, Irish oatmeal, the staple food of hounds, had risen about this time to a price unheard of since the war with France; and it was with no little alarm that many an M.F.H. found himself compelled to give £16, or even £18 per ton, for what he could have purchased aforetime at the lower sum of £12. Not a few, accordingly, with an eye to economy, turned their attention to Indian meal, hoping to find in it, though a cheaper article, still a satisfactory substitute for the more expensive food. But experience soon proved that, much as it was at first vaunted, it lacked that rare muscle-giving aliment, that stand-by quality, so bountifully possessed by sound oatmeal.

Russell never would try it during the season; but, knowing that a friend of his had done so, and hearing that his hounds rarely ended with a kill, he exclaimed, "No wonder; it's that Indian meal that does it. The hounds are as good as they ever were; but fed on that wishy-washy 'trade,' I'll defy them, or any hounds on earth, to kill a good fox."

Russell's independence in the field with respect to the services of a regular whip having been already alluded to, it may be mentioned that enthusiastic, amateur aspirants would now and again volunteer to act in that capacity, and take upon themselves the full duties of a hired servant. One especially, Mr. Houlditch, a Somersetshire gentleman, hearing almost fabulous tales of the sport shown by the N.D.H., migrated from his own into Russell's country, and at once offered his services, proposing to act as field-adjutant, and undertake, as far as his ability would permit, the ordinary work of a regular whip.

The offer at the time happened to be most opportune, and was gratefully accepted on

Russell's part; but, alas! on the very first day that Mr. Houlditch appeared in his official capacity, Russell discovered, by the most unmistakable signs, that his knowledge of the "noble science" was simply that of the veriest tyro, and that in reality he knew just as much as Billy Button, or a Tooley Street tailor, might be supposed to know about such matters. Still Mr. Houlditch, in spite of all difficulties, persevered, paying the closest attention to the lessons—nay, it may be said, the lectures—which his chief so frequently bestowed on him, not in the field, but on returning from their day's work. Many a time was it said to Russell, "Do what you will, you'll never make a sportsman of Houlditch; he hasn't it in him, and is too old to learn."

But so long as the pupil was anxious to improve, so long did his master do his utmost to instruct and encourage him in the sylvan duties he had undertaken to perform, till at length, after a season or two of continuous drill, the perseverance of both was crowned with complete success; and it must have been as gratifying for Russell to say as for the other to hear, that "Houlditch understood his work as well as most men, and had become a most useful and obliging whip." He served in that capacity for six consecutive years, and when he left created a blank which Russell was never able in like fashion to fill again.

Much has been said of the active service which Russell expected from his curates in the hunting-field, when parochial duties did not absolutely require their attendance at home; but, of course, some of the stories told in that respect were utterly untrue. One, for instance, describes him as testing the voices of two rival applicants aspiring to become his curate, by making them give "view-holloas," and then accepting the one whose voice sounded the most penetrating and most sonorous—a capital story, no doubt, for those who cultivate charity by believing and circulating such tales; but, as a matter of fact, it is one which rests on as baseless a fabric as the fleecy clouds that float through the sky.

That he never objected to the company and help of his curate in the hunting-field is quite true, provided always that the parochial duty, for which he was responsible, was first attended to and duly fulfilled; nay, if his curate had a taste for hunting, Russell would even encourage him to enjoy the pastime, maintaining, with Dr. Watts, that Satan would find him something worse to do, if he remained idle at home.

The following anecdote, however, is beyond all doubt a true one, and shall be given in the very words of an ear-witness, the late Rev. William Hocker, vicar of Buckerell, who related it to the writer of this memoir soon after the incident occurred. Mr. Hocker was standing at a shop-door in Barnstaple on a market-day, when Will Chapple, the parish clerk of Swymbridge, entered the shop, and while his business was being attended to, the grocer thus interrogated him :—

"Well, Mr. Chapple, and have 'ee got a coorate yet for Swymbridge?"

"Not yet, sir—master's nation partic'ler; 'tisn't this man nor 'tisn't that as'll suit un; but here's his advertisement" (pulling out a copy of the *North Devon Journal*), "so I reckon he'll soon get one now.

"'Wanted, a curate for Swymbridge; must be a gentleman of moderate and orthodox views.'"

"Orthodox! Mr. Chapple; what doth he mean by that?" inquired the grocer.

"Well," said the clerk, in some perplexity, knowing the double nature of the curate's work, secular as well as sacred, "I can't exactly say; but I reckon 'tis a man as can *ride* pretty well."

An old curate of his gives the following grateful but very brief record of the kindness and hospitality he received both from Mr. and Mrs. Russell during his residence at Swymbridge :—"My first reception by Russell I shall never forget. I had ridden a long distance, the latter part of it by devious lanes and countless cross-roads, which, as they were all strange to me, perplexed and jaded me far more than even the length of the ride, when at nightfall I reached the modest lodgings taken for me in the village at Swymbridge. My landlady, Mrs. Burgess, a most respectable woman, besides two sets of apartments let to myself and another gentleman, dear old Walter Radcliffe, kept also in the same house a general shop, where any article of food, from a double Glo'ster to a flitch of bacon, or a penny loaf to a packet of tea, might be had at a moment's notice; so that for the cravings of nature the wherewithal was at hand to satisfy my utmost wants. I had just quitted a happy home, broken up by my family migrating to Dresden for education; consequently, notwithstanding the kindly manner of my hostess, and her anxiety to make me comfortable, a sense of loneliness crept over me such as I had not felt for many a year, and I turned away from the savoury broiled rasher set before me as if I had been a Hebrew of the Hebrews, and hated the sight of the unhallowed food. At that moment a man's voice at the door aroused my attention —he was inquiring for me—and before I could rise from my seat Russell stalked in, grasped my hand without ceremony, and bid me welcome to his parish in so cheery a tone that in an instant my depressed spirits, rising like a mist in the morning, took wing and passed away.

"'Holloa,' he said, looking at the table, 'this won't do; you must come up and dine with us. Come as you are, plain fare and no formality.'

"I pleaded the necessity of unpacking my portmanteau, and devoting a few minutes to the Graces; but he wouldn't hear of it.

"'No,' he said, 'come along; you're quite smart enough. Mrs. Russell won't look at your coat, if you'll only eat a good dinner.'

"The invitation, I felt, was tantamount to a command, and accordingly, without further objection, I rose and obeyed.

"The dinner, an ample one, was yet simplicity itself—a cod's head and shoulders, the produce of Barnstaple Bay, a haunch of Exmoor mutton, hung to an hour; then an apple pudding, flavoured with lemon peel, and boiled to perfection. '"*Carpe diem*," which, freely translated, means "keep cutting,"' said Russell, calling for a hot plate, and inviting me to take another slice of the delicious moor mutton. He then asked how I had reached Swymbridge, and by what route I had come.

"'Across country,' I replied; 'by way of Cobbaton and Umberleigh Bridge.'

"'An awkward line for a stranger,' he remarked. 'But you rode, of course; and pray what's become of your horse?'

"'Gone to the village inn,' I said, 'where I saw him fed and bedded up for the night. He's my sole stand-by; does the double work of hack and hunter, so I hope will be well cared for, as I value him greatly.'

"'Then he musn't stay there another minute, or, in all probability, he'll be kicked by some farmer's horse before the night's over,' said Russell, rising to ring the bell, and giving orders that the horse should be fetched and brought to his stable at once. 'To-morrow,' he continued, 'you'll have no difficulty in finding a quiet little box in the village, and you must go to Barnstaple next market day and buy your hay and corn, for at Swymbridge you'll get none.'

"The next morning, as I was about to sit down to breakfast, to my great surprise a cart, heavily laden with hay and corn, stood at the door of my lodgings, and before I could make any inquiry as to its ownership, the man in charge, seeing me at an open window, thus addressed me: 'If yeu plaise, sir, this here hay and woats be for yeu, wi' maister's compliments.

"Had I possessed the cap of Fortunatus, I could scarcely have wished for a more welcome gift, as the business of buying good upland hay and old oats in Devonshire, at that season of the year, was, as I knew from experience, a most difficult job. Now, however, through

Russell's kindness and liberality, I had ample time before me to look around and suit myself in that respect. But I will not recount the similar acts of kind consideration in various ways, especially in those of hospitality, which I received from him and Mrs. Russell during that happy and unclouded period of my early life passed at Swymbridge.

"Once, and once only," continues the same curate, "did a slight skirmish take place between us, and that was on the wild open moor near Lanacre Bridge. It was a cold biting day in February. We had found in Twitchen Town Wood, and the hounds with a grand scent, having brought their fox up to the bridge, had there come to a check. A hound called Castor, however, hitting the fox under the archway of the bridge, through which the flood had carried him, dashed into the angry river, and by some means became unable either to pass under the arch or land on the opposite bank. 'The hound will be drowned; jump in and save him,' shouted Russell to me, in a state of the wildest panic; 'jump in, I say.'

"But, in truth, I saw no danger for the hound; whereas a plunge into the roaring Barle, forbiddingly keen as the wind blew, was likely to be one for me. I hesitated for an instant, and as I did so Castor struggled out, and, like a brave hound, threw his tongue manfully on the opposite side of the river. Directly afterwards, on my rating a hound for some fault he had committed, Russell turned sharply round, and said, "That's a puppy, let him alone; don't rate him, or you'll ruin him.'

"'Don't speak to me in that way,' I said, fairly roused this time by his peremptory manner, 'or I'll never turn a hound for you again.'

"It remains to be added that we killed our fox soon afterwards; and no two men could have jogged home together on better terms than Russell and I did after that event. My act of rebellion, however, was not forgotten by him; for to this day, when the hounds pass near Lanacre Bridge, he is wont to tell the tale with infinite zest and humour, pointing out the very spot to those around him, 'Where Davies mutinied; threatening, if I dared to rate him, that he'd never turn a hound for me again.'"

## CHAPTER XI.

The South Molton Club—Stopping out the Foxes—"Beatrice and Barbara"—Russell and Radcliffe's Stories—The "Little Specklety Hen"—Russell's Ducking in the Barle—Mallard and Cat snapped up by Foxes in Chase.

"Glorious West country! . . . you must not despise their accent, for it is the remains of a purer and nobler dialect than our own; and you will be surprised to hear me, when I am merry, burst out into pure unintelligible Devonshire: when I am very childish, my own country's language comes to me like a dream of old days! . . ."—Charles Kingsley.

In 1845-46 a project for starting a new fox-hunting club in the north of Devon, the rules and arrangements of which should be identical with those of the old Chulmleigh meetings, being warmly approved by Russell, it was resolved to establish it forthwith at South Molton, that town being a convenient centre for the accommodation of all parties. Accordingly by Russell's invitation, the packs of Sir Walter Carew and Mr. Trelawny were appointed, together with his own, to hunt the country for a whole fortnight in spring and autumn; while the George Inn was fixed upon as head-quarters for the mess and the numerous hunting men who, it was expected, would flock to the little town from all parts of Devon and Cornwall.

Nor was this expectation a delusive one. Throughout the county, north and south, the new club was looked upon as a kind of phœnix, rising, with renewed vigour in its wings, from the smouldering ashes of the Chulmleigh Club; the triumvirate alone, to whom its revival was due, namely, Mr. Russell, Sir Walter Carew, and Mr. Trelawny, of Coldrenick, being an ample guarantee that success would certainly follow upon such a combination.

Accordingly, on the occasion of the meetings, not only were the country-houses in the neighbourhood thrown open to friends from a distance, but every available bed and stall in South Molton was secured for weeks beforehand by gentlemen who, preferring the freedom of a hostelry to private hospitality, deemed it a matter of loyalty to the club to live at headquarters and support the mess.

Foxes, as Russell well knew, were just sufficiently plentiful, though not one too many to warrant the strain on his country necessitated by two exotic packs, which, besides his own, were about to hunt it for twelve days, twice in the year. But that it was so stocked appeared a marvel to all; for, occupying in the very heart of it an extensive area, comprising many square miles of cultivated farms, moors, and deep woodlands, in which game was strictly preserved, dwelt a magnate of the land, and one whose hostility, on political grounds, Russell had been unfortunate enough to provoke.

Tenants and keepers, accordingly, had received peremptory orders not only to forbid Russell from drawing the covers, but to wage an exterminating war against foxes, old and young, by trapping and digging them out at all seasons of the year; still, notwithstanding that edict, Russell found means to keep up a fair stock on every side of that wide domain—indeed, now and again, the very tenants themselves hesitated not, on discovering a litter laid up on the grounds, to take measures for securing its safety, either by smoking the earth, or warning some friend to fox-hunting that the sooner the cubs were disturbed the better it would be for their lives.

About a month before the first meeting of the club at South Molton, in November, 1845, a farmer living near Exford, a parish in Somersetshire beyond the left bank of the Barle, foreboding ill to a litter he had long guarded as the apple of his eye, wrote a letter to Russell, beseeching him, in short but pithy terms, to bring his hounds over and scatter the cubs. It ran thus:—

"HONOR'D SIR,

"Do ee plaise bring up the dogs first chance; us a got a fine litter, sure enough, up to Hollacomb brake. They'm up full-growed, a month agone; and last night was a week, what must em do but kill Mistiss' old gander & seven more wi' un—her's most gone mazed owing to't—so do ee plaise come up Sir and gi 'em a rattle—they'm rale beauties, they be, as ever you clapped your eyes on."

Russell lost no time in obeying the summons; he went off alone, slept, and kennelled the hounds for the night at Hawkridge Rectory, the hospitable residence of the Rev. Joseph Jekyll, a gentleman pronounced by Russell to be one of the finest and hardest riders in that or any other country; a direct descendant, too, of the eminent anti-Jacobite judge, and nephew to the witty lawyer of that historic name. The digression may not be an unwelcome one, if an example be quoted of the rare readiness with which the latter could toss off impromptu verses at the spur of the moment; for Russell is probably the only man who could remember the humorous lines here given, and which, so far as he was aware, were never published.

Towards the end of last century, Carry Ourry, a great Cornish beauty, and an ancestress of the

Trebys, of Goodamoor, had walked into the Assize Court at Bodmin, when Jekyll, catching sight of her, wrote the following lines and handed them up to the judge:—

"My lord, and gemmen of the jury,
I come to prosecute before ye
A noted felon, I'll assure ye,
Known by the name of Carry Ourry;
Known by a guilty pair of eyes,
Known by a thousand felonies,
Known to push her crime still further,
Guilty of killing, stabbing, murder;
But to be brief and cut it shorter,
I'll but indict her for manslaughter."

The next morning, crossing the Barle at Tarrsteps, and the wild heathery waste lying between it and Exford, Russell threw his hounds into the cover indicated by the farmer: in one minute a lot of cubs were on their legs; then followed a crash, till, on every side, the whole cover seemed to be on fire. A brace of cubs soon succumbed, and their brushes being handed to the farmer, he carried them home in triumph to his wife, declaring that now she would have no further grievance to complain of, "leastways, from they two foxes."

But Russell had not finished with them yet; after a short pause, casting his hounds round the outside of the cover, they dropped their sterns and away they went, pelting like a storm of hail after the old dog, twelve miles straight on end, over the wildest part of Exmoor. On reaching the Bray covers they were hard on his back; but Russell, fearing a change, deemed it advisable to stop the pack; and so the gallant fellow lived to fight again another day: that day, however, was not long deferred.

In the following November the new club met for their fortnight's sport at South Molton; and Yard Down being the first fixture, Mr. Trelawny's hounds proceeded to draw Sherracombe Brake, hard by. Russell, from a spot of open ground on the opposite side of the combe, stood watching the action of the hounds intently, as, without a vestige of drag, Limpetty, the huntsman, was doing his utmost to encourage them to face the strong gorse that opposed their entrance at every point. At length he passed on to draw another cover; but Russell stopped him, shouting at the top of his voice—

"You've left that fox behind you, Limpetty!"

"No, I ha'nt," responded he, in the habitual blunt, outspoken style that characterised the man.

"Yes, you have," repeated Russell; "not a hound has touched the comb of that hedge, and he may be there."

At that moment a hound spoke, and almost before Limpetty could look round, a screeching "tally-ho" from one of the field announced a view. The fox was on foot, a flyer, too, beyond all doubt, the next instant he was out

Mrs. Russell leads the Field.

on the open moor, a good lanyard clear of the brake.

"That's the same grey fox—I know it is," said Russell to Mr. Houlditch, who was standing near him at the time; "the very fox I brought away from Exford, twelve miles off, a month ago."

Houlditch shook his head.

"I own, Russell," said he, "you know a good many things; but as to knowing *that* to be the same fox you brought from Exford, you must pardon me if I venture to doubt it."

It would have taken Russell more time than was then convenient to explain his reasons for expressing that opinion; he knew, too, it would have been a mere waste of words on his part, and that Houlditch would only have exemplified the old saying—

> "He that complies against his will
> Is of his own opinion still."

So, turning to Mrs. Russell, who was mounted on her favourite horse, called "The Tickler," he said—

"Come along, Penelope, he's going for Whitefield Down, and catch them we must, or we shall never see them again."

Away they went up wind and over the hill to Sittaborough, when, the pace being tremendous, the fox turned and sank the wind down for Simonsbath, then on to the Warren, Badgeworthy, and up to Gallon House, where he broke out over the moor wall, a boundary fence big enough to stop the course of a native red deer.

And now it was that Mrs. Russell, a wee bit anxious, perhaps, to rival the renown so justly earned by Mrs. Horndon as a forward and intrepid rider, not only "set" that lady, but every man in the field: for, putting Tickler without a moment's hesitation at the formidable barrier, and landing safely over the deep trench on the off side, away she went with the leading hounds for a considerable distance, literally alone in her glory. They were then within less than a mile of the very cover, near Exford, from which Russell had brought the dog-fox in the previous month; and he was now pointing directly for it, when a terrific shower of hail and rain fell like a waterspout around them, washing away every particle of scent, and compelling the baffled hounds to put down their noses in vain.

So, this Hector of the moor, having once beaten Russell's hounds, and again, by the intervention of Jupiter himself, triumphed over the crack pack of the South, was toasted that night, during the symposium at the George Inn, with mighty enthusiasm; the identity of the gallant animal being no longer questioned even by the doubting Houlditch.

During these meetings at South Molton, which continued to flourish under Russell's immediate auspices for many successive years, it was admitted on all sides by the Nestors of the field, that the sport shown was fully equal to that of the most brilliant period of the Chulmleigh Hunt; and that it was due, in no small measure, to a plan adopted by him with respect to the main earths in the neighbourhood of the moor, there can be no doubt. About a week before each meeting, Will Rawle, his trusty kennel-man, was regularly sent with a couple of terriers, to rattle and turmoil every stronghold visited by the foxes, far and near. That being thoroughly done, a few drops of a certain strong-scenting liquid were sprinkled over the entrance of each earth, which was then stopped. The name of the liquid neither Russell nor Will Rawle would ever divulge; but its object was to prevent the foxes from digging themselves in again, before the meeting had come to a close. Directly afterwards, however, the earths were unstopped, and allowed to assume, as they soon did, their pristine and natural appearance.

The success of the plan exceeded even Russell's expectations; for, however stormy the nights might have been, the foxes were not only to be found above ground, but were undoubtedly much bothered by the blockade so ubiquitously maintained against them. They proved this unmistakably, by the strange line of country they were so often driven to take—

a great advantage to the hounds—which, day after day, whether Russell's, Trelawny's, or Sir Walter Carew's rarely returned to their kennels without showing a fine wild run, and crowning it with a kill.

One day, a brace of foxes were found by Sir Walter Carew's hounds, the first in Twitchen Town Wood, the second near Lanacre Bridge, and both were killed, the latter in forty, the former in thirty-six minutes, without the shadow of a check in either case from first to last, every inch of the run being over the wild rough heather of Exmoor; some idea may thus be formed of the style of sport that, as a rule, marked the South Molton meetings at that period.

Speaking of that day in particular, Sir Walter Carew, a well-known man with the Quorn about that time, and a rare judge of hound's pace, was wont to declare that he had never seen two such brilliant runs in one day, even in Leicestershire, or any other country.

Russell would have almost given the eyes out of his head for a couple of bitches called Beatrice and Barbara, which, figuring in front and always abreast with the leading hounds, distinguished themselves greatly in both runs. Scarcely above twenty-one inches in height, they were yet models of strength, length, and symmetry; dark tan, or, rather, hare-pied in colour, and never idle, they were, as Russell had already discovered, equally good all round, in chase, line-hunting, and road work.

A story went the rounds, but how it came to be known will ever remain a mystery, that he was heard to whisper the names of Beatrice and Barbara in his dreams that night. It was therefore shrewdly suspected that his object was not altogether a disinterested one, when, jogging alongside John Beale a few days afterwards, he was reported to have said, "What a pity 'tis, John, those hounds are not an inch or two higher; Sir Walter, I know, likes a level lot, and the pack, I think, would look all the better if he were to draft them."

"What! draft they tew beauties, Mr. Rissell?" replied the veteran; "nit he, if I know'th it. Why, they'm the flower of the flock, they be, and will do more work in a day than some hounds in a wick."

Sir Walter, too, prized Beatrice and Barbara as the pearls of his pack; but not more, perhaps, for their intrinsic merits than for the blood they carried in their veins. He had bred them himself at Haccombe, and being from his Bashful by Mr. Bulteel's Justice, a son of the famous Beaufort hound of that name, they had come from a sort stout as steel on both sides, and real hard drivers, even on a half scent. Consequently, the Furrier blood could scarcely have been more valued by Osbaldeston, nor that of the Warwickshire Trojan by Mr. Corbet, than the strain of those hounds by Sir Walter Carew.

The South Molton Club acquired in a short time immense popularity throughout the county, and the names of the members and visitors who supported its merry meetings are for the most part included in the following list: Sir Walter P. Carew, Sir Arthur Chichester, Sir John Duntze, Messrs. Charles Trelawny, J. Russell, Frederick and Charles Knight, William Horndon, James and Henry Deacon, John King, of Fowelscombe, William and Henry Rayer, T. Carew, of Collipriest, W. B. Fortescue, William Erving S. Clark, Walter C. Radcliffe, R. S. Bryan, Joseph Jekyll, Colwell Roe, Stucley Lucas, H. Tyrrel, G. Woodleigh, Rev. George Owen, Chichester and Chichester Nagle, Houlditch, Sleeman, E. W. L. Davies, William Hole, Courtenay Bulteel, Kingson, Willesford, Edwin Scoble, Bassett, Pinkett, Sherard Clay, J. Bawden, Reginald James and his brother, Karslake, Dene, two Riccards, and Bury Russell.

To this imperfect list might be added a host of hard-riding farmers, with George Toms at their head, whose devotion to fox-hunting and the master of the hunt it would be difficult to match in any other country.

After a fine day's sport over those heathery, scent-holding moors, when the whole party, "amid brightening bumpers" elated, with

Trelawny, John King, or Russell for their chairman, were discussing the incidents of the run, and killing their fox over and over again, then it was that the "fun of the fair" began. The ring of a shilling popped into a wine-glass gave notice that, with or without the knowledge of the owner, the sale by auction of his horse was about to take place, he himself being only allowed one bid; so that if satisfied with the price offered, and he said nothing, his horse then became the property of the last bidder; but if on the contrary, he had no wish to part with the animal, he took care to protect himself by naming a sum that at once put an end to further competition.

A chestnut pony by Pandarus, called "Stunning Joe," scarcely fourteen hands high, had so distinguished himself over the moor during these meetings, that on two or three occasions he was persistently put up, and large sums were bid for him with the hope of obtaining so rare an animal. But Reginald James, his owner, knew the value of the little horse too well to part with him; for when the bidding had risen to its top figure—an exceptionally high one—he invariably took a jump which at once extinguished the aspirations of the most spirited competitors.

A young squire, however, from the southern division of the county, who had indulged rather in "the flow of soul," than "the feast of reason," took, on one festive night, so active a part in the matter of bidding for his neighbours' property that, on awaking next morning, he found himself in possession of a "string" of nags which, as his groom was heard to say, "he no more wanted than a cat wanted two tails."

Another gentleman, the Rev. Thomas Carew, father to the present Squire of Collipriest, at the end of one meeting lamented to Russell that he had not a horse left to ride home on: "I came here," he said, "with six useful horses; and now I'm left with a pocketful of money, but without a single horse: I should like to buy them all back again."

Russell, as before stated, preferring early rest and an unclouded brain for the full enjoyment of the morrow, rarely remained in the guest-chamber to a late hour; nor could the most pressing request prevail on him to take a hand at whist at these meetings, or indeed on any other occasion. "I've no money to lose myself," he would say, "and should be very sorry to risk injuring my neighbour by winning his." But if there was one festive attraction which he could not resist, and which fairly glued him to his seat, it was that of a hunting song—and if trolled forth by that most hearty and genial of men, Walter Radcliffe, of Warleigh,

Russell would remain a willing and delighted listener to the very last note.

There was one song especially, written by Radcliffe himself, which, from the clear and stirring style in which he sang it, never failed to elicit rounds of applause, not only from Russell, but from every member of that jovial board. It was called the "Ivybridge Hunt-Song," and described a run with the Lyneham—then Mr. Bulteel's—so graphically that, if published, it would be found little, if at all, inferior to the best hunting songs, either of Mr. Egerton-Warburton or Mr. Whyte-Melville. To not a few of our readers, too, it would bring back to memory the bright scenes of a bygone day—ay, and the form of many a kind familiar face; of many an old friend long passed away, but still, to the mind's eye, blessed with the same unclouded brow, the same happy features which then, in the morning of life,

"Joy used to wear."

At one meeting of the club, which can never be forgotten by those who were present, a lively passage of arms took place between Russell and Radcliffe, not exactly in singing songs, but in telling Devonshire stories, which they told alternately.

Radcliffe's stories chiefly turned on a Cornish Squireen, whose eccentricities of character and speech were imitated to the life. This gentleman dearly loved fox-hunting, and possessing a clever "whit-faced horse," which carried him brilliantly over Roughtor and Brownwilly, he valued him more than gold. Being attacked by serious illness, which brought him face to face with an enemy he could no longer escape, and having lived a free-and-easy kind of life, with more thought for the present than for a future world, the clergyman of his parish deemed it his duty to visit him, and impress him with a serious view of his coming end.

"You are going on a long journey, sir," said the good parson, "and surely you should make some preparation for it, before it be too late."

"I've no wish to travel," replied the sick man; "this place suits me well enough."

"But, sir, 'tis to a better country I would direct your thoughts, where——"

"A better country, did you say?" interrupted the other, impatiently. "Give me only a thousand a year and my old whit-faced horse, and I'd never wish to see a better country than our Cornish moors."

Finding him impracticable, the parson took his leave, with manifest but unavailing "signs of sorrow."

In a very short time afterwards, being dressed in his top boots and scarlet hunting-coat, he was carried down to a settle near the kitchen fire, where, as volumes of smoke curled up from his lighted pipe, the spirit of this hardy Cornishman passed away, and, let us hope, in spite of himself, took its flight to a better land.

To give even a sketch of the many amusing stories that were fired off in rapid succession by the one or the other, in that continuous fusillade, would be to fill a small volume ; nor, at this distance of time, would it be a light task to gather together the fragments of that memorable encounter. One or two of Russell's, however, bearing on Devonshire parish-clerks in his early days, when George III. was king, can scarcely have escaped the memory of any one who was fortunate enough to hear them then—told as they were by him with infinite humour and in the purest vernacular of that favoured county.

John Boyce, the rector of Sherwell, wishing to have a day's hunting with the staghounds on the Porlock side of the moor, told his clerk to give notice in the morning that there would be no service in the afternoon at their church, as he was going off to hunt with Sir Thomas Acland over the moor on the following day. The mandate was obeyed to the letter, the clerk making the announcement in the following terms :—

"This is vor to give notiss—there be no sarvice to this church this arternewn ; caus' maester is a-going over the moor a stag-hunting wi' Sir Thomas."

Again, at Stockleigh-Pomeroy parish, the rector, Roope Ilbert, a well-known name in Devonshire, desired his clerk to give notice that there would be one service a day only at that church for a month, as he was going to take duty at Stockleigh-English alternately with his own. The clerk did so in the following words:—

"This is vor to give notiss—there'll be no sarvice to thes church but wance a wick, caus' maester's a-going to sarve t'other Stockleigh and thes church to all-etarnity."

It seems to have been a very common fashion in Devonshire, in Russell's early days, for gentlemen of standing in the county to adopt the native dialect, especially when conversing with the country-folk—a habit arising either from carelessness, or perhaps because their speech in that provincial form was best understood and most natural to the generality of their neighbours. Russell relates, for instance, that he was present when a colonel of the North Devon Militia was reviewing his regiment, and seeing a hare jump up in the midst of the men, he shouted out wildly, "There he go'th, boys, a lashing great shaver." Then, forgetting the exact point at which he had ceased to give the word of command, he turned round and said, "Where wor I, drummer-boy?"

"Present arms, sir," responded the youth; and the inspection went on.

Again, a yeomanry regiment were enacting a sham fight among themselves, when a Captain Prettyjohn was ordered to retreat before a charge of the enemy. "Retrait! what doth that mane?" inquired the captain. "Retrait mean'th rinning away, I zim; then, it shall never be told up to Dodbrook Market that Cap'n Prid'gen and his brave troop rinned away."

Accordingly, as the enemy came on, bearing down upon him at a rapid trot, he shouted to his troop, "Charge, my brave boys, charge; us bain't voxes, and they bain't hounds; us'll face 'em like men."

The collision was awful—men, horses, and accoutrements strewing the ground on every side; several troopers being more or less injured, while one positively refused to mount again, saying, "I've a brok'd my breeches already, Cap'n, and I won't mount no more."

The last time Russell heard Lord —— speak, was at a Chulmleigh meeting; when, being called upon to give a toast, he did so in the following words: "Gen'lemen, I wish to propose a toast; and that there is this here 'Fox-hunting.'"

But these Devonshire stories should be heard to be fully appreciated; for, seasoned and served up as they were by Russell and Radcliffe, with all the trimmings and peculiarities of the purest native accent, their piquancy is absolutely lost lacking such condiments.

No schoolboy ever enjoyed his hours of play more than Russell did these South Molton meetings, the lively and pleasant sociality of which, independently of the day's sport, was in no small measure due to the sparkling gaiety and telling effect of his own conversational power — a power not only of saying things humorously, but of communicating the humour to all around him. The hearty dinner which he rarely failed to make after the severest run, seemed rather to stimulate his social energies than suffer them to subside into that somnolescent mood which, with ordinary mortals, is so apt to follow a full meal after a hard day's work. Nor, till his head was on his pillow, did he ever indulge in a wink of sleep; but then, once there, ordinarily he slept like a top. "Tria sunt necessaria ad humanam vitam; cibus, somnus et jocus," was the favourite saying of a sensible Archbishop in former days; and certainly if any one ever did full justice to each and all of those three requirements, Russell was that man.

The business of the day being over, and the Homeric feast duly disposed of, then commenced the

> "Sport that wrinkled care derides,
> And laughter holding both his sides;"

then flashes of humour and good-fellowship enjoyed their full swing, and literally reigned supreme. So Dr. Doran was quite right when he said, "A good dinner sharpens wit; while a hungry man is as slow at a joke as he is at a favour."

"On one occasion, and one only," writes an old member of the club, "do I remember a breach of the peace taking place at those merry meetings. Somebody, utterly ignoring that precept of St. Peter, which warns us not to 'speak evil of dignities,' was abusing the Bishop of Exeter (Phillpotts) in round terms, when a young squire (Tom Carew, of Collipriest) a staunch friend and admirer of that stout-hearted prelate, seized a pound of butter and threw it with all his force at the speaker's head. 'There! take that,' he said; 'and don't attack in his absence a better man than yourself; I'll not hear him abused by you or any other man with impunity!'"

To most men whose years have been chiefly spent amid the stirring scenes of a sportsman's life, some adventures have occurred which, being so exceptional in their character, can scarcely be written or related without causing the shadow of doubt to darken their credibility. Many such have happened to Russell; but there is one he is wont to tell, which, at any risk, claims a passing notice in this memoir. It is the story of a wild fox taking his prey while hotly pursued by hounds—a circumstance not likely to be forgotten by the Rev. J. Bryan, the rector of Cliddesden, near Basingstoke, as he was present on that occasion.

Russell had found a fox one fine-scenting morning on the outskirts of the moor, and was bringing him at a trimming pace over the wide heathery waste of Hawkridge Common, and thence into the hanging woods that crown the Barle with such majestic scenery, when Russell's ear was attracted by the wild screams of a woman, apparently in the greatest distress. The hounds at that moment were running exactly in the direction of the hubbub; and as Russell rode up to the spot, he beheld a woman rushing frantically after them, and catching sight of him, she exclaimed in a voice of agony, "Oh! Mr. Rissell! that there fox hath a tookt away our little specklety hen; I seed un snap un up, and away to go, I did!"

"Then," said Russell, "I'll kill him and give you another hen;" and on he went with the hounds.

The woman was the wife of a poor charcoal-burner, living in a turf cabin, and passing a lonely existence in the solitude of those wild woods. On that one hen and her lively cackle, announcing the good news of a fresh-laid egg, depended, perhaps for days together, her sole supply of animal food; it had been as a pet lamb to her; had shared the crumbs of her scanty meal, and had been her companion in many a lonesome hour, when no other living creature was near.

But the avengers were on the track; and, with no refuge at hand, die Reynard must for his heartless theft. And die he did directly afterwards, for, within two gunshots of the spot, just over the Barle, the hounds ran into him; while the dishevelled carcase of the "poor little speckletty hen," still warm with life, was picked up by the disconsolate owner, bringing the deed home, without a shadow of doubt, to the rapacity of that hunted fox.

Here, however, Russell's sport was well-nigh brought to a serious and untimely end. "My horse Rattler," he writes, "in crossing the Barle, which was much swollen, missed his footing among the rocks, and, being carried off his legs, rolled headlong into the river, leaving me to get out as best I could—a labour of no little difficulty; but, with the assistance of Houlditch, a couple of masons, and a long pole, I escaped with only a good ducking. The old horse, however, would not leave the river till he had drunk his fill—at least three pails of water. We found in Twitchen Town Wood, ran him to South Molton, six miles; back through the same wood again and then straight over the Molland and Anstey commons, to the Barle, under Jekyll's house; time, one hour and forty minutes, without a check, and no harm happened to Rattler, notwithstanding his copious libation."

It will be anticipated that Russell did not forget to return to the hut, and console the woman, not only with an immediate half-crown, but with the promise of another hen at an early date.

"Dining at the late Sir Robert Sheffield's, at Normanby, some years ago," writes an old friend of Russell's, "I met Lord Henry Bentinck; and the subject of conversation turning on the habits of wild foxes, I related a story told me by Mr. John King, of Fowelscombe, the circumstances of which he witnessed when Master of the Hambledon hounds. He had been running a fox merrily for upwards of forty minutes; and coming up to a farmyard, by which he was making a short cut, he saw the fox dash into a flock of ducks, seize a mallard just below the green of his neck, and carry him off across a large field when, the hounds running into him, Mr. King picked up the mallard, then quivering in its last gasp, and restored it to its owner.

"'Mr. King must be a bold man to tell such a story,' remarked Lord Henry, dryly, as if he utterly disbelieved it.

"'I had the pleasure of knowing Mr. King intimately,' replied I; 'and he was a man quite as unlikely to tell an untruth as your lordship;' a rejoinder that brought the conversation to an abrupt close.

"Years afterwards I repeated to Russell what Lord Henry had said; on which he replied, 'I only wish I had been there; I could have told his lordship that a very similar circumstance happened to myself (that of the charcoal-burner's little speckletv hen), and I think *he* would have been the bold man, had he doubted that fact.'"

Russell's thoughts must have carried him back, at that instant, to the time when he blacked Bulteel's eye at Plympton School; or, later on, perhaps, to those days of muscular Christianity at Oxford, when, if any one had been rash enough to doubt his word, or that of his friend Denne, either of them would have knocked him down like a ninepin on a skittle-alley. Still, it must be owned that antics like these by foxes, when hunted, are most exceptional; two or three only having been witnessed once, during each of their lives, by men of such long and varied experience as Mr. King and the subject of this memoir.

Another incident is equally remarkable:—"During a Chulmleigh meeting," said Russell, "I was enjoying a day's sport with Sir Walter Carew's hounds. They found—I forget exactly where—and were running him sharply near

Romansleigh village, when I saw the fox catch up a large yellow cat in his mouth and carry him on as far as I could view him. The fox was killed, but what became of the poor cat I am unable to say."

## CHAPTER XII.

The South Molton Meetings—Limpetty, Mr. Trelawny's Huntsman, rides over a Flood-Hatch on "Jack Sheppard"—Russell Ceases to be a Master of Hounds—His Long Devotion to the "Antient Sport of Kings"—A Brief Sketch of the Staghounds—A Barrister and his Gallant Grey brought to grief in an Exmoor Bog—Anecdote of Hind and Calf.

> Magnificent creature! so stately and bright!
> In the pride of thy spirit pursuing thy flight!
> For what hath the child of the desert to dread,
> Wafting up his own mountains the far-beaming head;
> Or borne like a whirlwind down on the vale!
> Hail! king of the wild and the beautiful—hail!
>
> *  *  *  *  *  *
>
> In the wide raging torrent that lends thee its roar—
> In the cliff that once trod must be trodden no more—
> Thy trust, 'mid the dangers that threaten thy reign:
> But what if the stag on the mountain be slain?
> On the brink of the rock—lo! he standeth at bay,
> Like a victor that falls at the close of the day.
>
> John Wilson.

Under the immediate auspices of Russell himself, backed up by Mr. Trelawny and Sir Walter Carew, the meetings at South Molton continued to flourish, season after season, with unqualified success; the stout foxes, the undeniable hounds, and the rough heathery wastes, over which the chase from day to day swept like a hurricane, giving a wild character to the sport, and establishing its popularity throughout the western counties. Consequently, from all quarters between the Quantock Hills and the Bodmin Moors, between the South Hams and Hartland Point, every man who possessed a horse and loved hunting found himself, sooner or later, partaking as a guest, if not as a member, of the attractive and varied *menu* provided by that club.

Of course, a considerable amount of rivalry was exhibited, ever and anon, among sundry of the partisans attached to the three hunts, not only as to the merits of the respective packs and the style in which their work was done, but with reference to the staying powers of the horses and feats of audacious horsemanship performed by their riders. One gentleman, for instance, a member of Russell's hunt, was so determined not to be beaten or outdone by any competitor, native or stranger, that he rode in the most reckless manner, charging without a scruple of fear the most impracticable fences, and shouting to his horse as he did so, "*L'un ou l'autre*;" meaning that his own neck, or that of his steed, must be risked at such a time. It was his watchword, like that of a Knight Templar entering the lists; and so fiercely did he use the portentous motto, when the fence was an ugly one that, long after his own name had been forgotten by the members of Mr. Trelawny's hunt, he was always spoken of and readily remembered as that daring rider "*L'un ou l'autre.*"

From the southern side of the county, by none perhaps, was this rivalry in riding carried to a higher pitch than, much against his wish, by Mr. Trelawny's servants. Limpetty, the huntsman, on a wonderful little animal called Jack Sheppard, was utterly uncontrollable on such occasions; go he would, if hounds were running hard, at a castle wall or over the mouth of a coal-pit; while poor Jack Cumming, the whip, who afterwards broke his neck with the Grafton hounds, if not under the immediate eye of his master, was equally fearless and equally headstrong.

On one occasion, Russell had intimated to Mr. Trelawny that, if he met at Cuzzicombe Post and drew an acre of gorse hard by, he would probably find a flyer. Accordingly, meeting there, a trimming run after Trelawny's own heart—one of forty minutes—proved to be the happy result. The fox was in view, the hounds running into him and Limpetty "home to their sterns," when a barrier interposed, which no man with a heart less intrepid than his own would have dared to encounter. It was a flood-hatch, broad, deep, and dangerous; and a thrilling sight it was to see him on Jack

Sheppard flying over it, like a dragon on wings, looking back as he did so over his shoulder, and singing out to Jack Cumming, "Where be they Knights to now, I should like to knaw;" alluding to Mr. Frederick and Lewis Knight, of Simonsbath; two well-known brilliant performers over any country, but especially hard to catch over Exmoor.

Paradoxical though it may appear, never were the prospects of fox-hunting brighter in the north of Devon than when those happy and successful meetings at South Molton were at length brought to a close. For the flame that had first kindled them, and the fuel on which they had fed, had neither burned out nor smouldered away; but, on the contrary, had spread with a vitality that laid hold of the heart of the country, and continued to gain fresh vigour in every succeeding year.

After the expiration of that club it is not a little remarkable that, within a circuit of thirty miles, taking Russell's country as a centre, two or three packs, whose fame had hitherto been little known beyond the limits of the western counties, should have rapidly acquired a prominence which, in point of blood, looks, and efficiency, would have borne a comparison with the most renowned packs of the present age.

In the Chulmleigh country, for example, the hounds of the present Earl of Portsmouth, soon after his accession to the title, speedily assumed a very different aspect from that of former days, insomuch that the pack has since been pronounced, by no mean judge, to be "infinitely superior to anything that has ever been seen in the West of England: their hunting attributes being on a par with their other merits."

Living within twenty miles of Eggesford, and hunting with that pack on every available occasion, Russell must have known the history and character of every individual hound in it almost as well as the huntsman himself; moreover, being on the most friendly terms with Lord Portsmouth, even from his earliest youth, who so competent, who so ready as Russell, if consulted by him, to aid the young master with all the judgment and experience of his riper years?

That his lordship did so consult him in the first days of his hunting career is quite certain; although from his early association with a kennel, his hereditary love of hounds, and the power of close observation he has since shown with respect to the breeding and selection of puppies, Lord Portsmouth's judgment must very soon have developed into maturity, and needed little help from any man, even from Russell himself. And as to his knowledge of hunting, it is not very long since that, at a large breakfast-party given by Mr. Trelawny,

Russell was asked by a gentleman present which of the two he considered the better sportsman, the Duke of Beaufort or Lord Portsmouth? His reply was, "They are the two best in England—you cannot give a wrinkle to either; and if I place the Duke of Beaufort first, it is only in deference to his rank."

Again, in West Devon, the Honourable Mark Rolle, on the retirement of Mr. John Moore Stevens in 1858, took possession of the Torrington country; and, with the help of some valuable hounds from the Cleveland and Rufford kennels, established by degrees the noble pack which has since attained so much celebrity.

Then, about the same time, there arose a third pack, which, started by Lord Poltimore, with Russell as his chief counsellor, acquired so wide-spread a fame during the short time they hunted the country that, when they were sold, the price they fetched astonished even "Tom Pain" himself. His lordship, in reference to the subject of this memoir, thus writes of him: "When I first began keeping hounds, in 1857, he taught me much, and was of the greatest possible assistance to me; but, on removing into Dorsetshire and taking my hounds with me, I then saw less of him, except when he came on his annual visits, than in former days. His intuitive knowledge of the run of a fox, even in a country strange to Russell, was marvellous. I remember well that, on one occasion in Dorset, after a fast and straight run from Thresher's Gorse, in the Buckland Vale, over the Monument country, the fox was headed and the hounds brought to a slight check. At that moment a fresh fox was halloed ahead, while some of the field who viewed him did their best to get the hounds on to his line. Russell never moved; and some one remarking that he was taking matters very coolly (being so well placed in so good a run up to that point), he quietly answered, 'The hunted fox is behind; that is a fresh fox.' My huntsman was of the same opinion; and while he was making his cast, I viewed the hunted fox, which had laid down; we got on him again, and, in a sharp burst of ten minutes more, rolled him over in the open. Many of the field—a large one—had galloped off to the halloa of the fresh fox, and, being on those downs where hounds can race, were thrown out, nor did they make their appearance till many minutes after the fox was killed. One man on coming up remarked to my huntsman, 'Where have you been? Why didn't you come to my halloa?' 'Eating my fox,' was the answer; Russell, who was close by, adding to the man, 'I told you, sir, it was a fresh fox you halloed; the hunted fox was headed, and had laid down behind us.'"

That the extra impetus thus given to fox-hunting in the north of Devon may be attributed in no small degree to Russell's example, energy, and never-failing advocacy in its favour, no one conversant with its past and present history can for a moment doubt. Among all classes now, from the peer to the peasant in that country, the one feeling is to respect a fox; whereas in the early days of Russell's career, as already shown, the very church bells were used not only to announce public worship, or the passing away of a Christian soul, but the death-knell of a fox.

It is on record, that Mr. Mervyn Marshall, while attending divine service at Welcome Church, near Clovelly, a fall of snow having occurred during the night, was not a little startled by a man putting his head twice inside the church door, and shouting aloud each time, "I've a-got un;" on which almost every man of the congregation, knowing a fox had been traced to ground, seized his hat and quitted the church.

No such barbarisms exist in the north of Devon at present; bells do no more than the legitimate work for which their pious donors intended them—no more than that most devoted campanologist, the Rev. H. T. Ellacombe, could wish; and as for foxes, they have fair play shown them, and if they can only beat hounds, they live in no danger of worse enemies.

Fox-hunting, therefore, being now established on a sound and satisfactory footing throughout the north of Devon, Russell, in 1871, parted with his last pack, as the reader is already aware, to that distinguished sportsman, Mr. H. Villebois, of Marham Hall, Norfolk; and thenceforth he ceased to be a Master of Hounds. It was a wrench, however, which told upon him painfully at the time, and it could hardly have been otherwise; he had kept hounds, lived with them, and hunted them himself for half a century, nor did the old love cease, for many a day afterwards, to assert its long and strong hold on Russell's heart.

Still, there were not a few among his old friends who refused to believe that life, apart from the company of his hounds, could be longer enjoyed by him; and who consequently urged him, though in the seventy-sixth year of his age, to take to them again. But this time, much as he missed them under the old tree at Tordown, he remained firm.

As a scientific master of woodcraft, his great points may be thus summarized:—A thorough knowledge of the wild animal and his habits; his mode of drawing covers and finding his fox, working him in big woodlands incessantly, so that he was a beaten fox before he went away; letting his hounds alone at a check, and when they failed, making a grand cast on the line far ahead, his intuition as to the run of a fox guiding him aright in almost every case. His command over hounds—two or three of which he always had near him—so that with a tricky fox in a deep woodland, the moment he caught a view he could clap them on instantly. By this method he often drove a fox away from his old haunts and country, and so forced a run on a strange line—a grand point in favour of hounds. Then, his feeding—he knew the constitution of every hound in his kennel.

So far, then, as to Russell's life with his own hounds; but there is another and a no less remarkable phase of it—his long devotion to the "Antient Sport of Kings"—a phase which, before we part with him, claims to be seen and described, however imperfectly, through the medium of this memoir.

With the exception of that memorable day, the 30th September, 1814, when, with Lord Fortescue's hounds, Russell saw his first red deer found at Padwells; and then, after a thrilling chase, helped to collar the noble beast in the depths of the roaring Barle, no allusion has been as yet made to his love of Stag-hunting, a sport he followed through a long life with an ardour worthy of a boy—always fresh but never sated, and with an untiring consistency positively unparalleled. Mr. Charles Palk Collyns, of Dulverton, long looked upon as the Nestor of the moor, hunted, he tells us, "with the staghounds for forty-six years"; while the experience of Mr. Boyse, of Withypoole, his predecessor as a chronicler of that sport, does not appear to have extended beyond forty years, that is, from 1776 to 1816, when Mr. Collyns took up the running, and "regularly noted the chases" down to 1860.

Russell, then, dating his entry from 1814, with constant attendance, season after season, from that day to 1882, a period of sixty-eight years, had a far longer experience with that noble and unique sport than either of those gentlemen.

"Accordingly, down to that year, Russell, it appears, followed the chase of the wild red deer under at least a dozen different dynasties; the following being a recorded list of the masters, and the dates of their succession, during that period:—

In 1812 the late Lord Fortescue became Master of the Staghounds for the second time; but resigned them again in 1818, during which period of six years, as before stated, they killed ninety deer — forty-two stags, and forty-eight hinds.

Mr. Stucley Lucas, of Baron's Down, next took the command; his tenure of office being also brought to a close at the end of six years, when, in 1825, to Russell's great regret, the old-fashioned staghounds—a grand pack, that stood nearly twenty-seven inches high, and for more than a century had been bred expressly for that sport—were sold at Tattersall's, and for ever lost to the country. "They went to Germany," writes Russell; "but I kept three bitches for twelve months, hoping some one would begin again; then, having only £80 a year to live upon, I gave them to 'Smash Lewis' for a Welsh friend of his—a Mr. John Dillwyn Llewelyn, of Penllergare, near Swansea; and thirty years afterwards I picked out their descendants in his kennel."

With all Russell's love for the dash of a foxhound, he regarded those magnificent hounds with the most unbounded admiration; declaring them to have been, as they certainly were, peculiarly adapted for the chase of the wild red deer; so perfect were they in water, so driving on scent, and so sonorous in tongue, the latter, indeed, reminding him of a tenor bell,

> "Over some wide-water'd shore,
> Swinging slow with sullen roar."

Mr. Collyns, too, was in despair at their loss, and speaks of it with almost tearful regret: "A nobler pack of hounds," he says, "no man ever saw—alas! that they should now be consigned to the kennel of a German baron! For courage, strength, speed and tongue, they were unrivalled. Like the game they pursued, they never appeared to be putting forth all their powers of speed, and yet few horses could live with them on the open. Their rarest quality, perhaps, was their sagacity in hunting in the water—every pebble, every overhanging bush or twig which the deer might have touched, was quested as they passed up or down the stream, and the crash with which the scent, if detected, was acknowledged and announced, made the whole country echo again.

"Nor must I forget to notice the staunchness with which they pursued their game, even when the scent had been stained by the deer passing through a herd of his own species, or through fallow-deer in a park. Wonderful, indeed, was the unerring instinct they displayed in carrying on the scent, disregarding the lines, which, spreading right and left around the track of the hunted deer, would, it might well be supposed, have been fatal to their power of keeping on the foot of their quarry."

Again, "The importance of the two qualifications of staghounds above mentioned, viz.: sagacity in hunting in the water, and staunchness in pursuing a hunted deer through the herd and upon stained ground, is well known to every man accustomed to the sport. They are important, nay, indispensable, in consequence of the habits of the deer; for a stag is seldom, I might almost say never, roused without 'taking soil' in the course of the run; and he rarely neglects the opportunity of seeking for safety by joining the herd, if he has the good fortune to be able to do so."

After two years of mourning, the spirit of the country again revived, when, in 1827, the late Sir Arthur Chichester, of Youlston, brought a pack of hounds into the field, and once more restored the "antient sport," no less to Russell's delight than to that of the whole country.

On Sir Arthur's resignation in 1833, the "sport of kings" again fell into abeyance, and but for the exertion of Mr. Collyns would probably then have disappeared for ever. He, however, established a committee, of which Russell, who lived fifty miles from Dulverton, was not a member, although doing all in his power to promote the object it had in view; and under its management the country was hunted from 1837 to 1842.

The Hon. Newton Fellowes then came forward and gave most efficient aid "in the hour of need;" the hounds being under his able management till 1847, when the present Sir Arthur Chichester became the master for one season only.

In 1849 Mr. Theobald, and after him Mr. George Luxton, of Winkleigh, took the helm for a season each; when Captain West succeeded to that honourable post, and was followed by Mr. Tom Carew, of Collipriest, with John Beale for his huntsman; he, however, resigned the command in 1853, to the general regret of all classes. Captain West then came forward a second time, but only to stop a gap, which, happily, was destined soon to be long and most efficiently filled by Mr. Fenwick-Bisset, who, taking the command in 1855, held it to the entire satisfaction of the whole country to the year 1881, when he was succeeded by Lord Ebrington, the present Master.

Nor will the work done by Mr. S. H. Warren, who for so many years and with so much tact acted as honorary secretary to the Devon and Somerset Hunt, be readily forgotten; for long, able, and gratuitous were the services of that gentleman in behalf of the noble sport peculiar to that country.

Russell could not speak too highly in praise either of the management or of the sport Mr. Bisset had shown; the latter he considered equal to anything he remembered in the palmy days of old, when "the halls of Castle Hill rang merrily with the wassail of the hunters;" and as to the former, he would say that no man ever handled the farmers with more consummate tact, nor did more to establish the noble sport on a sure and permanent footing than he had done.

Mr. Collyns, to whose able and graphic work on "The Chase of the Wild Red Deer" the writer is beholden for so much information on that subject, thus alludes to Mr. Bisset: "The sport has now the countenance and support of the landlords and the enthusiastic good wishes of the farmers. Mr. Bisset knows how to take the command of a pack and of a country; and hunting as he does on the most improved principles, observing the rules from which in days of yore no sportsman ever deviated, having his deer carefully harboured, drawing with tufters and not with the pack, and so avoiding the danger of destroying deer out of season or unwarrantable, I have no doubt he will find the owners of coverts continue to rally round him as they have done; and that, if it should be our good fortune to keep him amongst us, he will again re-establish the sport and place it on such a footing as to make it vie with that which our forefathers witnessed, and the history of which they recounted and handed down to their sons and sons' sons with pride. Woe betide the stag which the present pack pursue! Well may he tremble when he hears the twang of John Babbage's horn, and catches the sound of his able coadjutor's, Arthur Heal's, shrill 'hark together,' as he cheers the eager hounds on their quarry. Not all his wiles, his fleetness, or his cunning, can save him from his well-trained foes."

It is to Russell, no doubt, and probably to Mr. Jekyll, the rector of Hawkridge, that Mr. Collyns alludes, when, observing that the recreation of the chase is deemed incompatible with the duties of clerical life, he thus adds: "For myself, I will say that, without wishing to see the dignitaries of the Church again maintaining their kennels of hounds, I should feel regret if I were to miss from the field the familiar faces of some of those members of the clergy who now join in the sport of our country, and whose presence is always welcomed at the covert side."

Without records of any kind to refer to, beyond those dependent on memory and oral tradition alone, the attempt to give anything like a detailed account of Russell's sport and doings with the staghounds would be at once a difficult and most thankless task. Local descriptions, however wild and grand the scenery may be, don't suit the general reader, and are too often followed with difficulty, even by those to whom the landmarks of the country are well known.

The "sport of kings," however, has formed so considerable a portion of Russell's hunting life, that to make no reference to it in this memoir would be an omission which not only modern Actæons, but many a fair follower of the buskined queen, would look upon as unpardonable. For has not he, from time beyond their ken, been one of the prominent features, and to many the guiding star, of that gay and brilliant meeting which, year after year, inaugurates the opening-day on Cloutsham Ball? Nay, with his knowledge of the forest, extending as it does to every bridle-path and sheep-track; to every ford, clam, and safe crossing-place during the stormiest state of the moorland floods; to the readiest inlets and outlets of every woodland combe from the Quantock Hills to Mole's Chamber—has he not scores of times picked up the waifs and strays of the hunting-field; and then, as "guide, philosopher, and friend," led them in their sorest need into safer and happier grounds?

Yes! countless are the heroes and fair women, too, who have been thrown out in that wild chase, and who, but for his pilotage, knowledge of the moor, and, above all, the experience he has had in the running and wiles of the hunted deer, would never have seen a hound again. It is not very long since that a gentleman, better versed in the intricate ways of the law than in those of Exmoor, came down for a month's hunting to Porlock. The first meet was at Brendon Barton; and the harbourer having reported a "warrantable deer" in Parsonage Wood, the tufters were trotted off to that point, and no sooner laid on than up jumped the grand beast, breaking away in view by Fairleigh,

DIFFICULTIES OF AN EXMOOR BOG.

and putting his head straight for the distant Chains of Exmoor.

The rouse was magnificent, and the hounds being clapped on at once, away they went at best pace for the wild waste on Exehead; crossing the brook above Cornham, they raced thence up to Acland's Allotment and Five-barrows, through the deep ground of which none but the stoutest horses and most experienced men could now hold their own and live with the hounds. Among these, however, was our friend the barrister, well mounted and well forward on a thoroughbred grey, but riding a little wide of the pack and following a well-known member of the hunt, on whom he had been told to keep his eye. Never was a field in greater discomfiture; some scattered for miles over the dusky moor, some floundering in the bog like flies in treacle; others brought to a dead standstill, as the chase swept on to Yard Down, Bray, Challacombe, Showlesborough Castle, and thence to Woodbarrow, where the gallant grey and his rider, having left their pilot miles behind, came to grief, and bid fair, in the absence of all human aid, to pass the night amid the swamps and jack-o'-lanterns of that solitary waste.

The man had, of course, quitted his saddle; and, with bridle in hand, was doing his utmost to help the horse forward, as he now struggled hock-deep through the spongy soil. With a few more plunges in the same direction, the brave beast must have come to its girths in another half-minute; when a ringing shout, such as no one but Russell could have given, reached the rider's ears: "Back for your life, man; back, I tell you!"

Instantly obeying the mandate, he managed with a mighty effort to get the grey's head fairly round; then with a few frantic plunges the gallant animal stood once more on sound ground.

"Now then," said Russell, who had lingered near him to see if he needed further help, "the deer's going to Woolhanger; and if you stick to me, we shall probably catch them again."

He *did* stick to him like his shadow, and caught the pack in the covers below; when the deer, hard pressed, broke away and took to sea; but being blanched by a boat, soon landed again, and after a short chevy was finally run into amid the surf and shingle of that loud-sounding shore.

The habits of a deer by night and at early dawn were perhaps never better understood by any man than by Jem Blackmore, harbourer to the staghounds for so many years; but it may well be doubted if by day, even he knew half as much as Russell did about the shifts and running of a deer when once roused and away. The former, indeed, had details to study, the perfect knowledge of which could only be acquired by long experience and the keenest and nicest observation. With the perceptive faculty of a prairie-hunter, he had to note carefully every trace, slot, or sign of the wary game, whose haunts and ambush it was his object to discover. How difficult the lesson, but how well it may be learned, may be gathered from the picture of a harbourer so artistically painted by Mr. Whyte-Melville in "Katerfelto." "The ground," he writes, "must indeed be hard, and the 'slot' or print of the animal's feet, many hours old to baffle Red Rube, who, stooping to the line like a bloodhound, reads off, as from a book, the size, sex, weight, and age of the passing deer, the pace at which it was travelling, its distance ahead, and the probability of its affording a run."

Russell's pursuit however, of the noble animal commenced only with the uncoupling of the tufters—the point at which the other has brought his labours to a close. But from that moment, although simply a looker-on like the rest of the field, yet owing to his intimate knowledge of the dodges which, before breaking cover, an old deer will adopt to save his haunches, many a needless sacrifice has been averted and many a glorious run obtained. An old stag, for instance, rarely if ever goes to lair without having a brocket, or young stag, within reach of him, which, when he is pressed by hounds, he turns out and instantly lies down in his bed—a sight once witnessed by Russell himself. The substitute then, till the trick is discovered, is compelled to do penance for his noble friend, the monarch of the glen. Thus the changes, which are constantly occurring before the right animal can be driven to face the open and exhibit his beam and branches to the gaze of a crowd, are so frequent and so puzzling that, in the absence of a view, it often requires judgment of the most acute order to discriminate whether the tufters are flinging their tongues so merrily on the right or the wrong game; on a hind, a brocket, or a warrantable deer.

Not once, nor twice, but a hundred times and more, has Russell done good service in that way. To him again, beyond all doubt, does Mr. Collyns allude when he describes the tufters at work, and the "hark back," to which so frequently they are compelled to submit. "Shiner," he says, "is close upon them (two hinds and a calf), and the rest of the tufters following him. A little rating and a few cracks of the whip, and their heads are up: they know that they are not on the 'real animal;' and as soon as Sam's horn summons them, back they go, and resume their labour. Again they open, and again we are on the alert. The cry increases; they run merrily, and we are high in hope. 'Ware fox!' says a M.F.H. the best sportsman in the west, as he views Charley slinking along towards the gap on the hedgerow. Then, with his stentorian voice, he calls out to Sam, 'Your hounds are on a fox, Sam.' Sam does not hear, but rides up within a hundred yards of us. 'What, sir?' 'Your hounds are on a fox, Sam,' repeats the M.F.H. 'Think not, sir,' says Sam; 'my hounds won't hunt fox!' 'I tell you that they are on a fox, Sam; call them off,' says the foxhunter. Sam looks vicious, but he obeys, saying in a voice which could be heard by the Master of Foxhounds, but certainly not by the tufters, 'Get away, hounds, get away; ain't you ashamed of hunting of a stinking little warmint not half the size of yourselves? Get away!' Sam still maintains his creed that his tufters were not on the fox, and two minutes afterwards a yell announced that a different sort of animal was afoot. Another tally; Tom Webber's voice; a guarantee that it is the right thing, for the good yeoman is the best and truest stag-hunter that ever cheered a hound. Every one is on the alert; we ride forward, and presently in the distance, view, not a stag, alas! but a hind breaking towards the moor. 'How is this, Tom? You were wrong for once.' 'No, sir; not I. I'll swear it was a stag, and a good one, but you see he has pushed up the hind and gone down, and we must have him up again. So the tufters are stopped again, and sent back on heel; and by-and-bye that unmistakable 'yell' which announces a view is heard, and this time the antlered monarch reveals himself to the whole of the assembled multitude."

Then again, on the water, which almost invariably is the last refuge of a deer in distress, the countless wiles he will adopt to elude his pursuers have been so often witnessed by Russell, that it is no figure of speech to say he was familiar with them all. More than sixty years of experience, the keenest observation, and a thorough acquaintance with the habits of the animal, at least in chase, gave him a power which, when appealed to, generally proved more than a match for the craftiest stratagem practised by a deer.

In early days, when Russell kept his otter-hounds at South Molton, and earned the gratitude of all fly-fishermen in that country by ridding the rivers of five-and-thirty otters in a couple of seasons, he must have learned many a useful lesson in studying the watery ways of those mysterious animals. The subtlety of their habits, when closely pressed by hounds, must have shown him how marvellous is the power of instinct to elude pursuit, if life be at stake, and water at hand—that almost natural element to which, for refuge, they are wont to fly.

It was a rare apprenticeship for him, that time with the otter-hounds; every kill developing fresh dodges, and qualifying him in after years to solve those most puzzling of all problems in the Art of Venerie—the wiles of a deer when he comes to "soil." It is a fact known to all followers of that noble sport, that, short of diving, a deer will take as much advantage of water as an otter does; wading and swimming for a mile or two, sinking himself to his nostrils, with the topmost tine of his antlers effectually submerged, and often quitting the stream at one point to return to it at another. "It not unfrequently happens," says Mr. Collyns, "that the cunning animal has merely 'soiled' when he entered the stream and then backed it on his foil, and laid fast in the covert."

Mr. Whyte-Melville, too, in "Katerfelto," describes the famous harbourer, Red Rube, as being utterly perplexed by what a deer may do when forced to its last move at the end of a chase: "Who shall say that all this calculation, this strategy, this reflection, is so far below reason to be called instinct? Even Red Rube, many a mile behind on his pony, taxing his resources of intellect and cunning, backed by the observation of fifty years, that he may arrive somehow at the finish in time to hear the 'bay,' confesses he is but a fool when his wits are pitted against those of a deer driven to its last shifts."

But, however marvellous may be the shifts of a deer to save its own life, the animal is equally adroit in saving that of its young. "I have heard Russell relate," says an old friend, "that on one occasion he witnessed a curious manœuvre on the part of a hind, which, with true maternal care, successfully managed to conceal and protect her calf, when pursued by hounds. But let him tell his own tale. 'We had been driving,' said he, 'for some time in cover what all supposed to be a barren hind; when, just in front of me, at the head of the combe, out came a hind and her little calf breaking away together over the open moor. After travelling for some distance side by side, I observed their pace slacken, as the young one appeared to be flagging and unable to hold on with her dam. The hounds were now gaining rapidly on them, when I said to Stucley Lucas, "They'll kill that poor calf to a certainty." "No they won't," he replied; "she'll kick it down." In another instant, on passing over some furzy ground, I distinctly saw the hind give the calf a sharp kick with her heel, and down went the little one as if she were shot with a gun. It was the signal for her to keep close—a signal no sooner given than at once instinctively obeyed. There she lay, crouched up like a hare in her form; while the hounds, pressing on and keeping the hind in view, swept over the spot without indicating the slightest suspicion of the trick they had been so artfully played. We ran that hind over the moor for twenty miles, by North Molton to Nadrid Ford, where Tout, the huntsman, and myself being the only two men up, he turned and said "Mr. Russell, what had we better do; we are close to Brembridge Wood; hadn't we better stop them?" "Certainly," I replied, "stop them at once; for if you get them in there, every hound will have his deer, and you'll never get them out again. Go back on the same line, and you'll pick up the stragglers."

"'This happened on a Tuesday, very early in the season, and before the regular hunting had commenced. Two days afterwards, on the way to Porlock, I was hailed by a turf-cutter, who said, "The hind you hunted on Tuesday last has only just gone back, not an hour ago." "How do you know it is the same hind?" I inquired, doubtingly. "Because, sir, she was a light-coloured one, and had a very big udder." The next day (Friday), the hounds were no sooner thrown into cover than, to our utter surprise, out came the same hind and calf again. The latter quickly disappeared, but the former took precisely the same line over the moor which she had taken on the previous Tuesday, gave us a glorious run, and at length fairly beat us by gaining Brembridge Wood and joining the herd; and I doubt not' Russell added, 'that in a day or two afterwards the loving pair were together again.'"

# CHAPTER XIII.

Russell and His Friend, the Rev. A. F. Luttrell, of Quantockshead—The Danger of Handling a Stag at Bay—Man and Hound Injured, and both Saved by Russell—Ladies to the Front over Exmoor—Mrs. Cholmondeley's Perilous Fall.

> He knows the best line for each cover,
> He knows where to stand for a start,
> And long may he live to ride over
> The country he loves in his heart.
>
> Egerton-Warburton.

Valuing the companionship of Russell not less than his long and untiring devotion to the sport, Mr. Fenwick-Bisset, the well-known Master of the Devon and Somerset Staghounds, sent him, in April, 1877, a couple of stags' heads, with the following letter :—

"I have sent you two heads to-day, one taken in Sheardown Water on the 6th of October last, the other that of a deer which, you may remember, stole away from Hawkcombe, and we hunted up to, and fresh found in Badgeworthy Wood, ran him back and killed him in Avon Pool, below Bossington. They are not very big heads, but not the less memorable on that account.

"I was greatly struck by your exuberant spirits in the hunting-field; much more like a schoolboy than a man of eighty. May you live to see many more such runs as these afforded; and when you can no longer *see* them, may you *talk* them over, like your rare old friend, Alec Luttrell."

The following communication from a lady, a near relative of Mr. Luttrell's, is so interesting that, with her kind permission, it may well find a place in this memoir:—

"On the 28th December, 1876, Mr. Russell was on a visit to his old college friend, the Rev. A. F. Luttrell, of East Quantockshead, then in his eighty-third year; and on the following day (after going on the Quantock Hills on foot, to look for the hounds of Mr. Luttrell, of Dunster, who was hunting near) he (Russell) went on to St. Audries, the seat of Sir Alexander Acland Hood, to dine and sleep, and to be present at the tenants' ball on that evening the 29th. During dinner he mentioned as a curious coincidence that, on looking over some family papers, he found that in the Christmas week of 1776 his father had made a journey on horseback from Meath, near Hatherleigh, to Dunster, to pass a few days at the Castle, with his old friend and schoolfellow Mr. Luttrell, the then 'Squire' of Dunster; and now, in the Christmas week of 1876, their two sons were passing some days together, both over fourscore years, and the next generation only, though a hundred years had passed since that visit of their fathers. Mr. Russell was then sitting at table with several of the grandchildren and great-grandchildren of his father's host and friend; among them, the present possessor of the Castle, a grandson, and his eldest son, who had attained his majority six months before, when Mr. Russell had been one of the many old friends assembled at Dunster on that joyous occasion.

"At the tenants' ball the same night, Mr. Russell was among the most active dancers, joining in quadrilles, lancers, and country dances, with the prettiest girls in the room (all *delighted* to have him for a partner), and greeting all his old friends in his hearty manner. He retired to bed at three a.m., regretting the necessity of leaving the festive scene before Sir Roger de Coverley began; but he had to start at eight a.m., on a journey of over forty miles, as, he said, 'Lord Portsmouth's hounds were to meet near his place in Devonshire, and he had promised his lordship to be back soon after twelve o'clock to show him his second fox'—which he did. The previous Monday had been his eighty-first birthday."

Mr. Stucley Lucas, the present owner of Baron's Down, whose father succeeded the late

Earl Fortescue, in 1818, as Master of the Dulverton Staghounds, and from whose house, it will be remembered, Russell saw his first stag killed in 1814, has kindly favoured the writer with the following letter :—

"So long ago as I can remember—and that is not far from half a century—down to the present year, Russell has always stuck to the staghounds with a consistency unequalled by any living man ; no matter where they met, how long they ran, nor where they finished at the end of the day. Our entrance hall, as you know, is pretty well decorated with stags' heads, trophies of the chase in my father's time, when the woods and combes of Exmoor resounded with the music of those grand old-fashioned hounds, which he kept for six years.

"Well, it would charm your heart to hear the fine old fellow when he drops in upon us, as he now and then does, still throwing his tongue with all the vigour and animation of youth, and pointing out, as if it had happened yesterday, how this deer or that had fought his last fight to the bitter end ; how, with brow-antler, piercing like a bayonet, another had killed the bravest young hound in all the pack, knocked over the huntsman, or old Joe the whip, or perhaps Russell himself, and held his own against all odds, till the death-stroke fell, and his life-blood crimsoned the ground.

"Then he would tell of one, whose royal crown of beam and branches proclaimed him king of the forest—a deer so savage that, when he was brought to bay in a farmyard, no one for some time dared to approach him. At length, as he shifted his quarters closer to the house, Russell was let out of a window, and with the aid of a rope was able to secure the noble beast and avert the danger that threatened the hounds.

"I see in my father's stag-hunting note-book," continues Mr. Lucas, "an instance recorded of Russell's indomitable pluck: the stag had crossed the Taw, when, coming to the bank of that turbulent stream, Russell, without hesitation dashed into it and swam to the opposite shore; while, of all the field, one man only was bold enough to face the stream and follow the hounds.

"Again, I myself, witnessed an act of courage on Russell's part which I can never forget. We had driven our stag, after a long run, to the foot of the Quantock Hills; and there, with five or six couple of hounds only, had brought him to bay in a small stream, just deep enough to compel them to swim, while he stood firm on his legs. What was to be done, for there was no one up but Russell and myself? The situation was a most critical one, as, with lowered beam and defiant air, the deer's charge appeared to be imminent, and then some of the best hounds would either have been killed on the spot, or have had their hides seamed from shoulder to stern. Russell jumped off his pony (Fox by name, a wonderful little animal, which, by-the-bye, immediately ran away and gave me no end of trouble to catch him), rushed in upon the deer, caught him by the horns and held him till a third man came to his aid; who, so far as I can recollect, was poor old Tom Webber, long since dead. Luckily for Russell, the deer (a four-year old) was not a very savage one; so, while I held the horses, the two, after a sharp tussle, managed to secure him. Several of the field then made their appearance—a little too late, however, to witness the last act of the play, the crowning scene of the day's sport.

"Russell and I started home soon afterwards; and, long as the distance was, reached Baron's Down before nightfall. I need not tell you that Russell has been out with the staghounds, to the best of my belief, every day during the past season (1877); that is to say, when a stag was to be hunted; for hinds he doesn't care so much about. Let me add, that he generally sees as much of the run as any one out; stays to the finish, and rides incredible distances back to his home—no trifling feat for a man in the vigour of youth; but for one of his age a truly wonderful performance."

Even to one well accustomed to the sport the business of collaring an old deer when he is "set up" by hounds, is a task that, to do it safely, requires at times all the skill and adroitness of a matador; but to the inexperienced hunter, no matter how quick, active, and strong he may be, the stag, with those long, pointed brow-antlers of his, which he is wont to use with such terrible effect, is an awkward customer to approach, when driven to his last resource and confronting his foes on some vantage-ground.

Many a narrow escape has Russell had, first and last, at such times; but fortune, aided by his physical power and thorough acquaintance with every mode of handling the animal in that the final ceremony, carried him scathless through numerous close and fierce encounters.

One day, during the mastership of Mr. Stucley Lucas, who, it will be remembered, was the last man to use the fine old-fashioned stag-hounds of that country, he was more than once exposed to imminent peril in saving a peasant, partly intoxicated, from certain death. They had found in Brembridge Wood, near Castle Hill, a noble deer, strong and swift as the winds of the moor, and bearing a grand head with "three upon top" on each horn. After a sharp burst of two and a half hours, they brought him to bay in a small brook near Bratton Mill; and there for a considerable time, he defended himself against all odds with so much vigour and effect, that several of the most adventurous hounds were more or less severely maimed in the repeated and desperate charges he made upon them.

And now the struggle had all but taken a more serious turn: an old man, muddled with cider, in spite of all warning, went up, and attempted to caress the infuriated animal, addressing it thus: "Sober, now, sober, don't 'ee be scared, my pretty dear." On which the deer, mistrusting his motive, made a fierce lunge at him; but missing a vital spot, drove his brow-antler right through the old fellow's hand; and, then and there, would have certainly killed him but for Russell's immediate help. He rushed in, collared the deer by the root of his near-side antler, dragged the man's hand off the reeking tine, and then rolled over and over with the deer into the bed of the brook; the animal forcing him under a foot-bridge and kneeling upon him in the water.

At length the deer shifted his position, releasing Russell, and bringing his back to bear against the wall of a thatched house, where, like a Turk entrenched, he again stood his ground with a lowered beam and defiant air. But "the race is not to the swift, nor the battle to the strong;" for anon a farmer, called

Skinner, mounting the roof in his rear, with rope in hand, gave token that the curtain was about to fall and bring the last act to its tragic end.

And here most touching was the spectacle which the poor beast presented; as, winding the man on the roof behind him, he turned round, stood on his hind legs against the side of the house, and looked his enemy in the face; as if he would have said, in the extremity of despair, "Ah! that's foul play—a cowardly trick to win your game."

The noose then fell; but his noble head—which may still be seen adorning the hall of Baron's Down—yet exists to tell the tale and remind Mr. Lucas and his friends of the perilous incidents which occasionally attend the chase of the wild red deer.

Mr. Collyns, although he gives neither date nor minute particulars, probably alludes to the same event at Bratton Mill, where, he says, "I remember seeing a deer, when 'set up' by hounds, thrust his brow-antler through the hand of a man who attempted to secure him;" and then he adds: "On one occasion when I was out, the late Sir Arthur Chichester, then the Master of the Hounds, had a very narrow escape from serious injury. We had brought to bay an old stag, after a severe chase. The deer posted himself on a high bank, from which exalted position he set the hounds at defiance. No rope was at hand, and whilst some of the party were absent in quest of one, the master rode up, and tried to dislodge the deer from his vantage-ground with his whip. I saw the animal gather himself for a charge, and had just time to successfully warn Sir Arthur against the danger he was in. He turned aside, and in a moment the deer leapt from the bank, just missed the horse's head, as it was being turned away, and with tremendous force plunged his antlers deep into the ground."

Short of death, one of the most frightful injuries ever witnessed by Russell was inflicted on a hound bred by Lord Portsmouth, and called Falconer, in taking an old stag at Watersmeet. Standing at bay above his knees, in the East Lynn river, he drove his long brow-antler up to its hilt in the hound's side; and then, in withdrawing it, brought out that portion of the interior known as "the apron" clinging to the rough inequalities of the blood-stained horn. Almost sickened by the sight, Russell put his whip around the hound's neck, led him aside, and having drawn out the apron as far as it would come, he cut it off with a pair of scissors. He then inquired if any gentleman or lady present happened to have a needle and thread about them; on which a gentleman immediately came forward and produced a huswife well furnished with the said articles.

"Any surgeon present," again inquired Russell, "who will sew up the wound?"

"I am one," responded another readily, "and will do my best for the poor hound."

The operation having been quickly and well performed, Falconer was then conveyed to Simonsbath by a passing cart; and, wonderful to relate, at the end of a fortnight from that day, was taken out again as a tufter by the huntsman, John Babbage, who pleaded that he absolutely needed his services, at the same time pronouncing him to be "fit as a fiddle" for that or any other work. Nor did the hound ever afterwards appear a pin the worse for the cruel treatment he had so bravely survived.

The open and often stormy Severn-sea being the last refuge of a deer when driven by hounds to the rock-bound coast of his native wilds, it has been Russell's lot, first and last, to witness many a remarkable instance of buoyancy and strength exhibited both by the stag and hind in battling with the waves and struggling to reach the opposite shore. On the 22nd of October, 1876, Russell wrote :—

"Letters just come in—one from Mrs. Kinglake, who, with her husband, son, and daughters has been staying at Porlock for staghunting since August—to say that a stag we ran to sea above Porlock Weir, a fortnight ago, was drowned; that the body was washed across the Channel and picked up on the Welsh coast. He didn't run three miles before he went to sea, and I saw him battling with the waves, now riding on their topmost crest, and now lost in foam; there was a very heavy sea on, not half a minute before he went down. William Deane was by my side, and said, 'He has sunk.' My reply was, 'If he has, 'tis a very unusual circumstance; for I have known a deer out in the sea for four hours, after he has stood two hours before the hounds; and have seen him come in again apparently quite fresh.' He was drowned, however, if he did not sink; and so ends my tale."

The buoyancy of a deer in water, even when dead, is not a little remarkable. His body, though the lungs are no longer inflated with air, will still float on the surface; while that of an otter, an animal commonly but falsely supposed to be amphibious, will sink to the bottom like a lump of lead. Mr. Collyns relates that a stag "getting on Slippery Rock fell over the cliffs and killed himself; fortunately no hound followed him. The tide was up, and he was carried out to sea for a considerable distance; and the boat sent out to secure him arrived just in time to save him from the hands of those on board a smack going up Channel, who had all but reached him."

Russell corroborated the fact: "Collyns' version is quite a correct one. A deer will float—not 'swim'—for a long time after he is dead, both in the sea and in a river. I have witnessed it often, and so have many other Devonshire sportsmen; but I have never seen an otter float after he was dead."

Russell, in alluding to a deer that went to sea for four hours and returned all the better for his cruise, refers to a gallant old stag found by Sir Arthur Chichester's hounds and driven through Badgeworthy, over the moor to Lynmouth. Six or eight couple of hounds were pressing him sorely, when he managed by a few mighty bounds to reach the pinnacle of an isolated rock, from which, with a firm footing for himself, he bid defiance to all his foes.

A man, however, with a well-aimed pebble, dislodged him at length from his perilous perch; and, as the deer bounded off like an eagle into space, Russell shut his eyes, that he might not see him, as he fully expected, dashed to atoms. On looking again, however, to his great delight he saw the animal striding away towards the sea, where he remained for four hours, standing boldly out for the opposite coast. But he was taken and brought back long before he reached it.

Another stag, less fortunate in his jump, was so beset by men and hounds, near the same romantic spot, that he bounded over a road-wall, and fell hundreds of feet, down into the rocky Lynn, every bone in his body being smashed by the fall.

Again, Russell speaks of a deer which, after a grand run from Badgeworthy, went to sea near Countisbury Church; when a sloop bound for Swansea fell in with him, the men of which threw a rope over his antlers and carried him captive into that port. Alas! a week afterwards, the noble animal is said to have suffered the ignominy of being "uncarted" and turned out before a Welsh pack of hounds.

Nor was this act of piracy an exceptional case. Russell, on another occasion, saw a hind picked up by a fishing-smack in the face of all the hunters, who, posted on the cliff above, shouted and signalled in vain to the daring thieves. The animal was carried to Pill, sold there, and turned into venison.

In the rough and imperfect sketch of Russell set forth in this memoir, his devotion to the chase and its attendant mysteries has thus far purposely formed its chief foreground; but there is another feature of his character which, though not yet touched upon, is entitled to equal prominence in the picture; and that is, his devotion to women and children. In a spirited article, entitled "A Day with the Devon and Somerset Staghounds," contributed to *Baily's Magazine* of September, 1874, the writer ("E. K.") alludes very pleasantly to one of the numerous instances in which Russell has taken children under his especial tutelage, and literally guided their first steps in the hunting-field. It runs thus:

"Then comes the parson of the hunt—what west countryman does not know, without my naming him, the best and keenest of sportsmen? Up he comes, with a smile and a joke for all. As he answers the numerous greetings he receives, I catch his cheery acknowledgments: 'Very well, thank ye.' 'How's the missis? Long ride for an old fellow like me, eh? rode all the way from home this morning—a good thirty mile, and more.' 'Going to ride all the way back too?' 'Yes, the old horse looks well, don't he?' Doesn't change much more than his master—last my time, anyhow. Hullo! that's your little girl? Your first day, my dear? Then we must blood you; follow me, and you shall see the kill. Oh! I'll take care of her, never fear!' So I see the plucky little girl made utterly happy—she is to be piloted over the moor by the Rev. ——, and her joy is complete."

And as to women, it boots not where, how, or when; but his gallantry to them, in the field or out of it, at home or abroad, has been through life that of a Launcelot, anxious ever to serve, succour, and defend them to the best of his manly power. "God bless them all!" he might say with Sterne; "there is not a man upon earth who loves them *better* than I do."

Nor has the sentiment been ill-requited on their part; for no matter in what class of life the maid or matron may be, if haply she have seen much of his company, her eye will kindle evermore with a look of sympathy and pleasant memories at the bare mention of Russell's name.

His readiness and ability to help ladies in the stag-hunting field have been already alluded to; and from the eulogistic terms in which he never failed to speak of a few as "elegant and accomplished horsewomen," who, whatever the pace, were wont to take a brilliant lead and look to no one for help, so long as their horses could gallop and they could help themselves, the writer is sanguine enough to hope that the liberty will be condoned, if he venture to bracket a very imperfect list of their names in company with that of their devoted and staunchest admirer. First and foremost, then, comes Miss Kinglake, now the Hon. Mrs. T. Fitzwilliam; "one of the best," as Russell writes, "I ever saw, from find to finish, on

Exmoor." Then, her promising young sister, Miss Beata Kinglake, Lady Lovelace, Mrs. Henry Dene, Mrs. Pulsford Browne, of Kirk Bramwith, near Doncaster—"a lady who lived for many years at East Anstey, near Dulverton, and hunted with Lord Portsmouth's and the Staghounds—a very fine rider and one who went as straight over a country as a bird on wing. She always called me 'Uncle John'; and once or twice in a moor fog did me the honour to accept my pilotage."

Then there was Miss Clara Jekyll, Miss Hole, now Mrs. Wynch, Mrs. John Luttrell, Miss Leslie, the three Miss Taylors, of Dulverton, Miss Julia Carwithen, now Mrs. Pyne-Coffin, Miss Luttrell, Miss Widborne, Mrs. Louis and Mrs. Russell Riccard, Mrs. James Turner, Miss Vibart, Lady Lindsay, Mrs. Proctor-Baker, Miss Constance Baxendale, and Mrs. Lock-Roe, an elegant horsewoman, and one of Russell's dearest friends. Then, last in the list, but rarely so in the chase, come Mrs. Granville Somerset and her sister Mrs. Cholmondeley, two ladies whom Russell describes "as worthy of niches in the grandest temple ever dedicated to the Forest Queen."

Of a fall that befell Mrs. Cholmondeley, where the two streams meet above Badgeworthy—once, as Mr. Blackmore tells us, the stronghold of the Doones—Russell always spoke with a shudder. The hounds had found in Hawkcombe; and, in spite of a hurricane of wind that was blowing at the time, had brought their stag at a trimming pace over the moor down to that old point where so many have "soiled" or sought refuge in the surrounding combes.

Mrs. Cholmondeley, with Lord Cork near her, was well in front, when Russell, at a short distance behind them, beheld the lady riding directly for the stream, and, to his dismay, attempting to cross it at a dangerous and impracticable spot. A high and almost perpendicular boulder stood erect on the opposite bank, bidding defiance to any steed short of Pegasus, and presenting a barrier only to be mounted by a scaling-ladder. Russell shouted till he was hoarse, but in vain—his warning was drowned in the storm; for, Mrs. Cholmondeley putting her horse resolutely at it, the gallant animal did his utmost; but, failing to reach the summit of the rock, fell heavily back into the boiling Lynn, and so saved his own bones; while the lady was hurled to the ground with an appalling thud.

Russell's blood curdled at the sight, but he leapt from his saddle and stood by her side in another instant. Anxiously awaiting the recovery of her breath, and being fully persuaded that some fracture of the limbs must have taken place, Russell said, "Move your right arm; now the other: your right foot; the other. Bravo! not a bone broken there. Now stand up."

The lady did so; and, though much bruised, in a short time was little the worse for her perilous adventure. Lord Cork—a hard man in his day, and who must have seen more bad falls than most men, if not during his Mastership of the Queen's Buckhounds, at least with the Christchurch drag—was so shocked by the sight that, on finding the lady was well attended to, he turned his horse's head and rode home.

In the fifth room of the Borghese Palace, at Rome, hangs an exquisite picture by Domenichino; the finest, perhaps, he ever painted on a mythical subject; it is entitled "The Chase of Diana." The figure of the goddess, who stands prominently forward, is the very personification of beauty. She is attended by a bevy of nymphs; and to one, whose superior skill as a huntress has just been tested, the goddess is awarding the appropriate prize of a bow and quiver.

But if, as of old in the valleys of Ida, the Forest Queen were at present to hold High Court in one of the ferny combes of Exmoor, attended, of course, by the fair votaries mentioned above, her Majesty would be sorely puzzled, so Russell thought, to decide on which of them to bestow the first prize—

> "For, all so good, 'twere hard indeed to tell
> Who figured first, or who should bear the bell."

## CHAPTER XIV.

Visits Marham Hall and Sandringham—Dances the Old Year out and the New Year in with the Princess of Wales—Manly Traits in the Young Princes—Sorrow at Home—His Clerical Life—Tiverton Old Boys' Meetings.

> Think you the chase unfits him for the Church?
> Attend him there, and you will find his tones
> Such as become the place; nay, you may search
> Through many counties from cathedral thrones,
> And lofty stalls where solemn prebends perch,
> To parish aisles which are not cells of drones,
> But echo the sweet sound of psalm and prayer,
> And you will hear no voice more earnest there.
>
> H. S. Stokes.

In the early autumn of 1877, Frank Goodall, the Queen's huntsman, accompanied by Mrs. Goodall, paid him a visit at Tordown; and on Tuesday, the 14th of August, Russell, who was to meet his guests at Cloutsham Ball—that being the first grand fixture for the season, the opening day of the Devon and Somerset Staghounds—varied his usual mode of going to cover by taking a servant with him and driving thither in a gig—a conveyance and attendant expressly meant for Mrs. Goodall's return to Tordown; while, at the same time, he led a spare horse to carry Goodall during the chase. Although now in the eighty-second year of his age, so unusual a sight as Russell upon wheels attracted, of course, universal attention among the large field assembled at the meet; some of whom jumped at once to the conclusion, not an unnatural one too, that the long distance to cover on horseback, just twenty five miles, had at length become too much even for him; others, with more humour, but with little ground for their advice, prescribed a list-shoe, giving him a broad hint that, if port wine were his liquor, the sooner he put on a muzzle the better.

An old stag-hunting farmer, however, whose feelings were really touched by the spectacle, created no little amusement, as he said, pathetically, "Zee! there he go'th, Passen Rissell in a chaise; never seed un afore off a horse's back, never. But there, us must all come to't; yeu can't have tew forenoons to one day."

Grand and striking, indeed, must have been the contrast to Frank Goodall's eye between the deep, romantic combes of that country and the gentle verdant slopes of Sunning Hill; between the wild, tumbling torrent of the Lynn and the "silver-winding way" of Father Thames; as, among water-lilies, weeping-willows, and

"Meadows trim with daisies pied,"

he glides gently and pensively seawards, lingering still on his downward course, as if loth to leave the peaceful and happy scene. Fair and graceful, however, as the landscape is in the region of Windsor, Frank Goodall must have been more than a philosopher if a twinge of envy did not seize him as he viewed the sparkling brooks, the ferny combes, and the open, heathery wastes of Exmoor, so attractively romantic, and, above all, so suitable to the chase of the wild red deer; and on comparing, as he must have done, these rough and almost trackless hunting-grounds in the west with the fair and cultivated enclosures enriching the valley of the Thames, how ardently he must have longed, on behalf of the latter, for a touch of old Nature as he saw her then, in her russet and untrimmed garb, in the solitude of the glens, and the grand, sweeping moorlands, "immeasurably spread" around him!

But it was far from Russell's object that his guest should moralize in such fashion; he brought him there to enjoy a good day's hunting; but that, unfortunately, Mr. Bisset and his hounds were, for a wonder, unable to show him. So many deer were on foot in Horner Wood, that, when at five p.m.,

"The antlered monarch of the waste"

did at length vouchsafe to exhibit his royal head to the public, he soon managed to beat the pack by a change in the depths of Badgeworthy. Consequently, the sport, on the whole, proving indifferent, Goodall and he turned homeward, but did not get back to Tordown before the late hour of eleven at night.

On the following Friday, August 17th, Russell again met the staghounds in Hawkcombe Head; and if, on the last occasion, he had enjoyed but scant opportunity of satisfying the "field," he must now have convinced them, beyond all doubt, that his power of endurance in the saddle was yet vigorous as ever; and that, notwithstanding the weight of years he carried so bravely, to challenge him in a long day's work on horseback would still be "more than the stoutest dare."

He had ridden nearly thirty miles to cover over highways and byways such as MacAdam would have blushed to own, remained with the hounds all day, and then, from a yet farther distance, had returned to his own homestead; where, at half-past ten, he sat down to dinner without a symptom of exhaustion, and then fed heartily, as a man might be expected to feed through the enclosure of whose lips no food had passed since seven o'clock that morning.

Having followed him thus far in his fox-and-stag-hunting career as closely as the scent would serve and materials permit, it will be necessary now to revert to a period somewhat previous to that with which the writer has latterly been dealing; and although Russell himself might have said that a for'rad cast is, as it ought to be, one of the golden rules of a foxhunter, still, exceptional cases do occur even in that go-ahead school, when its non-observance becomes not only admissible, but at times imperative.

Russell had found a fox on a certain occasion somewhere in the neighbourhood of High Bray, when, just before the hounds had killed him, he was joined by one John Zeal, a man who acted as factotum to Mr. T. Palmer Ackland, on whose business he was then going to Bideford. Now John, as Russell well knew, was an enthusiastic foxhunter, and chuckled cheerily over his good luck in having fallen in even with the tail-end of so pleasant an episode during his solitary ride.

Seeing him so elated, Russell said, "You'd better stop, John, and see me find another fox."

The man hesitated a moment, as if weighing the urgency of his mission against the prospect of sport—duty in one scale and pleasure in the other.

"But will you kill him, sir, if I stop?" inquired John, gradually yielding to the stronger impulse.

"Oh, yes! I'll kill him; so, come along."

"But will you promise to kill him?" repeated the man, still wavering; only say the word and I know you'll do it."

"Then," said Russell, I'll promise to kill him."

That was enough; up went the scale of duty to the beam; John instantly turned his horse's head and followed the hounds. Russell kept his word, had a fine run and killed his fox; but, alas! John Zeal found himself, when they finished, not only twenty long miles away from Bideford, but on a horse utterly used up and scarcely able to crawl back to his own stable.

The cause of his servant's detention became, of course, known to Mr. Palmer Ackland; nor is it at all unlikely that Russell's chance of promotion to a better living was more or less unfavourably affected by that circumstance. The rectory of High Bray had fallen vacant, and being in the gift of that gentleman, he was asked by a mutual friend to give it to Russell.

"No!" he said, somewhat curtly; "not to Russell; I shall be hunted to death if I give it to him."

Although living in times when cock-fighting was regarded as no crime, but, on the contrary, was upheld as a popular pastime, in which the squirearchy of Devon played a conspicuous part; when friends of his own, gentlemen of such standing in the county as the Hon. Newton Fellowes, Willoughby Stawell, Stucley Lucas, and Dr. Troyte, of Huntsham, held annual bouts for that purpose at their respective homes;

and when cocks of the choicest blood reared expressly for the pit, were put out to walk, as hounds are at the present day, Russell held aloof from the meetings, maintaining that he saw no sport in the fierce and savage exhibitions.

And with respect to the turf, perhaps no man ever loved to see an honest struggle between two good horses better than Russell; but on horse-racing in general, coupled as it is inseparably with betting and other dark doings, he has ever looked with a wary eye. In alluding to it he would say, "Have a care, my old friend; that is a game in which the best horse is not always the winner—very different from hunting, with twenty couple of hounds racing over the moor; there's no 'pulling' nor 'roping' then; every man does his best to get at them. That's the racing to my mind—nothing so honest under the sun."

It would be travelling beyond the compass and object of this memoir to tell of the various agricultural meetings and hound-shows at which Russell took a prominent part, as judge, during the last twenty years. Suffice it to say, with respect to the latter, that in Yorkshire he acted twice in that capacity; twice at Plymouth; once at the Crystal Palace, and lastly in Dorsetshire, where he was invited in March, 1878, to judge the puppies of the Blackmoor Vale Hunt.

At that meeting what reminiscences of fifty years ago must have rolled back on his memory! what thoughts of his two gifted friends, the Rev. Harry Farr Yeatman, of Stock, and George Templer, of Stover—the latter his beau-ideal of a gentleman huntsman, and the former the well-beloved master and founder of that hunt—each a consummate judge of all that pertained to hounds. He must have wondered, too, if one drop of the Old Stover blood—that of Guardsman or Pantaloon—could still be traced in the veins or looks of those young beauties, over which he now lingered with a fixed and loving eye. Nor could that memorable ride to Bath on the Warminster poster have been forgotten at such a time; nay, every incident of the journey must have recurred to him as freshly as on the dark night when he first crossed that garran's back.

At an agricultural meeting held at Exeter some years ago, Russell, while busily engaged in inspecting the blood-stock of a neighbouring squire, was told by an old friend that he had brought a young cousin to the show-yard who was very anxious to be introduced to him. "And let me tell you," said the friend, by way of commendation, the young man being close at his elbow, "that he is an ardent sportsman, and has already broken his leg by a fall in hunting."

"Then," said Russell, "he ought to be bred from," giving him, as he did so, a hearty shake by the hand.

When the Royal Agricultural Society of England held its meeting at Plymouth in 1865, Russell, by command of the Prince of Wales, was invited by Admiral Sir Henry Keppel to meet his Royal Highness at dinner, the Admiralty House at Devonport being the rendezvous for the distinguished party assembled on that occasion. The banquet appears to have been an unusually pleasant one; nor is it at all extraordinary that it should have been so, for, in addition to the Prince's wonted affability and love of hunting, the Admiral and his Flag-Lieut., Lord Charles Beresford, besides being the best of company, were both men after Russell's own heart—enthusiastic sportsmen, and regular attendants on Mr. Trelawny's hounds.

In strolling through the show-yard on the following day, Russell whispered to a friend that "The ship commanded by two such officers must be a jolly boat indeed, for they were the jolliest set of fellows he had met for many a day."

Sailors, when they take to hunting, proverbially do it *con amore*, and certainly it may be inferred that those gentlemen were no exception to that rule; for when they left Plymouth for other quarters, Mr. Trelawny could ill disguise the regret he felt at losing two members of his "field" whom he valued so much for their companionable qualities, not only with hounds, but at "table-board."

Russell, then, had fallen fairly on his legs by dropping into so genial a groove; and it is quite certain that, if form and ceremony had been the order of the day, instead of good-fellowship, seasoned, it may be, here and there, with a spice of horse-and-hound talk, he would never have enjoyed himself as he did, nor so cordially appreciated the honour done him by that gracious invitation.

Not long afterwards, however, he was destined to see something more of His Royal Highness's society than, from his position in life—that of a rural, west country parson, only known to fame within the limits of the hunting world—his homespun habits could have led him to expect.

In the winter of 1873, by the kindness of his friend, Mr. Harry Villebois, he was invited to spend a week at Marham Hall, the ancient seat of that gentleman's family, "to meet," as the invitation expressed it, "the Prince of Wales and a party of friends." It is doubtful, however, if even so fair a promise of hospitality, combined with the prospect of meeting such goodly company would alone have tempted him to turn his back for six hunting days on Lord Portsmouth's hounds, or Mr. Froude

Bellew's, or the "Stars of the West," and that, too, in mid-season; but when Mr. Villebois added, "and have a day or two, with the West Norfolk pack," he added a bait that was irresistible and Russell jumped at it as a trout would at a May-fly.

It boots not here to tell how rapidly that pleasant visit was brought to a close; the happiest moments have always the fleetest wings, and are apt to take flight ere we can well enjoy, or even realize, their presence. The day before the party broke up, however, a most agreeable surprise awaited Russell ere his steps were actually turned on his long journey homewards. The Prince, coming up to him, said, "How long are you going to stay here, Mr. Russell."

"I must be at home on Saturday, sir, without fail."

"Then," said the Prince, turning to Mr. Villebois, "you had better bring him over to our ball on Friday."

Accordingly, instead of returning on that day to Devonshire, as he meant to have done, Russell hunted with Mr. Villebois' hounds, dined at Marham, and at night, accompanied by his host, whisked off to the ball at Sandringham. It was a late and lively affair, the dancing being kept up with unflagging gaiety, and Russell taking an active part in it till four in the morning, when "God Save the Queen" sounded the signal to halt, and reminded the guests of that salutary hint so well given in Hudibras, that

> "Night is the sabbath of mankind
> To rest the body and the mind;"

a hint which all, with the exception of Russell, seemed quite ready to adopt forthwith; but he, at that chilly hour of the morn, buttoning on his top-coat—the wool of which had been grown at Eggesford, and, when manufactured into good broadcloth, had been presented to him by Lady Portsmouth—started for Lynn; and taking the first train thence for London, he reached home at a late hour that same night, "All the better," as he told his friends the next day, "for change of air and a pleasant outing."

That the Prince and Princess were not unfavourably impressed with their west-country guest, during his first flying visit, may be inferred from the circumstance that, shortly before his departure, the Prince sent Colonel Ellis to invite him again to Sandringham for the approaching Christmas week: "And, as we hope to hear him preach," said the Prince, "tell him to put a sermon in his pocket before he leaves home."

A story went the rounds of the London clubs, that Russell, on accepting the Prince's invitation, inquired of Colonel Ellis how he was to get to Sandringham from the Wolferton station?

"The Prince will send his carriage for you," replied the gallant equerry.

"Be good enough to write that down in my pocket-book," said Russell, "that there may be no mistake."

Colonel Ellis did so.

"Now," said Russell, "please to add your initials."

The tale travelled into Devonshire, and when it first reached Russell's ears he laughed aloud, saying, "A very good story against me, *if* only it were true."

The annual tenants' ball being about to take place on the last night of the year, a flutter of excitement pervaded the neighbourhood for many a mile round Sandringham, and expectation rose, not on tiptoe only, but to fever-heat, in anticipation of that joyous event. It was looked upon as the fête of the season, when the Prince and Princess were wont to mingle merrily in the dance, and delight their country guests not less by the welcome they received than by the simplicity, and almost homeliness of their own manners. No wonder, too, if Russell felt somewhat stirred by the coming event; nor if, remembering the seventy-eight winters of his life, he might have wished for the magic cauldron of Medea to restore him again to the vigour of youth, and bring back, at least for one night, that "freshness of morning" which, with "her clouds and her tears," the poet tells us is

"Worth evening's best light."

That would certainly have been his first wish had he foreseen the honour that awaited him at the forthcoming ball. On that night, a little before the clock struck twelve, and a few minutes before the old year had passed away for ever, Russell received an intimation that the Princess was about to favour him with her hand, and welcome the incoming year by taking him for her partner.

It would be trespassing beyond the due limits of this memoir to take more than a passing glance at the mysteries of that festive scene, the success of which, had the Muses been present, Terpsichore herself would have been charmed to witness. Russell, inspirited by his happy lot, and forgetting all time, except that of the music, stepped out like a four-year-old; and if, in the course of that brief enjoyment, he had not been the object of many longing, not to say envious, eyes, there must have been Anchorites in that assembly with whom he certainly would have had no sympathy.

It was whispered about by that little bird, to which, from our earliest years, we have all been indebted for so much authentic information, that Russell on hearing the tower clock announce the birth of the new year, turned to his fair partner and said, "Now I can say what no man else can ever say again."

"And what may that be?" inquired the Princess, with an interested look.

"That I've had the honour of dancing out the old year and dancing in the new (1874) with your Royal Highness."

"Quite true," replied the Princess; "no one else can say that but yourself."

But Fame, that worst of all gossips, relates of him on that occasion—though he himself stoutly repudiated the impeachment—that, in setting the Princess right as to some remark she had made, he forgot for the moment whom he was addressing and, said, "No, no, my dear; 'tisn't so." But if, in truth, his tongue did so slip, the pure Devonshire strain, in which he was wont to use that familiar expression in speaking to ladies, if it did not astonish, must have amused her Royal Highness amazingly.

At dinner, on the first day of that week's visit, Russell's country manners cropped out somewhat conspicuously. He had been helped to fish, and, wishing for more, had sent his plate off for a second "helping," when the Prince, observing the vacancy before him, asked if he didn't like fish.

"Yes, sir," replied Russell, "I'm very fond of fish. I've been helped once, and I've sent my plate up a second time; and now I remember, that's the very thing my wife charged me, on leaving home, not to do."

The Prince laughed, but took care that every day afterwards Russell should be helped a second time to his favourite dish.

Under the conviction, in which he was not far wrong, that his guest, like every orthodox parson of the old type, would prefer a glass of good "red port wine" to Bordeaux of the finest vintage, or to Falernian, though "kept with a hundred keys," the Prince called his attention to a bottle of '20 port, of which, on being invited to say how he liked it, he at once expressed his unqualified approval. The next day, however, a different and a somewhat thinner port was put before him, and again the Prince asked his opinion of that wine.

"Very good, sir," replied Russell; "but not quite so stout a wine as the port you gave me yesterday."

The Prince at once, inferring that his guest preferred the more generous wine, ordered the bottle to be changed, and thenceforth Russell enjoyed his glass of '20 port daily at the royal table. He was, however, no gourmet, plain food and sound home-grown cider having been the chief diet on which he depended through life; and these, sweetened by mountain air and strong exercise, appeared to agree with him admirably.

After dinner, on the first day of his arrival at Sandringham, a large party being present, Russell became the subject of a harmless, but very amusing, practical joke, which, as he said himself, "for the life of him he could not at first understand." Mr. Anthony Hamond's fox-hounds were appointed to meet in the neighbourhood on the following day, and that gentleman being then present, a telegram was brought in, which the Prince, amid the breathless silence of his guests, opened and read aloud. It ran thus :—

"Bill George, Canine Castle, Kensal Green, to Anthony Hamond, Esq., at Sandringham, Wolferton.—The Rev. John Russell having disappointed me in not calling for a bagman as he passed through London this afternoon, shall send him down to-morrow by first train to Wolferton. Hope he'll arrive fresh."

Such a telegram, as might be expected, called forth a peal of merriment at Russell's expense, but by whom it was concocted remains a mystery to the present day.

At table, the *carte-de-menu*, exquisitely designed, and very superior to anything Russell had ever yet seen, attracted his especial admiration. On the top appeared Sandringham House and the date, with a border on one side filled in with game, and all beautifully painted. "Isn't that very pretty?" said the Prince, observing his guest's eye fascinated by the design. "It was done by a bedridden girl, and you must take that home to Mrs. Russell from me."

On the Sunday, as requested to do so by their Royal Highnesses, he preached at Sandringham Church, the Rev. W. Lake Onslow, the rector, placing his pulpit at his service, and afterwards thanking him cordially for his able and interesting discourse. And that the Prince and Princess must have been equally impressed by the clear enunciation and earnest manner of the preacher there can be little doubt; though, on that point, if anything were said, history is silent.

Perhaps no portion of his time was more pleasantly spent than the quiet half-hour he passed one morning with the Princess, who, followed by her two eldest boys, then respectively nine and eight years of age, invited him to accompany them to the stables and inspect the stud. "It was a delightful sight," said Russell, relating the circumstance to an old friend, shortly afterwards, "to witness the utter freedom of the youngsters as they tumbled and plunged amongst the straw, and ever and anon begged for a bit of chopped carrot which the Princess carried in a basket, in order to feed some gentle favourite on which they had set their hearts. A more natural sight I never saw in my life; and, mark my words, those two boys will be as fond of horses as ever Castor and Pollux were."

The agreeable party at Sandringham, on that occasion, was brought to a close by the departure of the Prince, who, taking Russell with him as far as London, started off for St. Petersburg, to attend the wedding of his brother, H.R.H. the Duke of Edinburgh, an event that took place on the 23rd January, 1874.

Miss L. T——, a lady who had read a letter of Russell's describing the pleasure of his visit to Sandringham, wrote thus in allusion to it:

"What a list of things he got through in those ten days, and what a delightful picture he gives of the family circle at S.! I don't wonder the P. and P. made much of their guest, for all England may be proud of such a man as Mr. Russell. I only wish there were hundreds like him. 'Fox-hunting for ever!' say I, if it helps to make such men."

In the autumn of that year, 1874, a heavy sorrow awaited him—the heaviest he had known through life—by the serious illness and subsequent death of Mrs. Russell; with whom, had she lived but one year longer, he might have celebrated his golden wedding-day. On the 22nd of October, he thus wrote:—"The dear old missis is, I grieve to say, very ill; and I can't leave her for many hours together. Still, she is cheerful when anyone comes in, and *will*, as usual, 'stir her stumps' to make them comfortable. But that sort of exertion does her no good; and sometimes I am led to believe she can't live through the day."

On the first of January in the following year the long-dreaded blow fell at last; mercifully releasing the patient sufferer, but overwhelming Russell with unutterable grief.

Writing subsequently at intervals to an old friend, sometime his curate, he alludes thus painfully to his bereavement:—"I am at home again, though it no longer seems like home to me, for there is a vacant chair in every room, never again to be filled by her, the dear old soul, to whom I was united forty-nine years ago, come Sunday." Again:—"If the sympathy of friendship could soothe my grief, I possess it to a very great extent; for I have received upwards of a hundred letters of comfort and condolence from friends, far and near. Among them, one from the Prince of Wales, most kindly and feelingly expressed."

On hearing from the friend, already so often referred to, that he would like to see what the Prince had said, Russell wrote as follows:

"MY DEAR OLD FRIEND,

"I have sent a copy of the Prince's letter to Lady Westbury (*née* Luttrell) who will give it to you; but, please remember, not for publication, either before or after I 'sleep the sleep that knows not breaking.' Love to you all."

During a portion of that eventful year (1875) his time and thoughts were much occupied in preaching for charitable institutions, in behalf of which he not only took an active interest, but proved himself, as before mentioned, a most successful advocate. So truly, indeed, were his services appreciated, that, at the proposal of Earl Fortescue, he was constituted an honorary governor of the North Devon Hospital. "I am worked to death," he wrote, "at this season of the year (November); going about from church to church on working days as well as Sundays, preaching and begging for the N. D. Infirmary and similar institutions, and finding, when I come home, heaps of letters to answer, but no one there to cheer me in my labour—alone! alone!"

In the same year, as if well aware that occupation is one of the main secrets of life's happiness, he accepted the office of chaplain to the High Sheriff of Cornwall, Mr. George Williams, of Scorrier, who, in most complimentary terms, offered him the appointment. Of course, he rode to Bodmin, whence, in his epigrammatic style, he thus described the duty he had just performed:—"Here I am, doing chaplain to the High Sheriff of Cornwall, George Williams, M.F.H.; and am just returned from preaching before the Judges, Lush and Piggot, both of whom thanked me for my 'discoose.' I do like Cornwall and Cornish folk; but must be back in my old earth by the end of the week. A day with the Duke will be a real treat to me, when I come up to see you."

He alludes to the Duke of Beaufort, who, when Russell paid the promised visit to his old friend Davies, residing at Bath, very kindly wrote to say he would send a horse for him every morning to the cover side; but, alas! six days of hard-hearted weather forbad it; frost and snow covered the ground; and Russell, though rising each morn at seven to look at a vane and hope for a thaw, went back growling to bed. So, on that occasion, he never once saw the Duke's hounds.

In all his letters, terse and brief as they usually are, he displays to a remarkable degree the power of making all who read them feel and comprehend thoroughly what he himself feels and what he would describe—a power said to have been possessed by Nelson beyond any living man of his day. In writing to a young lady, Miss B. F. D., on the 6th of March, 1877, he says:—"Alas! my head and neck are now garnished with all the colours of the rainbow. The good old horse I have so long ridden, while galloping over a grass field, fell on his head, and pitched me I don't know where—but certainly on my head—for my hat was 'britted in,' and I saw more stars in the farmament than ever was a-put there. Ask your old daddy to explain that to you."

Again, in the same year, he writes thus to a brother sportsman, and claims his sympathy: "Last Thursday Lord Portsmouth's hounds met at Castle Hill; and, while they were running, I suffered such agony in my teeth that I requested a medical gentleman present to rid me of the chief offender. 'In lieu of a better instrument, a bit of whipcord,' he said, 'would serve the purpose'; and, verily, with that hempen appliance out he lugged the supposed culprit; but, alas! it proved to be a valuable friend—a tooth as sound as the day it was 'dropped.' You'll pity me, I know, when I say this is not the first time I have suffered a similar loss."

His habitual conversation, too, lacked nothing of the epigrammatic style so conspicuous in his letters; in it he went straight to the mark; and, if called upon to make a speech, he invariably did so in a few words, always pointed and often humorous. "If you have anything to say, get up and say it, and then sit down," was the advice of the great Iron Duke; and that was precisely Russell's plan.

While dining with his old curate at Bath, not long ago, with a party of gentlemen, most of them west-country friends, one, a most agreeable Cornishman, who was always on the move, wandering about from place to place, and never at home, complained to him that he did not feel at all well, and that he thought he should go away for change of air.

"Then," said Russell, "go home."

Had he studied the rules of "Lacon" all his life the pithiness of his advice could scarcely have been more complete.

In 1876 he again paid a visit to Sandringham; but this time there was no "dancing the old year out and the new year in." "The Prince's time is so occupied," he wrote, "by a house full of foreign grandees and other magnates, that I wonder he can find time to pay, as he does, the most minute attention to all." Among these Russell found himself little at home, and of course saw less of his royal hosts than on the former happy occasion. He left, however, in high spirits; the Prince promising to come down and enjoy a day or two with the Devon and Somerset staghounds, and see the red deer hunted in his native wilds.

But when the season for that sport had at length arrived, and Nature was now clothing the deep-wooded glens of the moor in varied and glorious apparel, burnishing the golden furze, the ruddy heather, and even the fern-clad rocks of Watersmeet with the loveliest of autumn hues; and now, when the "stag of ten," rudely wakened by the tufters from his long and idle summer dream, is roused from his leafy haunts and forced into view, displaying, to the hunter's delight, his big haunches, stately form, and magnificent head; the bad news reached Dunster Castle, where quarters had been prepared for him, that the Prince was unable to leave home, owing to the serious illness of one of his boys. So the project then fell through, to the great disappointment of Russell and every other stag-hunter, man and woman—from the fair maids of Taunton to the hardy yeomen of the Western moors.

To enter minutely into the abstract question of Russell's clerical life would scarcely be consonant with the general tenor of this memoir; still, as all his life he represented a phase of English character which, by the moderation of his opinions, and the unconventional manliness of his conduct, was a daily protest against the forms of one party and the cant of another—against Stiggins on one side and "dear Mr. Oriel" on the other—a brief allusion to it cannot be avoided.

To hold the line and maintain a steady middle course amid the host of skirters, now dividing and confounding their flocks, not less by the motley variety of their views than by the contempt they exhibit for the law of the land, is unquestionably a feature of the highest value in a clergyman's character at the present time; for never was the sectarian spirit more rampant in the Church of England than it now is within her pale; and, unless a larger element of secular ways and principles be infused into the clerical mind, woe awaits her at no very distant date.

The very union of Church and State depends mainly on men who, like Russell, are holding fast to English habits of thought and the text of the Reformation, guarding against divergence towards either extreme—that of the "self-willed" formalist on one side, and that of the shallow fanatic on the other. The narrow and exclusive grooves in which the latter move, Russell would have denounced as not only opposed to St. Paul's view of being "all things to all men," and hence anti-Catholic, but absolutely inconsistent with the simple and comprehensive religion of the New Testament.

"Our grand old Church," as a gentleman writing to Russell remarks, "like other old houses, will last a good many years yet, if it be left in the hands of its original architects; but it will not bear an incursion of amateur builders. . . . If then," he adds, "it has been the business of your life to maintain and exhibit sound and not ephemeral principles, and you have helped to sustain the reputation and power of the English character by simply cultivating the gifts (which we in our blindness call tastes) that God has given you, are you not 'a representative man?' But you will, I know, still sing 'Non nobis Domine,' and in your modesty confess yourself to be an 'unprofitable servant.'"

Notwithstanding the iron arm and Draconic rule of Dr. Richards, happy still are Russell's recollections of his school days at Tiverton; and thither he went periodically to promote the celebration of the "Old Boys' Day;" when he and all good Blundellians testified with gratitude to the beneficence of the founder, and to the high scholastic advantages conferred by that excellent institution. On one occasion he told the once-dreaded Doctor—then, however, no longer in authority, but a visitor like himself—that "he was the only man he was ever afraid of."

"Nonsense," said Richards, good-naturedly; "and was I so terrible?"

"Yes," replied Russell, "you were. I've set to with some of the hardest men in England, and never found one who could hit like you."

At a meeting of the "Old Boys" at Tiverton, Russell was once invited to preach the sermon, which he accordingly did; a local paper observing that "the discourse was a very able one." In addressing some remarks to the present boys, he especially alluded to the brilliant example of Dr. Temple, once a Tiverton scholar, and now the bishop of the diocese—a beacon, he told them, they should never lose sight of.

Tordown.

## CHAPTER XV.

### CONCLUSION.

In July, 1879, the valuable living of Black Torrington was kindly offered to him by Lord Poltimore, and with much perplexity was at length accepted for reasons which the following letter, written to Mr. Davies, will best explain:—

"Tell me, my dear old friend, what *shall* I do about Black Torrington? I cannot live on £220 a year, which is all I shall have after I have paid a certain annuity for another three or four years. Black Torrington is a clear £500 a year, and there is a good house; but then it is neither Tordown nor Exmoor, and by the time I have settled in there, I shall perhaps be called upon to leave it again for Swymbridge Churchyard! What shall I do? How can I leave my own people, with whom I have lived in peace and happiness for half a century? It will be a bitter pill to swallow, if it must be taken; but it will be my poverty, and not my will, that will consent to it."

Again, in October of the same year, he writes from Tordown:—

"The day of my departure from this my happy home draweth nigh, and I am fretting myself to death about leaving it. Old John Squire of Accot told me on Friday that if I went away from Swymbridge, it wouldn't be long before I should be brought back again. Cheering, very—eh? but possibly too true to be pleasant."

The leave-taking was a sad business between him and his parishioners; while their sympathy and that of his friends farther afield, including H.R.H. the Prince of Wales, was manifested by a handsome testimonial, which, amounting in value to nearly £800, was presented to him by Earl Fortescue, on behalf of all the subscribers. The ceremony took place at the Duke of Bedford's mansion in Eaton Square, kindly lent by His Grace on that interesting occasion.

Lord Fortescue said, "He had much pleasure in performing the pleasing duty of making the presentation; but the occasion was to him a sad one, owing to the removal of his old friend from Swymbridge to another parish—fortunately, still in the county of Devon. They would not therefore be losing him altogether. The presentation was a mark of their hearty regard, friendship, and respect for Mr. Russell, as a man, a sportsman, and a clergyman." His lordship then paid a high tribute to the reverend gentleman "for his kindly work as a clergyman in his late parish, and for his charity and Christian love."

Russell, after papering and painting the old rectory at Black Torrington, to which he had now removed, commenced building a set of new stables, at a heavy cost, and had just finished the work, when a fire broke out in them, and treated him to such a "house-warming" as he had never before encountered. "I had only just completed them," he wrote, "and at my own expense, when in less than a hour and a half they became a heap of ruins. There were two horses, Simon and a valuable Irish mare in them, besides two terriers. Alas! they are all dead."

On Friday, the 22nd of August, 1879, he was invited by Mr. Luttrell to meet the Prince of Wales at Dunster Castle; and on that day a noble stag, roused in the depths of Hawkcombe Head, lead them a glorious chase over the wildest region of Exmoor, the Prince, who was well up at the finish, being greatly delighted with his day's sport.

Then, in the same year, on Monday, the 3rd of November, that being the opening day of the Quorn Hounds, we find him at Kirby Gate, mounted by his friend, Mr. Pennell-Elmhirst, to whom he was paying a long-promised visit.

On Tuesday, the 4th, he hunted with the Cottesmore at Tilton Gate, and that evening Lord Carington, the Master, and Mr. George

Grey, the famous Northumberland sportsman and rider, now Master of the Glendale, were invited by Mr. Pennell-Elmhirst to meet him at dinner.

Talking of foxhounds, Mr. Grey asked Russell if he thought the foxhound was "a distinct species of dog from the first."

"Did he, in fact, come out of the ark?" explained Lord Carington.

"How could he?" returned Russell; "did not a brace of foxes come out alive?"

On Wednesday, the 5th, he joined the Belvoir hounds at Croxton Park, hunting that day upon wheels.

Thursday he devoted to travelling westward, and reaching Bath that evening, he managed to see the Duke of Beaufort's hounds find a fox next morning near Cross Hands; after which meet he started for home, intending to wind up the week by hunting with Lord Portsmouth's hounds the next day.

In 1881, a month or so before the Ascot week, Colonel J. Anstruther Thomson conceived the happy idea of bringing together under his own roof two kindred spirits, both old friends of his own, but living widely apart and hitherto personally unacquainted with each other. They were the Rev. John Russell and Mr. John Whyte-Melville, Master of the Fife Hounds in the early part of this century, and father of the late distinguished author, whom the patriarch lived to mourn as his only son and—

"Last scion of an antient Scottish line."

Mr. Whyte-Melville was 84, Russell in his 86th year, and so they numbered between them 170 years. Having regard to this fact Thomson, whose drag was to convey them to and fro from Slough to Ascot, deemed it advisable to consult his two venerable guests as to the days on which they would like to attend the races; thinking it just probable that going every day might be a turn too much for them. But not a bit of it; Whyte-Melville, who was first consulted, asked how many days the races lasted.

"Four," replied Thomson.

"Then," said he, "I should like to go every day."

The question being put to Russell, he said, "I too should like to go every day; but I have an engagement to meet a curate on the Thursday, and keep it I must."

The curate, however, did not turn up; and Russell knew it in time to take the box-seat beside Thomson, and go down to Ascot on that as on every other day.

Col. Anstruther Thomson declares that his two veterans were the life and soul of the party; and doubts if a coach-load so cheery and so congenial as his own could have been found on Ascot Heath.

Again, in the autumn of that year (1881), he

hunted as usual with the Devon and Somerset Staghounds. The meet on one occasion being at Culbone Stables, they soon found in Pitcombe, one of Lord Lovelace's covers; but the hounds dividing, the "field" followed the body of the pack, while Russell with one other man stuck to a couple of hounds, and with them brought the stag to bay near Badgery Water. "I can well remember seeing him," writes Mr. Nicholas Snow, the able Master of the Stars of the West, "as he crossed the moors from Culbone with the leading hounds, and shall never forget his ringing cheer as they broke from the river to Badgery, and on to Brendon Common. Several people passed the remark, 'Look at Russell leading across Badgery!'" In a little more than three months from that date he celebrated his 86th birthday, being still in fine health and robust form.

In the following February (1882) Russell again paid a visit to Sandringham, and was as before charmed with the consideration and kindness he met with from the Prince and Princess of Wales. On parting they presented him with a horse-shoe diamond scarf-pin, which the Prince put into the scarf himself, saying, as he did it, "There now, it looks quite clerical."

"But," said Russell, bowing to the royal pair, "may I ask if it is given conjointly?"

"Yes, of course, conjointly," replied the Princess with a charming smile.

Again, in 1882, the staghounds saw him booted and spurred at the cover-side, still cheery and enjoying the sport; but, as his friends observed, much broken, and showing manifest tokens of failing strength. With the fall of the leaf, however, on the 15th of October, he wrote as follows to his old friend at Bath:—"I am going to London on Tuesday morning to marry Mr. Curzon, the Duchess of Beaufort's nephew, to Miss Bassett-Williams, of Pilton House; the ceremony is to take place in Curzon Chapel, May Fair. When it is over I shall turn my head homewards, and should like, if you and the missus will have me, to break the journey at 26, Circus, for one night only. But I am more fit for bed than a railway carriage."

The wedding took place two days after, but the knot was tied by other hands. On that day, the 17th, a letter from his faithful housekeeper, Mary Cocking, reached Bath instead of Russell; it ran thus: "I am grieved to say my dear master is very unwell, and in bed since Sunday. Three doctors are attending him, and I fear they think him *very, very* ill."

The attack was a critical and a dangerous one—the beginning of the end, as his friends rightly conjectured—but such had been his temperate habits and fine constitution that, aided as he was by the assiduous and scientific attention of Dr. Linnington Ash, his medical man, he was able in January, 1883, to leave home and go for change of air to East Anstey; hoping to draw fresh life and vigour from those wild moors he had known and loved so long.

But the change did him no good; for on the 4th of February he thus wrote: "I fear we shall never meet again; I don't gain strength here, as I fancy I ought; and overwhelmed as I am by letters, it is pain and grief to me to write at all."

Then, on the 25th of March, having returned to Black Torrington, he wrote his last letter to the Author of this Memoir,—"Ten thousand thanks to you, my very dear old friend, for your hearty invitation to the Circus; but if I were to set out to-morrow in my little carriage, with George to drive, and Mary to keep me in my place, I shouldn't get to Bath in a fortnight, I am so very weak—a little trip of three miles to Buckland Filleigh House, and back again, quite knocked me up.

Soon afterwards he went to Bude; but, writes Dr. Ash, "it did him more harm than good, and I had to hasten his return home on Saturday—none too soon. He is weaker and worse than I have ever seen him, but happily is suffering no pain."

On the 24th of April the good doctor again writes to say: "Mr. Russell is much the same to-day. There is certainly no improvement in his condition, nor can there be, for he takes in literally nothing. He is, however, rather more conscious, I think, and has fully appreciated the kind message from the Prince received to-day."

Night and day he was tenderly watched by those around him, and all that human skill and devotion could do was done by Dr. Ash. But surely and rapidly the tide of life was now ebbing; the pulse fluttered, the keen eye became clouded with a film, and gradually, peacefully, and without pain, the spirit of that once manly frame stole from its tenement, took wing, "and returned unto God who gave it."

He died on the 28th of April, 1883, in his 88th year, and was buried at Swymbridge, where at least a thousand people attended the funeral. Royal and costly wreaths covered the coffin; but the most touching of all tributes were those of the poor cottagers, who, weeping as they went, brought their baskets and aprons full of wild flowers, and literally showered them into his grave.

> "No further seek his merits to disclose,
> Or draw his frailties from their dread abode—
> There they alike in trembling hope repose—
> The bosom of his Father and his God."

THE END.

# INDEX.

*Index.*

---

Exeter: W. J. Southwood & Co.

*With 75 illustrations crown 4to, handsomely bound, suitable for the library or for presentation, 16/- nett.*

# STAGHUNTING WITH THE "DEVON AND SOMERSET" 1887–1901

## AN ACCOUNT OF THE CHASE OF THE WILD RED DEER ON EXMOOR

BY

PHILIP EVERED.

ILLUSTRATED BY H. M. LOMAS

CHATTO & WINDUS
LONDON.

JAMES G. COMMIN
EXETER

1902

*OPINIONS OF THE PRESS ON*

# "Staghunting with the Devon and Somerset."

**The Times:**

Since Blackmore wrote "Lorna Doone," we have read nothing which gives a more vivid idea of the picturesque romance and sullen desolation of the wildest tracts in Southern England. Mr. Evered, though profoundly versed in venery and moorcraft, is something more than a zealous sportsman. He knows every rood of the ground and there could be no better guide to its beauties or to its innumerable perils and man-traps. He has a soul for scenery whether soft or sublime, he makes even the quagmires with their rank growth and the stone strewn "graveyard" attractive, and the charms of the wooded combes with the brawling brooks must be tempting alike to the tourist and artist. The volume is profusely illustrated with photographs of scenery, farmhouses, hounds, hunters and country folk and they are triumphs of the skilful use of the camera.

**The Spectator:**

Mr. Evered knows the country and the method of procedure thoroughly. His style is more agreeable than the common run of sporting writers, and he is imbued with a love of Exmoor, and a delight in the indescribable pleasures of the chase.

**The Literary World:**

With Mr. Evered for a guide we accompany the "harbourer," we share in the "tufting," we attend the brilliant meet at Cloutsham, we see the stag up and away with a bound, we hear the music of the pack, and admire the noble brute at bay.

**The Guardian:**

His account is instinct with the life and reality and eager force that only come to a writer who is dealing with a subject with which he is thoroughly familiar and which he really loves. The illustrations are numerous enabling the reader to realize the beauty and wildness of the haunts which the lordly red deer love.

**The Morning Post:**

Will be read with pleasure by all who have followed the famous pack of which it tells, and to the inexperienced it furnishes a complete guide and handbook.

**The Pall Mall Gazette:**

The numerous photographs are remarkable for their subject matter, they include more than one representation of a live and hunted deer.

**St. James Gazette:**

Mr. Evered writes not merely as one who rides to hounds, he is an observer of nature . . . he deals with the subject altogether in a picturesque way and his book comprises many interesting records of the famous Somerset Hunt.

**The World:**

Those who hold with that eccentric sportsman James Pigg that "there's nout like fox hunting" are rather apt to look with slight favour on the pursuit of wild red deer as being "slow" and lacking the excitement of jumping. They would probably be inclined to modify their views on the subject after reading Mr. Evered's delightful book on *Staghunting with the Devon and Somerset.* It is a book that will give pleasure not only to those who love the chase, but to all who appreciate spirited accounts of wild sport amid wild surroundings . . . . . it is scarcely too much to say that there is not from cover to cover a dull page in his book nor one that will not repay perusal. With a rare talent for picturesque description Mr. Evered tells of the varying incidents of the chase, touches in with an appreciative pen the local colouring that lends so much of its charm to the sport and the scenes portrayed among the wooded combes and wild woodland of Devon come vividly before the mind of the reader.

### Westminster Gazette:

Mr. Evered has done his part of the work in a way that will be keenly enjoyed and appreciated by all who have been out with the Devon and Somerset, and he has the exceptional advantage of having secured as illustrations a very remarkable series of photographs by Mr. H. M. Lomas.

### The Outlook:

The book generally is a capital one and will please all lovers of horse and hound. Some of the views of Exmoor are almost works of art.

### The Publisher's Circular:

With the aid of pen and camera he has produced a complete enthralling account of staghunting as it exists to-day which must take a conspicuous place in the literature of sport—and lovers of "Lorna Doone" will be grateful for the glimpses they obtain of the regions made famous by the genius of Blackmore—the illustrations are almost as much a part of the book as the text—they are numerous and beautiful.

### Somerset County Herald:

Such a well written and exquisitely got up work as this should be in the possession of every follower of "the Devon and Somerset" as well as the great number of general readers who take a keen interest in the chase of the wild red deer on Exmoor.

### North Devon Journal:

A book that will be treasured as a brilliant and faithful picture of the most glorious sport in England. Mr. Evered has given a picture of staghunting that is quite unique.

### The Scotsman:

The present handsomely and plentifully illustrated work is a delightful and instructive volume whether to look at or to read . . . . . the Devon and Somerset staghounds hunt a fairer country-side than any other in all England, and these pictures must awaken the liveliest associations of health, good spirits and open air adventure in the mind of any spectator who knows the look of the moor, the combes, the ferns, the cliffs and the foam within sight of Dunkery Beacon. Mr. Evered describes the country with a rare and catching heartiness in his appreciation. The literature of sport is sensibly the richer for the book.

THE END OF A GOOD RUN.—MINEHEAD CLIFFS.

On Haddon Hill.

# Opinions of the Press.

**The Field:**

The work is written by one who knows every yard of the moor, everybody about it, and all the details of hunting, the book is at once a record and a handbook of the most interesting kind. . . . . The book is exceedingly well got up, the title page is artistic while the printing reflects great credit on the firm of Southwood & Co., of Exeter, by whom it was executed.

**Illustrated Sporting and Dramatic News:**

Mr. Evered has made use of his opportunities to observe the manner of the red-deer and the methods of the men who follow the chase across the wild open moor when they can, down the sultry wooded combes when they must, and he tells in bright and graphic language the story of some of the best runs he has known.

**The Sporting Life:**

The reader is in the land of "Lorna Doone" and those who have been under the spell of that enchanting romance will find many a feature in Mr. Evered's description of the spacious, varied and majestic scenery he deals with, which recall Blackmore's pictorial touch. As a contribution to a select library of standard works on that phase of the noble science which only an enthusiastic follower of the wild red-deer from his lair to the death could have written the volume disarms criticism. It is written with manifest authority.

**The Ladies' Field:**

Staghunting on Exmoor has been fortunate in its historians. Dr. Collyns' book is a classic, Mr. John Fortescue's deserves to be, and Mr Philip Evered's volume on Staghunting on Exmoor which we have just read with the greatest pleasure is fully worthy of such good company . . . . to those who have been to Exmoor it is a treasury of delightful memories of past pleasures—to those who mean to go there it will be an indispensable guide.

**The County Gentleman:**

He not only depicts the wild beauties of the Devon and Somerset country but the genuine spirit of sport runs through every line he has written.

**Country Life:**

It is well written, and a valuable guide to those who have never hunted with these hounds, and a delightful recaller of happy memories to those who have—of the photographic illustrations by Mr. Lomas a word of high praise must be written. Not often have I seen more artistic or faithful landscape photography.

**The Academy:**

The wild red deer hunting of Somerset and Devon is a world of its own full of moor-craft and wood-craft and local lore. . . . You need not be a follower of these hunts or have ever seen an antlered deer pounding over Dunkery to enjoy these pages in which the breeze and the heather and the warmth of rocks and the music of hounds are recalled.

**The Athenæum:**

The get-up of the volume reflects great credit on all concerned, the type is good, the margins are ample.

Milton Keynes UK
Ingram Content Group UK Ltd.
UKHW041211231023
431175UK00004B/530

9 789354 022722